A JAZZ ODYSSEY

A JAZZ
ODYSSEY

THE LIFE OF
OSCAR PETERSON

OSCAR PETERSON

EDITOR AND CONSULTANT:

RICHARD PALMER

continuum
LONDON • NEW YORK

Continuum
The Tower Building, 11 York Road, London, SE1 7NX
370 Lexington Avenue, New York, NY 10017-6503

First published 2002 by Continuum by arrangement with Bayou Press Ltd

British Library Cataloguing-in-Publication Data
A catalogue record for this book is available from the British Library.

ISBN 0-8264-5807-6 (hardback)

Library of Congress Cataloging-in-Publication Data
The Library of Congress catalog card number for this book is 2002 141142.

Typeset by BookEns Ltd, Royston, Herts, England
Printed and bound in the United States

CONTENTS

NORMAN GRANZ

JAZZ PEOPLE

PREFATORY NOTE

Shortly after the manuscript that now forms this book was completed, my 52-year friendship with and musical commitment to Norman Granz came to an abrupt end. On Thursday November 22, 2001, he finally succumbed to the dreaded disease we all know as cancer. I still feel both personally bereaved and creatively drained.

In dedicating my book to Norman's memory, I am honouring not only my best friend and mentor, but also his monumental achievements. The history of jazz—and the lives and fortunes of many jazzmen—would have been very different without him. And that is why Richard Palmer and I have decided to leave the chapters on Norman in the present tense: Norman may have passed away but his spirit and influence will last as long as jazz itself.

Oscar Peterson

CAST OF CHARACTERS

It is hoped that this rudimentary "dramatis personae" will prove helpful to readers as a quick guide. A more detailed and comprehensive listing can be found in the Index.

First name	Surname	Nickname(s)	Instrument/significance
Julian	Adderley	Cannonball; Cannon	Alto saxophone
Monty	Alexander		Piano
Irving	Ashby		Guitar
Fred	Astaire		Dancer, singer
Bobby	Atchinson		Drums
William	Basie	Count	Piano, bandleader
Louie	Bellson		Drums
Richard Rodney	Bennett		Composer, piano
Shelley	Berman		Humorist
François	Bise		Chef
Art	Blakey	The Old Man; Mash	Drums
Jimmy	Blanton		Bass
Paul	Bocuse		Chef
Jorge	Bolet		Piano
John	Breen		Scientist/piano consultant
Bob	Brookmeyer		Valve trombone

First name	Surname	Nickname(s)	Instrument/significance
Bert	Brown		Bass
Ray	Brown	Mr Slick; Ice-Cream Charlie	Bass
Dave	Brubeck		Piano, composer
Lenny	Bruce		Humorist
Hans Georg	Brunner-Schwer		Recording engineer, entrepreneur
Milt	Buckner		Piano, organ
Anthony	Burgess		Writer
Kenny	Burrell		Guitar
Joe	Bushkin		Piano
Don	Byas		Tenor saxophone
Red	Callender		Bass
Ted and Chris	Campbell		Owners of restaurant/ jazz club, London, Ontario
Johnny	Carson		TV personality/host
Benny	Carter	The King	Alto saxophone, arranger
Lou	Carter		Piano
Dick	Cavett		TV personality/host
Charlie	Christian		Guitar
Alan	Claire	Mr Pretty	Piano
Sonny	Clark		Piano
Bill	Clifton		Piano
Nat	Cole	King	Piano, singer
John	Coltrane	Trane	Tenor and soprano saxophone
Charlie	Combe		Clergyman
Bill	Cosby		Humorist
Al	Cowans		Canadian bandleader
Dorothy	Dandridge		Actress
Eddie	Davis	Lockjaw; Jaws	Tenor saxophone
Rusty	Davis		Canadian TV producer
Paul	de Marky		Concert pianist, piano teacher
Buddy	DeFranco		Clarinet
Paul	Desmond		Alto saxophone
Martin	Drew		Drums
Bobby	Durham	Thug; Jeff	Drums
Clint	Eastwood		Actor, director

First name	Surname	Nickname(s)	Instrument/significance
Harry	Edison	Sweets	Trumpet
Roy	Eldridge	Speedy Gonzales; Little Jazz; The Midgets (*see also* Charlie Shavers)	Trumpet
Edward Kennedy	Ellington	Duke	Bandleader, composer
Herb	Ellis	Herbie	Guitar
Bill	Evans		Piano
Jon	Faddis		Trumpet
Tal	Farlow		Guitar
Maynard	Ferguson		Trumpet
Percy	Ferguson		Canadian bandleader
Ella	Fitzgerald	Fitz; Lady Fitz	Singer
Johnny	Frigo		Violin
Willie	Frukt		Lawyer
Chris	Gage		Piano
Gene	Gammage		Drums
Frank	Gariepy		Drums
Errol	Garner	Oooh-chi-cooo	Piano
George	Gershwin		Composer
Stan	Getz		Tenor saxophone
John Birks	Gillespie	Dizzy; Birks; DG	Trumpet
Fredy	Girardet		Chef
Ron	Goedvolk		Road manager
Al	Gold		Tailor
Paul	Gonsalves		Tenor saxophone
Benny	Goodman		Clarinet, bandleader
Norman	Granz	Smedley	Impresario
Benny	Green		Writer
Freddie	Green		Guitar
Merv	Griffin		TV personality/host
Jeff	Hamilton		Drums
John	Hammond		Impresario
Herbie	Hancock		Piano
Tommy	Harp		JATP road manager
Toni	Harper		Singer
Bill	Harris	The Sheriff	Trombone
(Mr)	Hata		Japanese promoter
Hampton	Hawes		Piano
Coleman	Hawkins	Bean; Hawk	Tenor saxophone

First name	Surname	Nickname(s)	Instrument/significance
Louis	Hayes		Drums
J. C.	Heard	Sweetie Dee	Drums
John	Heard		Bass
Edward	Heath		Statesman, piano
Woody	Herman		Clarinet, bandleader
Eddie	Higgins		Piano
Johnny	Hodges	Rabbit	Alto saxophone
Billie	Holiday	Lady Day	Singer
Major	Holley	Mule	Bass
Johnny	Holmes		Canadian bandleader
Louis	Hooper		Montreal piano teacher
Lesley	Hornby	Twiggy	Model
Lena	Horne		Singer
Freddie	Hubbard		Trumpet
Jim	Hughart		Bass
Milt	Jackson	Bags	Vibraphone
Jean-Baptiste	Jacquet	Illinois	Tenor saxophone
Benny	Johnson		Guitar
Herb	Johnson		Tenor saxophone
J. J.	Johnson		Trombone, composer
Clarence	Jones		Drums
Hank	Jones		Piano
Jimmy	Jones		Piano
Jo	Jones	Daddy	Drums
Quincy	Jones	Q	Trumpet, arranger, producer
Sam	Jones	Mutt	Bass
Buddy	Jordon		Trumpet
Hugh	Joseph		Boss, RCA-Victor (Canadian division)
Connie	Kay		Drums
Wynton	Kelly	Brimsha Man	Piano
Jerome	Kern		Composer
Barney	Kessel	Kess	Guitar
Gene	Krupa		Drums
Scott	LaFaro		Bass
Pinky	Lee		Dancer
Ramsey	Lewis		Piano
Sabine	Lovatelli		Promoter
B.T.	Lundy		Tenor saxophone

First name	Surname	Nickname(s)	Instrument/significance
Kenneth	MacKay		Lawyer
Alan	McLeod		Piano
Carmen	McRae		Singer
Johnny	Mandel		Composer, arranger
James	Mason		Actor
Louis	Metcalf		Bandleader
Charles	Mingus		Bass, composer
Red	Mitchell		Bass
Wes	Montgomery		Guitar
James	Moody		Alto and tenor saxophone, flute
Marlow	Morris		Piano
Art	Morrow		Alto saxophone
George	Mraz		Bass
Gerry	Mulligan		Baritone sax, composer
Phineas	Newborn		Piano
George	Nicholson	Big Nick	Tenor saxophone
Gene	Norman		Impresario
Red	Norvo		Vibraphone
Larry	Novak		Piano
Anita	O'Day		Singer
Claus	Ogerman		Arranger
Niels-Henning	Ørsted Pedersen	NHØP	Bass
Charlie	Parker	(Yard)Bird	Alto saxophone
Michael	Parkinson		TV personality/host
Joe	Pass		Guitar
Bert	Pearl		Singer, piano
Celine	Peterson		Daughter
Charles	Peterson	Chuck	Older brother
Charlotte	Peterson	Charlie	Third wife
Daisy	Peterson	Attila	Older sister
Daniel	Peterson		Father
Fred	Peterson		Oldest brother
Gay	Peterson		Daughter
Joel	Peterson		Son
Kelly	Peterson		Fourth wife
Lillian	Peterson	Big Scotia	First wife
Lynn	Peterson		Daughter
May	Peterson		Younger sister
Norman	Peterson		Son

First name	Surname	Nickname(s)	Instrument/significance
Olive	Peterson		Mother
Oscar Jr	Peterson		Son
Sandy	Peterson		Second wife
Sharon	Peterson		Daughter
Oscar	Pettiford		Bass
Flip	Phillips	Frick (of Frick and Frack— Flip and Oscar)	Tenor saxophone
Cole	Porter		Composer
Bud	Powell		Piano
Mel	Powell		Piano
André	Previn		Piano, composer, conductor
Ray	Price		Drums
Gene	Puerling		Singer, composer
Collie	Ramsay		Piano
Bobby	Redmonds		Tenor saxophone
Buddy	Rich		Drums
Max	Roach		Drums
Austin	Roberts	Vivy	Bass
Rufus	Rockhead		Montreal club-owner
Bob	Rudd		Bass
Mort	Sahl		Humorist
Ed	Sarkesian		Detroit club-owner
Bill	Sawyer		Clarinet
Bobby	Scott	Bobby Sox	Piano
Ronnie	Scott	The Rev	Tenor saxophone, humorist, club-owner
George	Sealy		Tenor saxophone
Hughie	Sealy		Alto saxophone
Charlie	Shavers	The Midgets (see also Roy Eldridge)	Trumpet
Horace	Silver		Piano
John Haley	Sims	Zoot, Scooter	Tenor saxophone
Charlie	Smith		Drums
Hezekiel Leroy Gordon	Smith	Stuff	Violin
Pat	Smythe		Piano
Jeri	Southern		Singer, piano
Sonny	Stitt	String	Alto and tenor saxophone

First name	Surname	Nickname(s)	Instrument/significance
Billy	Strayhorn	Sweetpea	Composer
Edwina	Swope	Mom	Landlady
Art	Tatum	T; Mr T	Piano
Billy	Taylor		Piano
Frank	Tenot		Promoter
Clark	Terry	Chief Bogen	Trumpet, flugelhorn
Ed	Thigpen	Thags	Drums
Billy	Thomas		Canadian bandmaster
Pierre	Trudeau		Canadian prime minister
Joe	Turner		Blues singer
Sarah	Vaughan	Sassy	Singer
Steep	Wade		Piano
Ulf	Wakenius		Guitar
Aaron	Walker	T-Bone	Blues singer, guitar
Thomas	Waller	Fats	Piano, composer
Jiro	Watanabe	Butch	Trombone
Ralph	Watkins		Owner, Basin Street East jazz club, NYC
Ben	Webster	Frog	Tenor saxophone
George	Wein		Impresario
Al	Williams		Restaurateur
John	Williams		Guitar
Gerald	Wilson		Composer, arranger
Teddy	Wilson		Piano
Jonathan	Winters		Humorist
Joe	Woldarsky		Manager, Alberta Lounge, Montreal
David	Young		Bass
Lester	Young	Pres	Tenor saxophone

To my mother and father, Olive and Daniel Peterson,

and to

Roy McMurtry, present Chief Justice of Ontario, who decisively
assisted my efforts to persuade TV companies to feature more
ethnics in their sponsorship programmes

and to

Norman Granz (1918–2001), my mentor and lifelong friend

PART ONE

THE KEY TO OSCAR

CANADA

1

BEGINNINGS

I can't truthfully recall my very first meeting with the piano but I am sure that it was characterized by the kind of practical curiosity prevalent in most five-year-old children, followed almost immediately by sheer uninterest. I say this simply because most children of that age, regardless of musical talents and capabilities, tend to look on any musical instrument as a passing fancy or perhaps something that should only be used as an attention-getter. They are keen to play at the precise time that visitors are in the home attempting to carry on a conversation, or Pop has high-tailed off to bed with an overpowering headache.

My view of the piano and my Dad's view differed: he had already decided that he was going to raise a musical family. This was decided on his own without any reference to the family's views, certainly not mine. As an immediate result all the members of the Peterson clan became his musical students. This included my oldest brother Fred, my older sister Daisy, my next older brother Charles, my younger sister May, and, of course, me. We were all started on the piano by Papa Peterson and were expected to make reasonable progress, based totally upon his evaluation.

My Dad was born in St Croix in the Virgin Islands and was a seaman by profession—a boatswain's mate to be exact. It was during his voyages that he bought himself a small organ for his own amusement and taught himself to play. On one of his journeys to Canada he met my mother, Olive, whose original home was St Kitts in the British West Indies. They decided to marry and settle in Montreal to raise a family. Mum had emigrated to Canada at the tender age of 16, at the request of an English family who wanted her to accompany them as their cook and housekeeper. This she did diligently, and continued to work until some of us reached our early teens. My mother was a hard-working person who took her employment very seriously, but most importantly she devoted countless hours to the rearing of her brood.

It is only now that I truly realize how much of her life she sacrificed in trying to be a good housewife and mother. She spared nothing in trying to establish total communication with her children. She was a woman of great sensitivity and understanding, with very deeply rooted religious beliefs. Those were the days when ministers and doctors visited homes on a regular basis, and it was always a very special occasion when our Reverend would come to the house to spend an hour or two drinking tea while reassuring my Mum about her beliefs in the religious system. If she knew in advance of his arrival, she would flutter around the house gathering "fresh apparel" for any of us who happened to be home during the intended visit. Then she would hurriedly refresh herself and, to put it in her vernacular, "throw on a clean dress" for his visit. This could sometimes even entail some ironing, and a lot of shaking out.

Somehow she managed her household with a firm yet loving hand —a feat that was not too easily done considering the fact that my Dad would be away on trips for the Canadian Pacific Railway, which was now his employer. He would be away, depending on his "run," for periods ranging from overnight to 14 days (Montreal–Vancouver–Montreal). During his time on the road my mother managed to keep everything running on some kind of schedule while meeting and overcoming any unforeseen obstacles that presented themselves.

During this period of my life I must confess, as I stated earlier, that my primary interests rested elsewhere than at the piano; important things like Cowboys and Indians, street baseball, and tag took precedence in my life over that brute of an instrument that stood in the living-room and dominated at least an hour a day of my precious free time. I took great exception to this and proceeded to conjure up ways of extricating myself from this irksome schedule that had been forced on me. And when I discovered that Dad's job involved his being away for such long periods, I realized that my practice burden was not insoluble after all! If I could somehow devise a plan which spared me such tedious routine, while also allowing me to escape all the lumps I knew would await me when Pop returned home, I would be, as the saying goes, "in front and running well."

Pop had set up a routine that involved all of us learning some scales, exercises, and pieces. It was this that made my scheme feasible. It would not work at all on the short one-to-three-day trips, but it would work beautifully on the long western trips to Winnipeg, Calgary, Edmonton, and Vancouver. We all had the same assignments and we all had to sign "the book" at the end of each of our hour's practice session. It was at this point that I noticed how extremely dedicated my sister Daisy seemed to be, and also how very exact she was in her mode of practice. She would go over each segment of the piece time and time again until she was note-perfect. By the same token I discovered that I had a very good memory and a pretty good ear. (It turned out later that I had what some people call absolute or perfect pitch, meaning that without looking at the keyboard I was able to tell exactly which notes had been played and in which order.) Because of these attributes I was able to leave any serious practice until perhaps two or three days before my Dad's return, thus allowing myself a lot more time for some of the more important things I had previously been unable to attend to.

As soon as Dad was back, he would call us one-by-one to the piano for the moment of truth, so to speak. He usually started with the oldest, Fred, and worked his way down to the youngest, May. I would generally sit and listen to the others go through their lessons, not only out of curiosity, but also to brush up mentally on any details that had become hazy in my last-minute rehearsals.

At one point Daisy came up with her own plan to defeat the licks that we received for wrong notes. One day she padded her back with newspapers and marched in for her lesson. Dad asked her to play her assignment and she launched into her performance. She was usually a bundle of nerves and even though she basically knew her work, she would make an uncharacteristic number of mistakes for which she would receive the appropriate number of licks from Pop. Quite naturally, like any other youngster, she would cry. However, on this day she proceeded to giggle with each hit until she was virtually in a fit of laughter. This dumbfounded Dad and he didn't know quite what route to take; it wasn't until he happened to hear the rustle of newspaper on one stroke that he became wise, and had to laugh himself.

My scheme stood me in good stead for quite some time and it was not until my mother insisted that I had been continually signing "the book" without practising that Dad finally decided to throw a monkey-wrench into the works. From that day on, he handed out different assignments to each of us and thus immediately negated my routine: not only was I no longer able to memorize Daisy's practice routines but I was also forced to really do my own practice periods or suffer the consequences. Oh well, the best-laid plans . . .

I have now come to realize how tight our family unit was in those early days (certainly compared to some family units I see today). For not only did we play with one another in a musical sense, but we also worked and helped one another over the rough spots. I can remember being in tears the night before my Dad's return because I was unable to figure out some part of my assignment. I can also vividly remember Daisy, or Fred, or someone in the family coming to my aid and spending the necessary time with me in order to set things straight.

Speaking of Fred, I have to say that in my estimation he was the most gifted pianist of all of us. It was from him that I received my first awareness of jazz, and I still feel that had he not been taken from us at the age of 16 through tuberculosis, he would have ruled the jazz-piano world to this day, had he so chosen. I can see him at the piano now, with his long, lean fingers playing to his heart's content, not even realizing how good he really was or, sadly, how sick he was at that time. I still look up to him today and still feel the loss of my big brother.

It was into this close family unit that a musician by the name of Billy Thomas made his entrance. All that I can remember about him was that he was a bandmaster and he was at that time the lightest-skinned Negro that I had ever seen. Relatively small, he nevertheless had a huge temper and when crossed would go cherry-red in the face, which never ceased to amaze me. No one ever made decisions for Bill. His word was final and so when he decided that I should be playing the cornet in the band, no one disputed him. (I should mention that all of us were tutored on more than one instrument at a time: I studied trumpet and piano, Daisy trombone and piano, and my brothers assorted brass instruments and piano.)

"The band" primarily comprised my family, augmented by a group of local people who had got together to form an orchestra of sorts and met almost every Thursday evening for rehearsal at our house. Please don't ask me why *our* house. That's probably what Bill decided! Nevertheless, I began to learn the cornet and became thoroughly entranced with this shiny instrument with all the tubes and the pearl-topped valves. It was always an instrument of wonder to me and I was forever toying with it even when I was not playing it. These instruments were loaned to us by the community centre and we were totally responsible for their upkeep. Once, however, my brother Chuck and I decided to repair some instruments that didn't need repair. We unscrewed the valves and tried exchanging them one with the other. Of course they didn't fit, so we decided that they were out of alignment. With the aid of my mother's wooden darning egg, we proceeded to bang the imaginary lumps that we thought we saw on the valves into proper shape. Needless to say, from that moment on nothing fit anything. Upon her return from work, my mother was horrified at the mess we'd made and darkly foresaw the bum-kicking we would receive when Dad returned from his latest journey.

The strange world of brass enchanted me. The first thing I noticed was that there was only one line of musical matter to contend with, compared with the two clefs that I had to deal with in learning the piano. I was also fascinated with the fact that a horn player could hold a note at one volume, or, if he desired at some point along the way, increase or decrease it. Not so on the piano. Also, I had the choice of using vibrato if desired, which also was not available on the keyboard. At this time such things seemed terribly romantic and mysterious. It was also an exhilarating experience to be a member of a brass section and to learn how to phrase along with other players. It gave me a tremendous sense of really belonging to the orchestra, as opposed to plunking away in isolation at a keyboard. Belonging was the name of the game for me at that age. This went on for some time during which, on various occasions, I became a featured soloist on certain numbers.

All seemed to be going well when suddenly the Peterson family had a major cave-in. Fred took ill with some mysterious disease that seemed to have the doctors baffled. Before I realized what was going on, the health authorities visited the house and almost immediately my sister Daisy and I were whisked off to the hospital. TB had ravaged our home. Things got rapidly worse: Fred succumbed to the disease, and I suddenly realized that my stay at the Montreal Children's Hospital was not going to be a short one.

A year and one month later I was finally released, and returned home to continue my musical studies. The first shock that I received was when my doctor informed my parents that the playing of any wind instrument was so unwise as to be out of the question. The second was that Dad's attitude about learning music had not changed and he appeared to be as hard-nosed as usual. I suppose he considered this a necessary part of my recovery. Deciding that it was not worth the struggle to try to best him, I reluctantly gave in to him. As I progressed in this next phase of my musical life a strange new attitude slowly seemed to be overcoming me, and I sensed a revitalized interest in the piano. Perhaps it was my total removal from the music world that made me realize how much it had become a part of my life, and how central it was to become in my existence. Whatever it was that took place, I decided to go along with it all and see exactly how it would work out for me. The answer was not long in coming.

2

EARLY TEACHERS

During my early childhood days I can't say that I had any real difficulties or periods of uneasiness. I spent the usual amount of time playing as any normal child did. I laughed, argued, and fought the battles that all children do. The only period that seemed unusual to me was my stay in the Montreal Children's Hospital. I had suddenly been displaced from my home and trundled into a strange antiseptic environment that I had no relation to or feeling for.

My first reaction was to sink into a period of detached non-communication, not only with the staff but also with the other youngsters in the ward. I remained almost totally silent, except for answering any necessary questions asked of me. I played quietly by myself and slept more than the other children, in order not to have to communicate. This brought on an even greater sense of caring from the staff and led them to conclude that I was just a silent well-behaved youngster. Around this time, a charitable organization donated a huge box of toys to our ward; the *pièce de résistance* was a large chrome tractor. The staff decided that it would go up on the table in the middle of the ward for a week, at the end of which it would be awarded to the best-behaved child. My strategy was simple: I continued the behaviour-pattern I'd adopted since my arrival—utter silence. Come the end of the week, it was unanimously agreed that I be given the tractor!

Shortly after this I became acclimatized to my new environment and resumed my normal behaviour. In the ward there was a box of wool that had been donated to help us learn how to knit. I didn't see myself as a knitting person, and thought that the wool could be put to better use; accordingly, I festooned the ward with it, diligently trimming every wall. This effort, and a few more anti-hospital acts, earned me my first spanking from one of the doctors.

The nurses all seemed to take to me; most of all, the night staff really loved me—partly due to my folding huge piles of dressings for them, saving them a fair bit of drudgery. I became very proficient at this and thus became their darling, being favoured with extra hot chocolate and biscuits after the other children had gone to sleep.

After my release from hospital I re-adjusted quickly and continued my life at home. It was then that my Dad decided that, musically, we were getting beyond his powers of instruction and needed outside help. I was leery of this new turn: for the life of me I couldn't understand why I had to be taught by a total stranger. It became a private sore in my musical life, and I suspiciously wondered what the eventual outcome would be.

My first teacher was a lady whom I found charming and pretty, but not to be taken very seriously. She seemed too easily impressed by what I already knew, and many of our lessons would start by my showing her what I was privately working on. She would half-heartedly ask for the scales and some of the exercises she had left for me to learn, only to curtail the lesson with "Oh well, I'm sure you've been through all these items," and ask me to go back to my own pieces. Often she would stop me, saying, "Wait, wait! Show me that once more." Initially this pleased me no end, but I soon got bored with it, and told my parents that I was not getting anything out of the lessons. Money was hard to come by in those days and waste could not be tolerated, so it was not long before I was introduced to my new piano teacher. Exit one bemused lady, enter Professor Louis Hooper Snr.

By the time he entered my life Professor Hooper was a distinguished figure in the Montreal music community, well known as a piano teacher and also actively engaged in jazz. It was this that made me particularly keen for our lessons to get under way. At last the day arrived; precisely at four o'clock on a Thursday afternoon, Lou Hooper arrived at my house for our first get-together.

He was a fairly tall man, immaculately but not over-dressed for the occasion, handsome, with slightly greying hair and a warm smile. He said a very friendly "Good afternoon, Oscar," seated himself in the chair next to the piano while motioning me to the piano seat, and immediately got down to business. "Let's see what we can learn about this marvellous instrument." Almost before I knew what was taking place, we were flying through major and minor scales and arpeggios at an unbelievable rate.

Then we came to the point in the lesson which dealt with actual pieces; it was here that I gained my first real insight about communicating with the instrument. Professor Hooper listened attentively to my performances, then politely asked me to allow him to sit to the piano. He replayed the pieces that I had just played (or so I thought!) and while effortlessly doing so offered comments such as, "You know, Oscar, I have always felt that Chopin was looking at a lovely landscape at the time he composed this piece because everything about it is so lush and green-like" or "Franz Liszt must have been feeling his own strength at this point because as we play it we can almost feel the transmission of power from his music to us."

These comments affected me deeply, causing me to take an entirely new look at what I had been playing. I have used this approach at various times with students whom I felt had lost that dimension in their playing, and it has proved gratifyingly successful. Thank you, Lou, wherever you are!

Before I had fully taken in all that had happened at my first lesson, Professor Hooper stood up, wrote out a receipt, shook my hand, smiled, and vanished from the building. Our lessons proceeded well, and once I had accepted the need to respond in full to his efforts by learning the assignments he left me, we enjoyed a great association. Eventually I plucked up the courage to ask him about his jazz playing; he gave that marvellous smile and said, "I've been waiting for you to get around to that, young man." He hesitated for a moment and then went on, "I'll tell you what: I'll play one of the jazz pieces that I know if you play one of yours in return. Agreed?"

Now uncontrollably curious, I of course said "Yes." He sat down and played one of the prettiest ballads I had ever heard, then got up: "It's your turn." I responded by playing a piece I felt comfortable with, and once into it gave it my all. At the end I turned and looked over my shoulder at Professor Hooper as he stood silent. He had his chin cupped in the palm of his right hand and was looking at me oddly. He simply said, "Interesting, interesting." Puzzled, I didn't pursue it further, but I felt he had made some kind of decision about me.

That turned out to be true, for several weeks later, at the end of another lesson, he asked to speak to my Dad. He told him that he didn't think he could take me any further in the direction that I should and would go. Despite Dad's pleas, he stuck to his decision, adding that it would be better for me to have some more specialized help and tuition, for that would allow me to attain the heights he thought me capable of.

This came as a shock to me. I had come to love this gentle, congenial statesman of the piano. He had brought into my life a new-found understanding of how best to interpret a musical selection; he had also made me much more aware of the delicacy and beauty of the instrument. Even today, when people are moved at my performance of a ballad, my thoughts go back to that debonair and subtle gentleman, for Professor Louis Hooper went out of my life, as the Ellington song has it, *All Too Soon*.

3

MY DAD: DANIEL PETERSON

Around the age of 10, I experienced quite a period of frustration and indecision. I was attempting to cope with schoolwork, friendships, and family relationships, while being discontented with my musical progress, particularly in the direction that I thought I should be going. I suppose like any other youngster I was suffering from the dawning of adolescence. My school years were, for the most part, enjoyable and even challenging; somehow I even managed to become an honour student and ended up in a three-way race for a scholarship to high school. I suppose that I have always enjoyed competition in any shape or form, with school being no exception.

During these years, my Dad kept a watchful eye on his children's progress—or lack thereof. As soon as he discovered that I had some scholastic prowess, he quietly zeroed in on exactly what was going on educationally with me, and of course he made it plain to me that he was watching my every move.

Needless to say, he oversaw all of his children's schoolwork with unwavering attention. He went out and bought a huge book on mathematics, from which he would assign work to each of us over and above our regular schoolwork. Tedious and unfair I thought then; it was not until later in my life that I grew to appreciate his thinking. Here was a man from another country so concerned about his kids' education that he was willing to spend his own precious time to try to ensure their musical and educational well-being, even after his wearing trips on the CPR. I wonder how many parents today stand ready to make that kind of commitment?

My Dad was a very special person to me because although he was quite a powerful man, he was in essence very gentle and quiet, choosing only to show his anger as a last resort. There is one thing I must say about him, however. When the breaking point was finally reached with him, there was no return.

For instance, at a relatively early age, I had learned some famous cuss words that kids sooner or later learn, and was dying to try them out on someone. As fate would have it I could not find anyone except—who else?—Mum! Upon my return home from school I had misgivings as to whether or not I would be able to try out my new-found treasures because Mum was in the highest of spirits. I waited and waited, and even attempted some antagonization. All to no avail. Mum just kept singing her favourite hymn, as was her custom, and went on her merry way. The opportunity finally presented itself just after supper, prior to bedtime. Mum would decide that it was necessary to perform a good wash job on us, especially in areas such as our ears and "privates," as she called our personal areas, and it was then that I decided to take offence at her efforts. I objected to being washed and opened up with a quick and terse volley of invectives that I am sure were all out of context, however convincing they sounded to me. To my shocked surprise absolutely nothing happened. Mum merely increased the volume of the hymn and continued on her sanitation task. After mulling this over I decided to really lay a volley on her, this time thinking that she would certainly jump up with surprise. No such thing. All that happened was that she merely clasped me even more tightly to her and, in a very loving way, murmured simply about how "God loves and forgives all." After which she put me to bed and kissed me goodnight, as was her custom.

The next day I was off to school to tell my closest friend how his "new vocabulary" had gone. At noon, as usual, I returned home for lunch and asked Mum for $2.00 to buy running shoes. She quietly replied that she was short of cash at the moment and I should go upstairs and ask Dad, who had returned from one of his journeys just that morning. I romped upstairs into Dad's bedroom, kissed him as he lay listening to the radio, and told him about the money I needed to take back to school for the shoes after lunch. He nodded and told me to take a seat. This I did unsuspectingly as he got up from the bed and proceeded to close the door. I still didn't think anything unusual about this until too late. I noticed that as the door swung shut "the strap" was on the back of the door knob. My only recourse was to make a headlong dive under the bed, which I did. My Dad calmly took a seat and asked me to repeat some of the language to him that I had used on my Mum the night before. Still being of sane mind, and wishing to remain so, I refused. He informed me that I had a choice. I could come out and take my lumps like a man or I could wait it out, be late for school (which meant death), and suffer the consequences. I refused both alternatives and decided to wait for the passing of the storm. Wrong move! All of a sudden Dad decided to take direct action, and reached down and in one move swept all of the covers from the bed (a double one at that). He then proceeded to remove the mattress and the spring-base effortlessly, or so it seemed to me, which then left me totally unprotected in what was now a corral of punishment. He methodically administered the licking I deserved, told me to get to school immediately before I was late, and pressed $2.00 in my hand for running shoes. My Dad was a man of few words.

He was also a direct man who dealt with things in the only way he knew how—head-on. He faced them squarely and accepted all the consequences of his actions. To understand him fully, one needs to know a bit about his background.

He was a man of very high ideals, which in my mother's view stemmed from his life having been a far from easy one. In later life he told me that he'd been forced to run away from school because of a fracas of some sort in the classroom in St Croix. He took to sea, eventually becoming a boatswain; I cannot remember the name of the shipping company he worked for, but from the things he told me it seems he sailed on some kind of freighter. This was in the 1920s, and for a black man to rise to the position of boatswain in a white shipping line was hardly normal.

During this time, as a relief from the rigours of work at sea, he bought that portable pump-organ mentioned earlier and taught himself the rudiments of music. Upon his arrival in Canada, he met my Mum, married her, and settled in Montreal. He took various jobs as a labourer until gravitating to the work that claimed or attracted so many blacks during that period in Canada: the railroad. Like many families they struggled through the Depression, and had just enough to start raising a family.

Dad's belief in his family was total, but his way of mobilizing its strength and power was far from obvious. As a youngster in school I had the usual problems with guys who were bigger and tougher than I was. Sometimes I had to take lumps, but increasingly I resorted to the solution most kids choose when frightened of getting their heads swollen: I ran. It was on one such Olympic run, while being pursued by a kid called Butch (his physique and presence fully lived up to his name) that my Dad appeared as if from nowhere, picked me up by the collar and inquired where I was going in such haste. When I explained what was going on, he put me down and said in an unruffled tone, "You've got your choice: either you whip him or you're going to have to find a way to whip me." Well, I couldn't figure any way of whipping Dad, so Butch reaped the harvest: the next time to took after me I doled out some awful lumps to him. That was Dad's way of protecting his family and ensuring his children's growth.

I recall that he came home once and started writing a "statement" for the railroad. Such a fully documented report was required when anything unusual had occurred during a trip. On this occasion Dad had travelled west on one of his regular runs for Canadian Pacific, and had been "bumped"—superseded by another porter with greater seniority who wanted that particular trip for himself. As a result, Dad had to "dead head" it, returning from Vancouver to Montreal without a car or passengers to look after—which, of course, meant no work to do and no tips.

Later, in war time, military personnel were often on board, and Dad ran up against a fairly high-ranking officer who had been really laying into the sauce. He kept coming into Dad's car and addressing him as "George"—the most hated racist insult at that time. Even though he was repeatedly informed that the car was not in service and that he was not supposed to be there anyway, he persisted in his taunting, and eventually drew his sidearm and threatened to blow Dad's head off. He continued his tirade as Dad quietly got up, walked to one end of the car, locked the door, returned, and did the same at the other end. The insults continued until, suddenly, Dad not only disarmed the officer, but also meted out a certain amount of physical pain in the process. I remember how proud I felt at Dad's handling of such racism, because by now, as a young man, I knew all too well that some of the taunts I received were a long way from being playful.

Beneath his serious exterior, Dad had a mischievous sense of humour which surfaced more than occasionally. He was a master of sleight of hand, and enjoyed causing friends' personal belongings to disappear. My great friend and musical confrère Ray Brown was one of the few to recognize the leprechaun that was part of Dad's nature, and they became great friends. Ray enjoyed nothing more than baiting my Dad verbally in a way I would never do; this led to various articles mysteriously disappearing from Ray's person, forcing him to go to my Dad and repent. They really cared for each other.

The only major sadness I feel about my relationship with Dad is that he died shortly before I really "got the handle" on my career. I took him on a trip to Toronto during the very early Trio days, and vividly remember how proud he was when people came over to see him after I'd announced his presence. He was in my view an outstanding man: although he wasn't able to fulfill his own dreams of success, he lived long enough to see his dreams fulfilled vicariously through his children's musical achievements and public recognition.

4

THE FORMATIVE YEARS

As mentioned earlier, my school years were basically happy. I managed to do well in my studies—because of rather than in spite of my efforts elsewhere, perhaps. I had an excellent rapport with most of my teachers. I believe that this was because children of West Indian heritage understood that to be disobedient in any way at school could quite possibly result in a stay at the intensive care unit of the nearest hospital! Obviously, that's an exaggeration; nevertheless, it was deeply imprinted on most West Indian kids' minds that any kind of disrespect at school would not be tolerated. We were taught that our teachers were people of special merit put there to enlighten us, and were to be given the same respect as our parents enjoyed from us. One of my most dreaded fears during my school days was that I might have to bring a note home to my parents from my teacher. Luckily for me it never happened!

My involvement in music never interfered with my days at school until I was into my teens. Most of my music teachers at school became aware that I had a greater understanding of what they were trying to teach than the other children did; however, they never made a big deal about it, but would simply try me out with a few further questions.

During most of this time I was without the aid of an outside teacher; my sister Daisy assumed that position almost without my noticing it. One would think that having been through the same practice hassle in earlier times, Daisy would handle my case leniently— but guess what? She immediately decided to go the other way on me, reading me a speech about being my older sister and not wanting me to think that I was going to slide by her with any tricks. I could hardly believe it: here was the lady who had padded her back with newspaper reading me the riot act about no fun and games! Nevertheless, after realizing that she was adamant, I settled down to study with her and found my working understanding of the instrument rapidly increased.

Daisy is a very special person. She is a member of that rare breed who believes that with hard work and an ability to fathom what you are working hard for, your goal can be achieved. In other words, Daisy gave me the one thing that has steadfastly sustained me throughout my career: dedication. While too nervous to perform publicly, she has a musical knowledge, talent, and sensitivity that enable her to instill the will to overcome the many pitfalls and mountains that litter the path of every striving and impatient student. To this very day this great gift of hers continues to nourish students and sustain their creative belief.

Her next step was typical: she enrolled not only herself but, without my knowledge, me too in the Conservatory of Music in Montreal. When I asked her what it involved, she blithely explained it all away by giving me the requirements for the entry exam (which I promptly put out of my mind), and proceeded to settle down for the summer to prepare herself. I, of course, had more important things to attend to.

Before I knew it the summer had passed, and there she was serving notice on me that I had approximately one week before the trials. Still no panic, plenty of time. Two days before the exam she tried to impress on me how late it was getting; somehow I still managed to tell myself that there was no sweat.

On the night before the tests, I decided to take a first look at the chosen performance pieces. At the piano I opened up the book, and for what seemed like an eternity I sat there, frozen. To my horror I was confronted by an array of notes set up in an order that defied playing, let alone memorizing. I could not play what I saw! Nevertheless, there they were and so I decided to take a peek at the following pages— perhaps there might be some help elsewhere. It got worse! Whoever composed this stuff was getting madder as they went along, and by the last page it was clear to me that the composer was a raving maniac. I closed the book and decided right there and then that it was all over for me. I went to Daisy and told her that there was no way, but with her usual undauntable resolve, she said, "Look, just go up there anyway and do your best. They cannot fault you for that." That's my Daisy!

Why I ever let her talk me into even appearing at the trials the next day I will never know, but the next morning found me sitting amongst the candidates. As I sat there a strange thing started to take place. I started to lose my nervousness and assume a kind of bravado: I was almost anxious for them to get to me. (Some people enjoy torture, they tell me.) However, when they finally called my name I was in a mood of rare antagonism towards the panel, and walked on with an air of belligerence.

That soon vanished when they called for the first selection, for I made the serious mistake of trying to sight-read it. Sight-reading had never been my strong suit anyway, and this particular task was not unlike attempting to unscramble a Tibetan marriage ritual word for word. After coming to a very abrupt stop from sheer frustration, I recall a voice in the darkened auditorium asking for the second selection. Did I learn anything from my experience? No, of course not! I went once more on the trail attempting to decipher the Galilean war codes—same ending!

Finally, after a deafening silence, a voice from the darkened room asked, "Is there any reason why you didn't learn your commitment?"

"Didn't have enough time," I replied.

"Why not?"

"I was busy playing another kind of music," was my proud reply.

"What kind of music?"

"Jazz." These snobs weren't going to put down my music.

To my surprise they asked me to play some of this special music for them, and I complied with a jazz version of a Gershwin tune. The voices from the dark then asked for more of my kind of music, and again I complied. There was a further silence, punctuated by intermittent whisperings, and then they asked me if I had pitch.

It was at this juncture that I decided that I should have my turn at bat. "Pitch?" I asked in my most puzzled tone. With this, a woman came to the rostrum and stood by the piano. Without any further questions, they explained to me the procedure they intended to use in the test, which entailed me standing apart from the piano with my back turned to it so that I could not see the keyboard. With some sort of signal the test began. The woman struck a note and they waited for my supposed guess. I played it for all it was worth time-wise and squeezed out a timid "C!" There was silence and then another note was struck— another pregnant pause; "F sharp?" came the answering question. Then another note, another hesitated answer, and so on until finally we got into the multiple notes. Finally an exasperated voice from the darkened hall said, "You may not know what pitch is, but you sure have it. Step down, please!" I left the stage knowing that I had failed the test, but feeling gratified that at least they knew I had great ears!

The result of that little examination to get into the classical world? I passed and yet they failed Daisy!

During the time that Daisy was working with me on the classical side of my training, I engaged in a massive struggle of my own to gain a better understanding of jazz piano. I felt that I had the ability to grasp the fundamental principles of the medium, but as an adolescent, impatient, and confused student of the form, it all became a huge maze in which I could not find a proper path. I spent many, many frustrated hours at the piano in an endeavour to put myself on course, but nothing worked. In the meantime, I became a devoted listener and fan of Teddy Wilson.

I found out through my Dad's love of the radio that bands such as Benny Goodman's were broadcast from various hotels late at night. One night Dad had dropped off to sleep and left his radio on, and I heard this incredible jazz solo being played. I strained in order to hear the name of the player, but the radio faded out for a moment or two and all that I managed to hear was that it was the Benny Goodman Orchestra, and they were broadcasting from the Sherman or some such hotel. I decided to wait until Pop was out on the road to try my luck at listening. Sure enough, a few nights later while he was away I tiptoed downstairs to the living-room and turned our large radio on ever-so-softly. With my ear pressed tightly against the speaker so I would not have to play it too loudly and waken everybody in the house, I ever-so-slowly started moving the dial, searching for the sound of that big band, for the announcer had said that they would be broadcasting all week from the hotel. Suddenly my search came to an end. Here without doubt was that beautiful soloist that I had heard just nights before. He was in the middle of a tune that I was hearing for the first time: *Where Or When*.

As a youngster who was in the throes of personal musical upheaval, I welcomed the discovery of Teddy Wilson as a guiding light in the midst of a gale. I could not believe the polished inventiveness of this man. His approach to the piano was the embodiment of all that Professor Lou Hooper had attempted to instill in me. Teddy had such a huge talent that even when he played and improvised on songs that I didn't know, I was given to believe that I had a working knowledge of them. When he played, I could feel his love of the instrument flowing through every phrase and run, that impeccable touch giving a crystalline sound to what he played. He could swing so hard at times that the pulsation was almost overwhelming. Yet on other occasions he would touch a song with such delicacy that each note became like a single raindrop. This was it! This was exactly the form and direction that I needed in order to continue on my own in the jazz world. It was a very special sort of talent that Teddy had on the instrument; I became a dedicated Teddy Wilson fan, and lived for those nights by myself in the living-room that came all too seldom and passed so quickly.

By now I approached my own practice sessions with a new vigour and resolve, and spent many hours working to achieve that subtle ease and delivery that seemed such a normal part of Teddy's being. I wanted it to be a part of mine also.

5

SUBCULTURES AND BIGOTRY

During my academic years, I became acquainted with the caste system. I was first taught that this system originally existed in India, and was a way of attaining position and economic superiority within that culture. I soon found that a similar system exists within the structure of most ethnic societies, although if we were to quiz the people within these groups I am almost positive they would deny its existence.

Originally I attended the Anglican Church over which Reverend Combe presided. This was essentially a white church with a mostly white congregation. Later I became more and more involved with the Union United Church, which was peopled by the black community. I attended Sunday school there, went to church picnics, performed at church concerts, and met the girl who would become my first bride.

Things seemed to run quite normally in the black community: like many other black youngsters, I participated in various events under the guidance of my parents, and regarded them with unremarkable adolescent naïveté. It was not until I took a much closer look that I came to realize there was a definite, albeit unspoken, pecking order in our own community, and I still remember the outrage I felt when I realized it was based on the tone of an individual's skin—exactly the same bigoted pattern that I was to experience later in the Caucasian business world, which operated on the premise of "White is bright." Substitute the word "light" for "white," and you have an approximation of what I sensed to be taking place in our community. An outstanding case in point was the Negro Community Centre's attempt to hold music classes under an appointed teacher. I became more and more incensed as I watched while my sister Daisy, whom I considered to be without peer as a qualified music teacher in the black community, was continually bypassed for other people whom I knew were less qualified and less accomplished.

I watched this take place not only in our church, but also in other aspects of community life; it served only to weaken and dissect the black community. At social functions, the controlling power usually rested with someone of a fairer skin tone, and I can recall hearing the varied rumblings about "He or she only got that appointment because they're light-skinned." This outlook siphoned its way down to the ritual of dating; most parents would caution their offspring about dating someone lighter than they were. Should the male happen to be mulatto, and his date darker than he was, the female would be warned not to allow herself to be debased, even though it might be expected of her simply because of her darker skin tone. In the case of the male being darker, the warning was that "She will take you for everything you've got and certainly will expect more of you because you are darker than she is." This was an outgrowth of bigotry that many blacks, regardless of their facial tone, expected within the white environment. I am sure that in those days many Negroes, very aware of their colour, were unable to understand where their inalienable human rights were, and learned to expect this inner cult suppression without reacting to it except in extreme cases of emotional strife or upheaval—a fundamental example of human disorientation and disenfranchisement within a social structure. The irony of it all is that not too many years later, the "in" motto became "Black Is Beautiful," and these same people suddenly began to experience a new-found pride in being a deeper shade. However, even such an increase in ego and dignity could not entirely wipe away the deeply rooted scars caused by not only white oppression, but also self-imposed gradations within the black community itself.

Sundays were ritualistic days in my family's life. It was a foregone conclusion that you arose and prepared yourself for church in the morning. All the good "Sunday-Come-To-Meeting" clothes came out on that day. It was also expected that your behaviour would be toned down—there would be no wild games or screaming or shouting around the house, in deference to the sanctity of the day. After church came lunch and then it was off to Sunday school, which never made any sense to me: after the early morning church service, Sunday school always seemed like overkill! Next on the agenda was preparing to attend the regular meeting at 4.30 p.m. at the UNIA, or, to give it its full name, the Universal Negro Improvement Association.

Our family became deeply immersed in this organization when its leaders discovered that we all played various musical instruments: we were then expected to perform a small musical portion of the Sunday program that preceded the various speeches. Like any youngster aged eight and over, I objected to my time being spoken for, especially when the good weather came and I knew that the other kids were out chasing baseballs and girls. The UNIA represented something of much greater importance and inspiration to the adults of that era than it did to many of us youngsters. I remember numerous discussions after these meetings by the adults in which it became very clear to me that their social consciences had been tweaked by several of the guest speakers. They had local speakers, others from more distant parts of Canada, and even some from the United States, England, and the West Indies. Of these, the most inspiring was without a doubt a man named Marcus Garvey.*

---

*Marcus Mosiah Garvey (1887–1940) was born in St Ann's Bay, Jamaica, and died in London. He founded and led the Universal Negro Improvement Association (UNIA), the largest black nationalist organization ever seen, with its headquarters in New York City and branches across the United States and Canada, with

I still remember my parents' excitedly expectant muttering prior to his arrival—"Marcus Garvey is coming to speak to us," they would say. "He'll find some solution to the wrongdoings and oppression that we suffer," was another comment one might easily hear before his visits. The UNIA was run by a dedicated couple by the name of Mr and Mrs Tucker. It became customary prior to Mr Garvey's visit for one or both of the Tuckers to drop by our home to make certain that some, if not all, of the Peterson children would be performing on that very auspicious Sunday afternoon. I vividly recall the pretty face of Mrs Tucker with her soft-spoken, slow, thoughtful, and carefully delivered words. "I hope we are going to be honoured with some of the marvellous Peterson music when Mr Garvey comes," she would say. After receiving assurances (and tea and cookies) she would depart, secure in the knowledge that the proper musical preface to the great words of Marcus Garvey had been arranged.

I couldn't fully recognize at that time what Marcus Garvey was all about, but I was aware of the fact that this man brought with him some sort of magical promise of better days for all blacks who had the devotion and desire to better themselves in what Garvey saw primarily as a white world.

His entrance into the hall on that first visit was curious. It had the pomp and ceremonial effect of a miniature coronation, and I watched as adults that I knew as ordinary working men and women, normally treading up and down St James Street, now became proud followers and standard-bearers in a parade that proceeded with silent deliberation up the main aisle of the UNIA to the stage. They seemed enriched, regal people taking their places on the podium behind Marcus Garvey. He was a man of medium height and stocky build, with a thick moustache and a strong, round face; the thing that remains with me

---

cont.
hundreds of chapters worldwide. A messianic figure, Garvey is remembered for preaching race pride and self-determination, and the liberation of Africa from white colonial rule.

most of all, however, is the measured tonal density and deep severity of his voice. I sat there and listened despite myself as he told us all that there could never be a real awakening for the Negro in Canada unless we ourselves awoke from the comfort of the jobs that we were "allowed" to have. He drove home that it would only be with the courage and determination to create and sustain our very own black industries, grocery stores, taxis, airlines, and even shipping lines that we would at last be truly free from the economic bondage that we endured. Intriguingly, if we thrust that form of thinking forward to today's world, Marcus Garvey was dead on the mark, for in many cases it has only been through the black boycott against the bigoted sections of the white business world that the market-place has been opened up to blacks. In those days of poverty and Depression, the chances of ever seeing a black airline or shipping company seemed remote to most of us, but we lived on the desire that this man created in all of us to have these things come to pass, no matter how distant they all seemed.

Marcus Garvey faded out of the picture—he never returned to Canada, and with the advent of various opportunities in the working world in Montreal, coupled with the intermingling of more and more black children with their white counterparts in the high schools and colleges, the need and thrust of the UNIA came to seem almost meaningless to blacks in the community. By the same token, let us not forget that just as Canada tends to mimic or mirror many political and social phenomena that occur in the United States, the impetus of the civil rights movement from the early days of Selma, coupled with the vivid and horrid pictures on television in the 1960s, caused many Canadians discomfort and guilt. Just as many white Canadians did not want to be aligned with the American stance on Vietnam, so they did not want to be, in many instances, blood brothers to the raging racist Klan members and bigots of the South. Not publicly, anyway.

Mr and Mrs Tucker doggedly held on to the UNIA building and did everything within their power to continue the Sunday meetings, even though the attendance scarcely warranted it. I can still picture Mr Tucker, after sitting around in the hall with perhaps six or eight people in attendance, resignedly getting to his feet, taking his watch out of his waistcoat pocket and, after checking it with the clock in the hall, saying in a very tired manner, "Well, brothers and sisters, there are only a few of us here, and it does not appear that more are coming. Our members are few, but our purpose remains great." He would then commence the meeting as though dealing with a full house.

When I think back to those countless Sunday afternoons, I realize that I got more from those meetings than I was aware of at the time. Not only did the repeated public performances in the hall increase my musical confidence, but—more importantly—I learned from Marcus Garvey and others the need for dedication and devotion to any cause that one sincerely believes in. Many of the young Montreal blacks of today may not even have heard of the UNIA; nevertheless, it served their forebears as a place of spiritual sustenance and personal reconstruction. It made believers and proud standard-bearers out of oppressed workers who now walked with their heads high, no longer weary and oppressed, and no longer prepared to be bent under a perverse racial system and the yoke of bigotry.

6

RUNS, CHORDS, AND GIRLS

During the period that I was attempting to develop on my own musically, I sat to the piano one day and came to the conclusion that the only way I would ever be able to play this instrument comfortably would be to remove as much of the technical hassle from it as possible. Having come to this conclusion, I spent the next so many days setting out things that seemed to be continually tripping me up along the way and made note of them. I even remember going to my mother one afternoon and telling her about my belief that one day I could really be a great pianist. She listened patiently to me, and after some deliberation said, "I am sure, Son, that if you work at it and ask God's help, you can do almost anything." I even recall at that time wondering if God could really play in the key of F sharp. I would love to hear that. Not many guys over the years got too heavy in that key, including yours truly! Nevertheless, I started putting all this analysis together and made a few personal yet to me important decisions.

First and foremost I decided that there were no such things as wrong notes. There were, however, misplayed notes. Big difference! Each note has a relationship to another and this is true of any chord (John Coltrane and others are evidence of this). It is merely a matter of correct placement within the movement of harmonic cadence. This decision was important, for it taught me that the harmonic structure was the governing factor in improvisation.

Next I looked at something that was increasingly causing me discomfort and loss of control: the problem of playing genuinely two-fisted piano. What was I to do about that? You can't very well carry out architectural surgery on your body in order to be able to play an instrument. I finally came up with a solution. There was no need for surgery: what was to prevent me from telling myself that my hands were capable of changing the digital position of my fingers when necessary? Nothing. I started thinking this way and before I knew it began to master the idea. I also found that as a result I became able to play virtually anything that I chose to in a two-handed fashion. This gave me another form of artistic expression that had hitherto been beyond me.

Another aspect of improvisation that I worked exceedingly hard at was building the ability to perform one phrase while formulating the next one in my mind—in other words, being able to think ahead of what I was playing at the moment. These were just some of the pianistic and jazz attributes that I decided I must master absolutely, so that I could relax and devote my time and concentration to the conceptual side—to harmonic and melodic ideas, and, of course, to rhythm. I vowed to spend as many waking hours as I could dedicating myself to this realization.

As a result of this intensive practice, I was not able to give of my time to too many other things. At high school I spent most of my free time conjuring up musical selections or practising in the auditorium, which had a good piano. I spent many lunchtime periods there. This had a two-fold benefit: not only was I improving my musical prowess, but once some of the girls found out that I was playing in the auditorium, they would somehow drift in at various times to listen and have a little chat with me—chats that blossomed into some fruitful dates later on. Don't ever knock practising! This all went well until the Vice-Rector found out what was happening and decided to curtail my "practice" sessions.

It was during my early high school years that I met Maynard Ferguson and his brother, Percy. Poor Maynard got selected to play for the mounting of the flag in the courtyard and I enjoyed going down to heckle him. In truth, however, I felt really sorry for him on some of those infamous Montreal mornings, because I could see his mouth-piece virtually freezing to his chops.

We became friends and one day he asked me if I would be interested in playing piano in his brother Percy's band. I thought this would be fun; however, I had to get permission from Mum and Pop. When asked about this new venture, Pop's major concern was not how much my salary would be, but what impact it would have on my studies at school. After giving him my assurances that it would not interfere, and also telling him that Maynard's Dad was a school principal himself, he decided that it would be okay for me to have a go at it. Consequently, the next tea dance that Percy Ferguson's Serenaders played, the piano spot in the orchestra was filled by the St James Street flash: me. It was a unique experience for me. Here I was, the only Negro in the band; not only that, I was being featured. We were all so young then! I can still see Maynard sitting in the trumpet section. I say "sitting," but when it came time for him to solo he had to stand on his chair! I still sometimes kid him about that.

This particular period of my life seemed to be moving at quite a clip, for it was during this time that sister Daisy (once again) submitted me for the *Ken Soble Amateur Hour*. This was a weekly radio show that went out every Sunday and drew on amateur performers from all parts of Canada. It featured almost every kind of talent—singers, tap dancers, instrumentalists, you name it. I managed to survive to the finals and by the luck of the gods, ended up winning my division. As a result of this victory I was given my first sustained exposure on radio: my own 15-minute show once every week. This had a tremendous impact on my life. Here I was, a snotty-nosed 15-year-old with his own radio show every week, coupled with appearances with the Percy Ferguson band!

I was riding the top of the world, or so one would think. In many ways, however, I found life quite confusing at this time. Things did seem to be falling right into place. On the other hand, I was still prone to great uncertainty about a number of aspects of my playing. I compensated for this inner unsettledness by adopting an air of brash overconfidence—something that soon cost me.

Significantly it was my Dad who made me pay the price. In those days, during the summer time, there was a fleet of ships known to us as the "Lady Boats"—cruise vessels that sailed between Canada and the West Indies. Being an "old salt," Dad knew some of the crew members of the various vessels, and one of his friends was a piano player of some skill; Dad brought him home one afternoon to let me hear him play.

As soon as he hit the first eight bars, I knew he was a Teddy Wilson devotee. However, admiring Teddy is one thing; being able to play like him is another. I smiled inwardly as I listened, because this cat couldn't handle any of Teddy's silken runs or lines, even though he did have his stride together and had also memorized some of Teddy's easier licks.

One thing that turned me against this man was his condescending attitude towards me. For some reason he seemed to have taken it for granted that I was thoroughly confused by what he was doing and enjoyed talking down to me as if I were a musical numskull. I'll never know if Pop did this because he'd deduced how I felt and wanted me to waste this cat, or whether he really didn't think that I could outplay him. Whatever the reason, after his friend had finished, he asked me to play something. By this time I was, as they say, "red of eye with anger" and I proceeded to take out whatever I could on this stud. I started with *Avalon* at a medium tempo, and when out of the corner of my eye I spied what I interpreted as a look of shock on the guy's face, I doubled the tempo and at once laid out one of Teddy's most awesome and difficult ascending runs. No contest. The cat grabbed Pop and started spouting off to him about how talented I was, and what was he going to do about it. My day was made. I had made my point via the piano; I had also unknowingly been involved in my first "cutting" session.*

Although I really feel that Pop was proud of the way I handled myself that day, I have also learned that he was worried that I was becoming just a little too sure of myself. Even with my radio show, he had a certain routine that he would work on me in order to keep me level, as they say. On the nights that I managed to screw up something musically, I would return home to find him awake and curious as to what had happened. On the nights that I felt I had really cooked, I would rush home to ask if he had heard the show, only to find him bleary-eyed as though I had awakened him from a deep sleep. In the end my mother blew the whistle on this little ruse by telling me that he had been awake all through the show and enjoyed it.

That was one method that he used to keep me from becoming too self-confident. But the one that really got me was when he brought home the Art Tatum recording.

One afternoon Pop walked in, called me as he wound up his gramophone and said, "Tell me what you think of this piano player." I later found out it was Art Tatum playing the *Tiger Rag*. My first reaction was to laugh, because here was my Dad trying to fool me with a recording of two piano players. He asked me what I was laughing at and I replied that I was on to his joke and that I knew it was two

---

*A "cutting" contest occurs when musicians attempt to upstage each other during a jam session in order to prove who is superior.

pianists. He seemed to take a lot of pleasure informing me that this was one man—and blind at that! A total sense of frustration came over me. First, it was unbelievable to me that this man could play that way. Second, it was obvious that, though blind, he had accomplished pianistically worlds more than I had been able to do with my sight. I sank into a morass of dejection and would not go near a piano for a month, so incredible was this music that I heard and so impressed was I at its performance. I can recall being encouraged to play by various members of my family, but I could not respond.*

I had a dear friend at the time by the name of George Sealy, who was Montreal's best tenor saxophonist, and had happened to be present that day when I first heard Tatum. George was one of the most jovial men that I have ever known, and was probably one of the most self-confident human beings I had known. It was his continued taunting (coupled with encouragement) that made me return to the piano. "You're not going to let Tatum stop you from playing as good as you can play," he said once. "You are just going to have to find some other way to go, that's all." To George it was all very simple. "He went that way, you go this way," was his summary of what was needed, and this fuelled a new resolve not to let anyone or anything deter me from my goal. No matter who stood in my way I firmly resolved to become the best jazz pianist in the world.

ART TATUM

> I once knew a man whose mind was so quick
> That to run through eight bars was like playing one lick.
> I once knew a man whose hands were so fast
> He could skate over the keyboard as tho' it were glass.

---

*To understand the situation fully one has to bear in mind that I had never heard Art Tatum play. He was seldom if ever played on the airways in Canada at that time—or if he was, I never knew of it.

I once knew a man whose thoughts were so deep
One would wonder how on earth it was possible to keep
All the thoughts, all the lines, all the rhythms, all the blues
In his mind at the ready for whenever he'd choose.

I once knew a man whose virtuosity I feared
And under whose stigma I was musically reared.
I once knew a man whom I dreaded to meet,
Who understood my shyness, and was gentle and sweet.

I once knew a man who taught me to hate him—
Musically, that is; for I loved Art Tatum.

7

DECISIONS, DECISIONS

A s my high school days progressed, I became more and more disenchanted with every passing day. Experiencing difficulty in concentrating on the various subjects I was taking, I found myself more devoted to music than to academic matters. I continued the daily struggle, telling myself it was all for a worthwhile purpose. I kept myself busy, appearing on weekends with Percy Ferguson's orchestra, doing the occasional guest slot on a slew of variety radio broadcasts, and once World War II commenced, a few troop shows and war bond drives.

My older brother Chuck entered the Army, and was stationed at Longueuil in the band. His greatest fear throughout his whole sojourn in that band was that I would be drafted into the Army, and immediately be assigned to that particular unit. Chuck knew the bandmaster was ambitious and possessive, and could be vengeful. He used the band to fulfill private dance engagements at night; if the musicians did not co-operate, they stood a high chance of being shipped overseas (and into combat), for he had high-echelon military connections. At this time I was attracted by the Air Force and went to join, but was turned down for health reasons. Shortly after that, a group from the Navy attempted to recruit me for their band; however, I envisioned myself in that tight-fitting naval uniform and decided to decline their offer.

By this time, my stint with the Ferguson band had just about drawn to a close, and I was looking for a new challenge. In the Army band with my brother was an alto saxophone player named Art Morrow; he was also considered to be one of the leading arrangers in Montreal, providing charts for the prestigious local dance orchestra led by Johnny Holmes. Johnny heard from Art that he was a friend of my brother, and invited me to audition for the band.

When I attended my first rehearsal, I was pleasantly surprised to find that the band used special written arrangements rather than the "stock charts" used in Percy Ferguson's orchestra. At the same time, I was filled with trepidation: I knew that my sight-reading was shaky, and I was worried about whether I could cope with such sophisticated writing. By the end of the first tune I was aware just how heavy it was, and also uncomfortably aware that my problems were all too evident to the members of the band.

Johnny came over during the band break and said, "Want a Coke, son?" and proceeded to guide me outside the hall to an anteroom. "Listen, son, there is nothing in there that we are doing that you can't handle. It's just a matter of relaxing, taking your time, and reading things over," he said, trying to reassure me. Little did he realize that there was a lot more worrying me besides nervousness. Not only was I the youngest member of the orchestra but I was also the only black in the band. To me these were not the best circumstances in which to join an orchestra. Ideally, I would have come into the band, and receded into the background without drawing any attention to myself. It was impossible for a lone Negro in an otherwise all-white aggregation to do this.

I think that my experience here was, in a number of respects, representative of how many Canadian Negroes must have felt in the various jobs they took in Canada at that time, and this is worth considering in detail.

Economic opportunities for Montreal blacks were limited. The majority worked for the railroad, like my Dad. This was seen as a normal and socially equitable job; it allowed a man with not too large a family and without too many aspirations to raise his family in moderate comfort—provided they were all content to live within the social structure provided by the income from the railroad. In the case of our family, which eventually grew to five offspring, it was not enough and had to be augmented by my mother taking work as a maid, housekeeper, and cook. And whenever Dad got "bumped" from one of his regular runs, times were really hard—full of need and aching.

The grim fact was that there were few other occupations for most black males to turn to if they could not find work on the railroad. If they were lucky they might land a job as a janitor or, in rare cases, as a general factory-hand, but such fortune was not common. Most other jobs, certainly in the blue-collar sector, were simply not available to blacks, no matter what their academic qualifications. Somehow, Negroes in Canada seemed in general to live peaceably (though not agreeably) with this stealthy form of oppression. They spoke quietly of being refused this job and that job, but never resorted to any visible uprising or resistance to such economic segregation.

Such an ethos characterized the world of music and entertainment as well. During my childhood years, there were just two black night clubs in Montreal. The larger and more famous was Rockhead's Paradise, owned by Rufus Rockhead, a very enterprising West Indian who ran the establishment with an iron hand and dedicated continuity. His club was located on the southeast corner of St Antoine and Mountain Streets; around the corner on the west side of the Mountain stood the Cafe St Michel, whose ownership was never quite known, although it was reputed to be subsidized by members of the underworld. Both clubs used primarily black orchestras and featured black entertainment. And that was it, apart from a few other east-end clubs that it was not then considered chic to go to; I know of no other establishment that regularly employed blacks in its bands. Moreover, when black players in the orchestras in those two clubs fell ill, they would often be replaced by white players. It was as if black musicians lived under an unwritten law: take what you're given, accept what happens, and don't ask any questions.

This was the enigma that confronted me as I grew up in the musical world in Montreal. None of this had entered my mind when I played with the Percy Ferguson Orchestra, for that seemed more like an appendage to my high school days; it certainly occurred to me, however, as I settled in with the Holmes Orchestra on my first night. But I was quietly determined not to be another victim of this subtle but profound black subjugation: I decided that since the early critiques of my playing had been very favourable, I would go for broke. And in all fairness, I must say that there wasn't anything other than words of encouragement and appreciation from the other guys in the band.

After that first rehearsal, I returned home with my ego slightly deflated but resolved that, no matter the cost, the piano chair in that band belonged to me. The following day, I received an early telephone call from Johnny inviting me to lunch uptown with him. We sat across from each other and bantered thoughts back and forth about the band and my place in it. Johnny explained to me that he wanted to have the best musical band in Canada, and yet he wanted to give people the pleasure and enjoyment of being able to dance to the band's music. He also envisioned having a small jazz group within the orchestra now that I was in the band, and said he wanted me to head it, so as to spotlight my solo work. We became extremely close friends, and I know how vigorously he tried to understand the frustrations and battles raging within me. Apart from all that, I fell totally in love with his wife, Norma, who just happened to be the maker of the best mincemeat pies in the world, not to mention the hard sauce that went with it!

My tenure with the band lasted roughly five years, during which time I enjoyed many memorable moments with Johnny. He was a man with very firm convictions about life. If I were to evaluate him using today's political terminology, I'd call him a middle-of-the-road conservative. He was of British descent and had a deep allegiance to the British way of thinking. We disagreed many times, during which some pretty heated arguments would take place. These never occurred in our musical relationship, however: we retained our own very personal feelings about music while respecting each other's views. When speaking about piano fills and solos he would often cite people like Joe Bushkin and Mel Powell as the models he wanted on certain tunes; I found it very hard to comply, even though I was willing, for I would subconsciously fashion them in Teddy Wilson/Nat Cole style, since that was my instinctive medium. One thing that Johnny and I concurred on was Art Tatum's genius. Flatteringly, he regarded my control of the instrument as every bit as good as Tatum's, and would urge me to use it to the full.

One day he walked up to me and said, "Why are you wasting all of those ideas?" When I asked what he meant, he said, "All those fantastic things that you play on the piano are great, but why don't you write some of them down so that the band can play them?" I had never given a thought to this aspect of music, and now I shied away, arguing that I did not have that facility. He brushed this excuse (and others) away as nonsense, produced a sheet of score paper, and said, "Sit down and play something for me ad lib." I began on an original melody; he rapidly jotted something down on paper and showed it to me. "Now, I would give this to the trumpets, and those chord clusters that you are playing with your left hand to the 'bones.'" In this low-key way Johnny introduced me to the world of arranging and writing. I did a few arrangements for the band from time to time; however, my primary writing interest centred on the small jazz group which was now flourishing. Our red-headed clarinetist, Bill Sawyer, had a great sound and improvisational flair, enabling us to offer a fair pastiche of the famous Benny Goodman Quartet.

I particularly admired Johnny's way of handling any situation that concerned his having a black in the orchestra. He refused to tolerate anyone telling him what he could or could not do with his orchestra, and would turn down flat any engagement in which my presence was any kind of a racial irritant. I feel good about my tenure with Johnny's orchestra; I learned a lot, not only about the music and the ways of a big band, but also how to deal with a large and heterogenous group of people, all with their individual emotions, quirks, and distrusts. Despite my personal success as a soloist, which gave me some kind of special status, my fellow players were entirely unenvious and warm: throughout I was treated as one of the guys. I can best sum this up by recalling one of our rehearsal nights.

I had been in the band for quite a while and had started accruing quite a snazzy wardrobe for myself. That evening I decided to wear a brand-new green suit that my tailor had just made in the latest cut and style. I was very apprehensive about what the band's reaction would be when I entered the rehearsal room, and with good reason: as I came through the door, Bobby Redmonds, a saxophonist, stopped dead in his tracks, dropped his music stand, and yelled, "Grab your cues, fellas, here comes the snooker table!"

It is my firm belief that the early and local experiences that any player is exposed to are just as important as later influences exerted by the bigger and better-known names; for one thing, the player is much more impressionable at this juncture, and very likely more unstable too. In my case, I was reared amongst some highly talented players, local and otherwise, and they certainly exerted a positive effect on my formative years. I grew up knowing that they were all of a special calibre.

Hughie Sealy, one of four brothers, played a dominant part in the shaping of much of my musical thinking. He was an alto saxophone player much respected in Montreal for his classic tone and command of the instrument, and also for his maturely business-like approach to the music scene. Unlike many others who had a come-what-may attitude towards their gigs, Hughie played no games. A hit (start) at nine o'clock meant a hit at nine o'clock, just as a 15-minute intermission was just that—15 minutes, no more, no less. This was only one part of Hughie Sealy. The part I knew was seldom shown to others, for he was a very proud man, dedicated to his music and his few true friends. He had an undying love and admiration for alto saxophone players like Benny Carter, Johnny Hodges, and Willie Smith, rightly regarding their rich tone as an endorsement of his approach to playing the instrument. Were Hughie alive today, when it is commonplace to see blacks occupying chairs in radio and television orchestras, he would undoubtedly be first call for the lead alto spot in any of them.

He believed that every black musician should be able to read music as well as he could (and he could read!), and he would stress this again and again to members of the band, particularly in view of the bigotry and segregation that disfigured the music scene in Montreal at that time. "You dumb bastards better hope you never get the call, because you won't be able to do anything about it once they lay that music down in front of you," he'd declare, his authoritative stance defying them to dispute him; they never did, because they knew they were listening to the truth. Unfortunately, his theory was never proven: in all my days in radio in Montreal and Toronto I cannot recall seeing a single black seated in any of the orchestras. Naturally, this was a major irritant to all black musicians of Hughie's class who knew they could cut it, but who also knew that the opportunity would never come their way.

My luck made me an exception, and I came to embody, I think, some of what Hughie had envisioned for himself; consequently, he invested some of his fierce pride in me. Although we were close friends, we seldom worked together. He took me under his wing and insisted that I meet some of the standards that he had set for himself. Shortly after my first marriage, our two families lived together for a while, and at home he would get out his horn and say, "Do me a favour and run this down with me." I noticed that as we went along the pieces became harder and harder. When I complained about this, his reply was "Shut up and play the God-damn music." And when I was in Johnny's orchestra, Hughie was even harder on me. "If you think you're going to go up there and embarrass us, you'd better think again."

The touching thing about all this was that whatever I attempted became, in Hughie's mind, symbolic of black community effort. It was always "We do not want this to happen," or "They should not be able to charge us with that." Consequently, he endowed me with a mantle of responsibility, making me understand that I had become some sort of role model for other Negroes in the community. He took a special interest in my personal life, and attempted to guide me around some of the pitfalls that night-club life can engender. Hughie also insisted, whenever I sat down to play for him, that I become and remain a two-handed pianist. He enjoyed all the bebop lines and ideas, but in the end he'd come out with the demand that I always think of as his trademark: "Now play me some of that pretty piano and never mind that other crap."

We remained close friends even after I'd left Canada and begun my US tours. I returned to Montreal fairly often with JATP* and for concerts of my own at Place des Arts, and on one such occasion I was informed that Hughie had not been too well. He did indeed look drawn when he came to the concert that night; full of concern, I told him to take care of himself as we parted. But the following year I came back for another concert, only to find that Hughie had passed away. That concert was the saddest I ever played in Place des Arts; his wife, Marguerite, attended it, and I dedicated to his memory Johnny Green's *Body And Soul*, a tune he loved, playing it with tears streaming down my face.

Hughie's younger brother, George, was a tenor saxophonist renowned for his rough-hewn sound and driving solos. George could improvise on anything at any given tempo, and in contrast to Hughie was a very happy-go-lucky, impish person. He and I played numerous gigs together, and countless afternoons jammed with just piano and sax. I gained a very early understanding of the true meaning of improvisation from George, for once he put that instrument to his lips,

---

*Jazz At The Philharmonic, an annual series of jazz concerts organized by Norman Granz in venues throughout America, which later toured abroad.

he became a free spirit, going off on fantastic flights of linear invention. He too would spring new tunes on me, but unlike Hughie he never showed up with any music, saying merely, "Follow me on this, kid." I learned an awful lot from these two men, who could have been giants in their own right had geography not been against them.

Montreal in this particular era was a melting pot for many musicians, who came from all over Canada (and sometimes the USA) to settle there. This "jazz mecca of Canada" had a marvellous flavour, mingling the flair of the French language with other dialects and cultures and a tremendous night life, for in those days putting on a show meant importing large-scale cabarets, complete with a master of ceremonies, at least one comedian, a vocalist, maybe a dance troupe, and often a complete chorus line. Those were marvellous days for musicians: they migrated from club to club as the opportunity presented itself. Often these shows would include a small jazz band, and the impact of one such outfit is still vividly remembered.

Al Cowans and the Tramp Band etched themselves indelibly on most people's memories after their first appearance in the Club St Michel. I sat through show after show, totally intrigued by how hard the group swung. Al Cowans, believe it or not, played washboard with a set of thimbles on his fingers, and created a musical framework for a talented dancer by the name of Pinky Lee, whose moves on the floor would make Michael Jackson's moonwalk look clumsy. He was dressed in a long coat, baggy pants that came to a fierce peg at the bottom, shoes with elongated toes on them and a tie that dragged on the floor while he walked around with what could almost be termed a stupid look on his face, as if he did not understand why he was there. All the while he would be executing incredibly silken moves, which brought not only laughter but gasps of awe from the audience. The set would culminate with Al (a tremendous dancer himself) joining Pinky for the finale, which evoked cheers from the crowded night-club audience. I learned the simple truth of the word "swing" from this group: they taught me how much you could move an audience through a fierce four–four momentum. This power was intensified by the arresting lines played by

B.T. Lundy on sax and Buddy Jordon on trumpet (all dressed as garishly as Pinky)—for these were the early days of bebop, and such work was new to most.

I was desperate to play in this wonderfully pulsating group, but was too shy to impose myself on what I believed to be a perfect unit. It all came together one night while I was sitting at ringside, and they had an unforgiving groove going on some blues thing. All of a sudden Al, who was standing just above my seat, looked down and said, "Come on, OP, I know you want a piece of this." He spoke truer than he knew: that tune continued for at least 15 minutes and ended only when the manager came down to the side of the stage, pulled on Al's pant leg, and pointed to his watch. That rhythm section was the epitome of simplicity, yet the time they laid down, punctuated by occasional bebop bombs from the drummer, built a tremendous steamroller effect that engulfed everyone within earshot.

That was a wondrous episode—but I had so many in Montreal. To attempt to log in full the names of all the players that I learned from and played with in Montreal would be futile; I can only say that people such as Alan Wilman, Steep Wade, Willy Wade, Willy Gerard, Rodney Millington, and any number of others were of incomparable value to my musical development, nourishing my every day as a jazz tyro.

8

FROM SIXTEEN TO THREE

The time that I spent in the Holmes Orchestra, along with the many hours that Johnny and I spent together as friends, all went to make up a large part of my life at that particular stage. Johnny also became my personal manager for a time, setting up various appearances and tours for me across Canada. It was on one of these tours that I got to meet another man who was to have a great effect on me.

At that time Canada's best-known radio show was a noon hour CBC presentation called *The Happy Gang*, which dominated the ratings with the Canadian public for many years. It was hosted by a diminutive, dapper, and quick-witted gentleman named Bert Pearl, a fine vocalist and also quite a pianist in his own right. On one of my appearances in Toronto, Bert asked if I would appear on the show and do a few tunes. This all sounds quite normal now, but then it was quite a step on Bert's part, for it was not a jazz show as such, but essentially a family show, with lots of warm humour that would appeal in a wholesome way to all members of the family, coupled with renditions of various standard songs and some of the more popular tunes of the time.

Bert took me under his wing, squiring me around Toronto to hear different people play, including a very gifted pianist by the name of Bill Clifton. Bill was then appearing on a major New York radio show called *Piano Playhouse*, networked on Sunday mornings. It featured, on a rotating basis, the most important pianists in both the jazz and classical fields, and Clifton became a regular on the show. Bill's playing was noticeably introspective, having an intuitive, languid Debussy-esque feel to it.

We used to get together at Bert's apartment and at other friends' homes for our little piano play-off sessions, in which Bert would be the instigator. He would start a given tune and then open things up with a remark such as, "There are so many different ways of going in this tune, aren't there?", upon which Bill would move his six-foot-odd frame over to the piano seat and go into his version of the song. At some point, he would stop and, holding a suspended harmonic cluster, turn to me with a "How do you hear this, Oscar?", thus bringing me into the musical discussion.

Bert had a great sense of timing in a performance and I still live with a phrase that I learned from him when someone on another show asked me to do an extra tune. I can still see Bert sitting on one side of the studio quietly swinging his head from side-to-side in a negative gesture, while his mouth formed the phrase, "Oh no, oh no." I took my cue and declined the extra tune, and of course he turned out to be totally correct in his appraisal of the timing of my slot. "You work by one rule in show business if you want to be great," he said. "Get on, do your act, and get off!" This remains my credo for performing to this day, for I always hear Bert's voice whenever I am asked to prolong a performance past the point to which I think it should go.

Although I was musically engrossed in my work with the Holmes band, plus my high school studies, sister Daisy once again made a decision for me. She had found a music teacher whom she admired and loved, decided that he should also teach me, and announced that I was expected at 4.00 p.m. at the studio of my now new teacher, Paul de Marky. Apart from natural curiosity about this man, whom I had already heard about, I was all too aware of the things about the instrument that I was still not properly acquainted with and passionately wanted to learn, so consequently at 4.00 p.m. on Thursday afternoon I rang Paul de Marky's doorbell. As the door opened I was faced with a small, almost frail-looking man, with intense eyes, sunken cheeks, and veined hands. "Come in, come in," he said in rapid fashion. "So you are Os-car," said he with a distinct European accent. "Your sister Daisy spoke most highly of you and I am anxious to hear you play." With this he gestured me to the piano, which sat in an alcove of what in reality was a somewhat small and very personal room. As I looked around I saw a phonograph with a stack of 78 rpm records next to it, various books of topical interest on a small book shelf in a corner, music, and manuscript paper galore strewn across various pieces of furniture. Mr de Marky walked with a very unusual gait—it was almost like a limp, favouring his right side.

I played one of my classical pieces for him, I believe something from Chopin, and he listened from his armchair with a gaze seemingly fixed on some other object in the room other than me. Out of the corner of my eye I was aware of his head moving ever so slightly as I entered the lyrical part of my selection, and as I approached the final section of the piece, he leapt up from his chair with a "No, no! That's not the way you play Chopin," and with this he easily dislodged me from the piano seat, slid himself into place, and commenced finishing the rhapsodic end of the piece. The emotions that I experienced from his playing of that segment continued during his instructions on how to play Chopin. "In this case you must be brilliant," he said, "for Chopin had many moments of great brilliance and you must make your listeners aware of that. Just as you play the very lyrical part of the piece with beautiful lyricism (his head nodding) so must you play the brilliant part of Chopin with a crystal-like performance." Somehow, I was not even aware that we were in the middle of a lesson, for we had slid into it through such an emotional entrance; it was as if I had been there discussing music with him for hours past.

I loved Paul de Marky, for he brought to me a great understanding of the respect and love needed to play that behemoth of an instrument that we call a piano. No less important, he imparted to me some of his secrets of tonal control, a gift he had in common with only a very few others. He was the early version in my life of Jorge Bolet. He always insisted on relating my playing to that of Franz Lizst, of whom he was a descendant. Both Paul and Jorge had the capacity of portraying every possible emotion, from utter joy to abysmal sadness, simply in the manner in which they touched the keys. Perhaps the best illustration of Paul de Marky's great understanding of music was given a few lessons later when I found out, to my great surprise and pleasure, that he was an absolute Art Tatum fan. He played me several of his Art Tatum records, and then proceeded to illustrate some of the points he wanted to make while mimicking his style. I found this feat remarkable; I considered Paul de Marky the foremost classical pianist in Canada, and to witness his sympathetic and expert facility in jazz made a great impression on me.

My great love and respect for my teacher notwithstanding, I once—and only once—attempted to deceive him. I appeared for my usual lesson one particular week, totally unprepared but determined to hoodwink him by diverting his attention to other things and sight-read the piece he had given me to learn. But I believe that Paul de Marky was hell and begone ahead of me! He did something that he'd never done before: he started at the very back end of the lesson by asking for the piece that I was supposed to have learned. My original theory was that by the time we had reached that point I would have engrossed him in a lot of other areas with questions about a multitude of things. Attempting to save my skin, I tried to interest him in the scales and exercises that ordinarily would precede the piece he had assigned to me. No go! He insisted on doing the piece, at which I point I began a routine not unlike the episode at the Conservatory. The only difference this time was that after perhaps six desecrated and mutilated bars, he strode over to his desk and wrote out the receipt for my lesson. Coming back to the piano he handed me the receipt and said, "Give me my money, I don't have time to waste." I embarrassedly handed him my Dad's hard-earned $15 and then he ushered me out of his home. This created a real problem for me in more than one way: I had only been in his studio for about five minutes and, with my lesson usually lasting one hour or thereabouts, I had quite a bit of time to kill. Not daring to go home, because my Dad would know right away what had happened (and that his money had disappeared), my only alternative was to spend the next hour-and-a-quarter wandering around Montreal hoping to not bump into my Dad, who just might be cruising somewhere!

After that experience I never again turned up unprepared for a lesson with Mr de Marky. To illustrate the depth of my love, respect, and, yes, even fear of Paul de Marky, we have to move ahead to the 1976 Olympics in Montreal, where I appeared at a hotel for a two-week engagement. His doctor came in one night and informed me that he would love to bring Paul down to hear me. The Trio I had at that time comprised Bobby Durham on drums and the Dane, Niels-Henning Ørsted Pedersen, on bass. I can remember Niels taunting me as we stood waiting to go on with that smile that he would wear when he intended to start something. "Well, I'd say you'd better not make any mistakes tonight," he said, as I stood there nervously flexing my fingers. He turned to Bobby and said, "I'm sure Mr Big and Bad isn't going to miss any parts tonight with his teacher out there," he continued, revelling in my nervous discomfort. Finally the time came for us to go on stage and I must confess that although I'm usually unperturbed before a performance, that night my stomach churned like a 1925 Maytag washing machine. At the conclusion of the show, I went over to say hello to the man I had not seen for at least 15 years (for during this time I had moved to Toronto), and was greeted by the same small figure on whom the years had evidently taken their toll: he looked even more fragile, and his silver hair accentuated his gaunt look, although those deep piercing eyes were unchanged. I embraced him and held him tightly to me as I called his name. The first thing he said to me was "Liszt ... Liszt! You are indeed a modern reincarnation." I was truly moved that my teacher and friend had come to hear me and was enthralled with what I had done musically. I was once again moved very deeply when he spoke about me on a television interview sometime later, saying that as soon as he heard me play, he felt I was blessed "with true genius." Paul de Marky passed away on May 16, 1982, nine days short of his 85th birthday.

I finally made my decision to leave Johnny Holmes' orchestra and form my own trio. I called on two local musicians to make up the other two-thirds of it. I selected Austin Roberts—or Vivy, as we used to call him—because he loved and was steeped in the Jimmy Blanton approach to the bass. Clarence Jones had a way with brushes that is fast becoming non-existent today. He grew into a bebopper of the first order, although we had at times to suppress his total devotion to Max Roach!

I began rehearsals at my house with these two men without a job in sight. Nevertheless, the word must have gone out to the right sources because one day I received a call from the manager of the Alberta Lounge, asking me to come up to talk to him. I found that they were about to open a recently finished brand-new room and wanted my trio as the musical group. It was possibly the most intimate room that I have ever worked in—seating about 50 to 65 people, dotted with maroon-covered, deeply upholstered sofas, and peripherally lit by huge colour transparencies of western Canada. The Alberta agreed to buy a new piano for me, and I decided that such a benevolent working environment would give us the incentive to work and rehearse all the harder. I accepted their offer, and the Trio opened in the fall of 1947 on a four-month contract.

The placement of the Alberta Lounge was interesting in that it was more or less in no-man's land. It was not as far south as St Antoine Street (home of the black jazz clubs), yet not as uptown as St Catherine Street (the main street), being located on Osborne Street. It was more or less equidistant between the two and thus became the musical Mason–Dixon line of Montreal, in that musicians from both sides of the tracks felt comfortable visiting or playing with us.

The Trio remained there with roaring success until September 1949. During this time we actually broke the racial barrier by appearing in several uptown clubs where black musicians had not gone previously. At the same time, Montreal started to grow up musically because other lounges, sensing the Alberta's success, started bringing in trios and quartets of both races in order to cash in on the new-found jazz era (for example Cyro's, Club Algiers, and the like).

I have to admit that by this time my only concern was to make the Trio work, and consequently I devoted almost every waking hour to this. I insisted on a certain dress code and was intolerant of any lateness, not to mention any intoxication while we were working. My penchant for a well-dressed trio got me into hot water one year: I was unable to meet the payments for the group's uniforms and the tailor, Al Gold, sent a bailiff with a summons for my arrest on Christmas Eve. This was a very painful experience because I had become a father earlier that year and I had visions of spending the holidays behind bars. Luckily Gold's lawyer, Kenneth MacKay, instructed the bailiff to bring me to his office rather than incarcerate me. As soon as I arrived he sat me down and laid a blistering attack on me for being such a great musician at the piano while being such a dumbbell to allow things to come to this point. He made a bargain with me: he would settle the account so I could spend Christmas with my family on the single condition that I be in his office at 9.00 a.m. the day after Boxing Day, along with all details of my financial status. The irony is that he eventually became my lawyer, accountant, and advisor and, most importantly, my friend. He eventually went on to success in the political arena in Montreal.

Towards the end of my time with the Holmes Orchestra I hit a low point in my career objectives. I became disoriented and depressed, both musically and personally, sliding into a malaise that prevented me from taking any initiatives. Morose and despondent, I even quit my music activities and went to work at the Nordine Aircraft Factory, trying to get a new perspective on my life. One day I sat down and expressed my disappointment and utter boredom to my Mum, telling her that I felt I had reached a dreadful cul-de-sac in my career. She asked me what there was in the musical field that I wanted to do and had not done. When I mentioned recording as an example, she calmly asked why I didn't call up the people that make records and simply tell them that I wanted to record. Here was that honest and down-to-earth—even naïve—approach that only loving mothers can have. Yet perhaps it is sometimes wise not to question these moments in life but rather to act on them.

Anyway, I followed Mum's suggestion, and it was not long before I found myself recording for RCA. My first records were made with Bert Brown on bass and Frank Gariepy on drums. They were strong boogie-woogie renditions of old standards such as the *Sheik Of Araby* and *I Got Rhythm*. I was not happy with the sessions musically, but I looked on them as an important opening for me in the record field and grabbed it. As time progressed, I managed to talk Hugh Joseph, head of the recording arm of RCA, Montreal, Canada, into slackening off some of the boogie-woogie, thereby allowing me to play something more representative of what my trio was doing. I also got his consent to record my real trio instead of presenting studio musicians to do the recordings. However, these developments, the liberating nature of my Mum's suggestion, and the early success of the recordings blinded me to what was actually going on at RCA.

After I called to speak to Hugh Joseph about recording, he arranged a meeting. He was a man with a nervous laugh and a way of talking to you without quite looking at you. When I arrived he asked me why I wanted to record and what I intended to record. He also asked if I thought the type of music I was playing would be accepted by the record-buying public. Strange questions from a man whose position, surely, demanded that he should have already worked out the answers! The meeting concluded with him saying, "I'll get in touch with you."

There then followed two or three more meetings spaced out over a period of two months or so, in which much of the same rhetoric was repeated, yet he never conclusively said RCA was going to record me. It was not until I talked to one of the managers in his office and another artist who was already recording for RCA that I realized he was sitting with a contract under the blotter on his desk the whole time. Another strange piece of information came my way: RCA's New York division had already asked for the right to record me if the Montreal division decided not to. I leave it to your imagination as to what exactly was taking place in the mind of this recording lord of the Canadian record industry.

9

COLLIE RAMSEY: MYSTERY
PIANO PLAYER

Sometime during 1947 Collie Ramsey appeared out of nowhere onto the Montreal music scene. I was introduced to him by the manager of a bar where an American trio was playing. He was a good-looking man, slim and of average height, and he was impeccably dressed—flawlessly tailored suit, daringly patterned tie, and matching muchoir. Every strand of his wavy black hair was in place, and he had one of the most dazzling and disarming smiles I've ever seen. His eyes sparkled and he talked with an easy and natural intimacy. A fair-sized diamond ring blazed on the little finger of his right hand, which caused you to notice more sharply that he had no index finger.

He had great presence, then; I also already knew that he had a heavy reputation as a pianist. The conversation quickly turned to piano, and inevitably we began sizing each other up. He let me know that he had heard there were guys up here who would love to see me smothered musically, but that he reckoned I was more than capable of looking after myself; furthermore, he was appointing himself my caretaker and would see to it that I wasn't bugged by the Titans. I quietly nodded assent, but made a mental note to beware of an attack from the rear spearheaded by one Collie Ramsey! Talk flowed from him endlessly, like the torrent from an icefield during a quick spring thaw, and it eventually wore me out. On my way home I remember thinking that if Collie could play as much as he could talk, I and all other Montreal pianists were in deep trouble.

A week later I got my chance to find out. Collie invited me up to the room he was playing "to listen to a funky old piano player with a crippled hand." He had chosen his territory well: as soon as I got there the manager told me his clientele had mushroomed since Collie's arrival, and it soon transpired that Collie was already planning exactly how the club should be redecorated to meet his requirements. The arrival of a new piano was imminent, and Collie outlined to me his arrangements with a local tailor concerning his wardrobe needs. He was resplendent enough as it was, in a maroon silk suit fashioned with a Spanish motif to it, and a shirt that displayed just enough of its lace cuffs to set off the entire outfit.

I was ushered to a table and almost immediately a Scotch and water materialized (my favourite drink at that time). Collie slid into the seat next to me and the drone commenced at once—how did I feel, how was my family, how "pretty" my attire was, what impeccable taste I had, how great my trio sounded, how I had set such high musical standards that other players feared for their continued livelihood, and on and on and on. I just nodded my way through the lot, and finally asked him when he was due on. He replied that it was up to him; however, if I really wanted him to play now, he would.

I settled in to listen, and before long realized that Collie's style was a blatant copy of Errol Garner. However, even more evident than this derivativeness was the fact that he could swing his can off—and when I say swing, I mean swing! Although his lines were delivered in Garner-esque three- or four-note harmonic clusters, Collie played much harder than Errol—and Garner sure played hard! His conception of time was flawless, without a hint of hesitation or deviation. The other intriguing thing was that he played almost everything in either D flat or G flat; a common occurrence in self-taught pianists or rank beginners, even though most trained players consider these keys awkward or difficult. The main reason for such an apparently strange choice is that the melody lines are fashioned on the black keys, of which there are fewer, allowing the pianist to count off the spaces between the notes more comfortably. In the keys of C, F, G, and the like, one is forced to use more of the white keys in succession, and to be more careful in counting up or down the melodic sequence; all that increases the chance of mistakes, since there are fewer "places to hide" and a narrower margin of error.

My reaction to his work was unusual. Normally a carbon-copy turns me off, but I really enjoyed Collie's music. Although deeply indebted to Garner, Collie had a mind and musical imagination of his own, and created lines that were his, not Errol's. And his swing was so formidable that I reflected, "I don't think Errol would want to face this stud head-to-head." His all-round musicality brought the room totally under his spell, and as he rose to acknowledge the raucous shouts of approval, the boyish smile appeared, the eyes sparkled, and he made his way back to my table. "I'm really ashamed to have embarrassed myself in front of you like that, OP," he said, his bright eyes darting from place to place in the room as he talked. "Now I know what all those other piano players you come across must go through. I'm just happy that you're my friend." I stayed for another set and then went home, declining Collie's offer of dinner.

I was beginning to suspect more and more that Collie had something in mind for me. His ingratiating manner and his disingenuous deprecation of his own playing made me very leery, and I resolved that he would not get ahead of me in any way. This strong undercurrent notwithstanding, our friendship continued as Collie branched out. He moved from club to club, ever more "upmarket" in the venues he worked in. He developed friendships within Montreal's top show-business crowd and also with leading politicians. Most of his closest associates, however, were women. As I've mentioned, Collie was a very good-looking man and he seemed to have easy access to women's affections. From time to time he'd show me an expensive piece of jewellery or article of clothing, commenting, "So-and-so said she wanted to see this on me and insisted on buying it." At other times he would bring me into it: "Much piano as you play, I should get _____ [naming one of his ladies] to buy you a nice diamond ring for your right hand. Fast as you move it, with a decent stone on there you could light up the room!" With this he'd throw his head back and roar with laughter. My taste wasn't in tune with that kind of thing, so I'd either laugh along with him, or just good-humouredly pooh-pooh his idea— and all the while staying very much on my guard!

Our friendship, and his entire approach to it, spanned several years. He constantly encouraged me to challenge and out-play other pianists; I'd ignore such goading and steer the conversation onto another track. Eventually, as I travelled more, I saw less of Collie. On my trips home I'd hear stories about him—that he'd fallen into bad odour with the underworld by informing on some of its members, that he was suspected of being a big trafficker on the dope market, and so on; I ignored these and continued to see him from time to time. Then, suddenly, in much the same manner as he'd appeared on the Montreal scene, he dropped out of sight. Stories of what had befallen him were as vague and as various as the accounts of where he had come from in the first place. A Mystery Man from first to last.

I really enjoyed Collie because I accepted him for what he was: a hell of a piano player who had decided to make the world his oyster and was well on the way to succeeding. And he brought one undoubted benefit to Montreal: a renewed and vigorous interest in lounge playing. Before Collie, there had simply been lounges in which there happened to be a piano player; he made it possible for pianists of ability and talent to take over a lounge, and draw people to it every night.

10

DEPARTURE AND ARRIVAL— PART ONE

From 1947 to 1949 my trios held forth in the Alberta Lounge. During that time there were a few changes; the most significant was the replacement of Clarence Jones on drums by Benny Johnson on guitar. Benny was a man several years older than both Austin Roberts and me, and who had high regard for what our previous trio had been doing musically. Once we gained another linear instrument in the group, the arrangements took on a different shape and feel. Almost immediately the interplay of piano-against-guitar lines came into play, which, coupled with three-way challenges between guitar, bass, and piano, gave our trio a new sound, different perspective, and increased fluidity, and was obviously the blueprint for later guitar trios with Barney Kessel, Irving Ashby, Herbie Ellis, Kenny Burrell, and, much later, Joe Pass. We put together an extensive library of arrangements and gained the reputation of being "the group" in Canada.

At the same time, curiously enough, we accrued an "underground status" throughout the United States simply because whenever big bands and small groups visited Montreal, their members and their leaders would often end up in the Alberta Lounge listening to us; it was not uncommon to see Woody Herman, Dizzy Gillespie, Benny Goodman, Coleman Hawkins, and the like sitting in the audience. I got to meet many of my future confrères on JATP in this very manner. Bill Basie came to hear us on one of his appearances, and invited me to come to the United States as his guest so that he could present me to the jazz world there. Dizzy Gillespie visited us, and after being invited to my home for supper, ended up excusing himself and falling asleep in my mother's bed upstairs!

It was on one of his pre-tour visits to Montreal that Norman Granz got to hear me in person. He recalls being told about me by people like Coleman Hawkins and Roy Eldridge; however, he may not remember inadvertently meeting me one night prior to that visit, under very difficult circumstances. JATP had performed its near-annual concert in Montreal, and as usual various members ended up at the Cafe St Michel where they were, as always, implored to sit in on a jam session with the Louis Metcalf Orchestra. Because that club operated much later than the Alberta Lounge, and knowing that this might take place, I wandered over to the St Michel. As I arrived in the lobby I could hear a screaming fracas taking place. There were the manager and the doorman telling Norman that they didn't care who he was, he could not go upstairs unless he paid the door charge. In return Norman was shouting to them that "Those are my God-damn musicians up there, and if you don't allow me in without paying like some ordinary customer, I am going to go up there and pull them off of the stage!" Sensing that this was not going to get any better I managed to grab the manager's arm, and taking him to one side explained to him exactly whom he was barring from his club. When he realized who Norman was, he attempted to apologize, inviting him to come upstairs. Norman's reply to this was, "Fuck you! You can take your club and shove it!" and off he went, disappearing into the nearest cab.

Intriguingly, the notion that Norman should not be allowed in to hear his musicians was something that seemed to dog him over the years. There were numerous occasions when we dined together prior to a concert, or he would simply say, "I'll pick you up for the hall," or "Meet you in the lobby," and off we would go to wherever JATP was performing that night. Most auditoria keep the entrance to the stage door a well-guarded secret, with the result that after walking around the building several times in growing frustration, we would head for the front entrance to simplify matters. The upshot was forever the same. Any performing artist such as myself coming through the turnstile would be allowed in, yet the moment it came to Norman, up would go the guard's hand and he would be asked to produce a ticket. No matter how much he entreated the guard to let him in because he was the impresario, his plea would fall on deaf ears; eventually one of us in the group would have to go back, rescue him, and arrange entrance for him into his own concert. After a while this became a running gag.

During the earlier years of JATP, I found that various jazz people had certain trademarks. There was Lester Young's legendary black pork pie fedora, Dizzy Gillespie's slanted horn, Buddy Rich's perennial scowl, Miles Davis' back, and Norman's white-and-brown buckskin college-kid shoes that were popular in the 1940s. He wore them relentlessly: whatever his attire elsewhere, those buckskins were ever-present down below. It was these same white-and-brown buckskin shoes that caught my eye one night in the Alberta Lounge and, as my gaze moved upwards and I reached the head on top of the body, there were the famous bushy eyebrows along with the curious, almost distracting stare. Norman Granz, the founder and presenter of JATP, was sitting in the Alberta Lounge listening to us!

11

DEPARTURE AND ARRIVAL—
PART TWO

At the conclusion of our set, I went over to welcome Mr Granz (as I called him then) and, to my surprise, found him to be the exact opposite of the gentleman I last saw in the foyer of the Cafe St Michel. Rather than the gruff, angry man that I remembered, he was a very calm, soft-spoken, and almost shy person. He told me that he had been on his way to the airport when he was struck by the music on the taxi driver's radio; finding out that it wasn't a recording but our 15-minute weekly broadcast from the Alberta Lounge, he decided to turn around and come down to hear us in person. "Hawk and Roy have been raving about you to me," he said in a leisurely, relaxed voice, a hint of a smile on his face. "You're really something! Why don't you let me present you in New York at my concert?" he continued, in a manner that gave me the feeling that he had already made up his mind about me. I must have stammered somewhat, but finally managed to tell him that I could not come down to perform without a proper visa. "Oh, don't worry about that, we'll get around that," he countered in a manner which suggested that US Immigration and Customs were non-existent.

We talked for quite a while and then he left for the airport. I felt an instinctive closeness and trust in this man. His directness smacked of an intense honesty; obviously my feelings were right, for we became fast friends.

This episode took place in mid-summer, 1949; my now-destined debut at Carnegie Hall would not take place till September, and the next few months saw me continuing our season at the Alberta. Naturally, I was very excited at the prospect, and there was an anticipatory buzz about it in Montreal's music world in general. Although it was difficult, I tried not to think about it too much. Most certainly, I didn't want to work myself into a nervous state by the time the date arrived, so I concentrated during those months on refining my playing as best I could. I looked ruthlessly at the weak points and attempted to strengthen the continuity of my musical thoughts. To hone up my competitive edge, I jammed as often as possible, especially with pianists whom I respected.

Number one amongst these was a local pianist by the name of Steep Wade, who at the time was playing in the Louis Metcalf Orchestra. Steep was a big, lovable man who elected himself my protector whenever I came into his ambit, which was roughly between the Cafe St Michel and Rockhead's Paradise. He not only made sure that I did not get into any trouble personally, but would also constantly challenge me with the names of other well-known jazz pianists in the United States—comments on the lines of "If you play like that in New York, Bud Powell is going to eat your ass up!" or "Arthur T can probably taste you right now, you'd better get your act together." Steep would from time to time send a message to me at the Alberta whenever some jazz pianist of any stature showed up at either of the two clubs, and would wait for me to come over. As soon as I arrived he'd take on the role of "trainer," much as you'd normally find in a heavyweight champion's corner. "This stud thinks he can play," he would say, "but he ain't got no kind of left hand. I figure you should take him out within a couple of choruses." After which he would invite the visiting pianist to sit in, and at some moment of his choosing, would relieve him of the piano and call me up to play. This routine continued over the whole span of my friendship with Steep, and culminated with my meeting—or should I say run-in—with a very brash and bellicose gentleman from New York.

Marlow Morris was a pianist that I had heard of, but never listened to. I had been off from the Alberta for a while and had been in and out of town doing concerts through Quebec and Ontario. One evening I returned from an afternoon concert nearby and ran into a couple of musicians who told me that Steep was looking all over town for me.

When I got to the Cafe St Michel, Steep leapt off the piano bench even though the band was still playing for the dancing, grabbed me and asked, "Where the hell have you been? Don't you know the man is looking for you? He is talking about kicking your ass." Seldom have I seen Steep so concerned; as a result I became worried about what was going to happen to me. "He's gone down the street to scoff [eat] but said he's coming back, and told me to get hold of you and get you in here!"

When I found out that it was Marlow Morris who was looking for me, I remembered a story of Bill Basie's. He'd told me that Marlow had such gruffness, anger, and boisterousness, along with a belief that he could play as well as anyone in the world, that he would walk into places where Art Tatum was playing, yelling at him to get up from the piano. Young though I was then, even I could not imagine anyone being quite that talented—stupid, yes; talented, no. It suggested someone with an unexplained urge towards self-annihilation.

I sat at one of the tables near the bandstand talking to Steep and Hughie Sealy when out of nowhere, a form appeared towering over me at the table. "So you're the kid that's supposed to play all that piano, are you?" He had to be Marlow Morris. "Sit down and learn something," he growled, and strode off towards the piano. By this time the word had spread not only between the two clubs but also to other places uptown that Marlow Morris was in town and about to give Oscar Peterson his lumps, for the room rapidly became crowded with curious onlookers. Marlow launched into *Body And Soul*; I was soon aware that my attitude was switching from that of prey to that of assailant.

"He can play, P, he can play," said Hughie Sealy, even though his voice at that moment sounded very distant.

"Yah, but you can take him!" I heard from Steep. "You better take him, or I am going to kick your ass off up and down Mountain Street for as loud as he's been tonight."

Marlow was now into his third chorus and as I sat there an obscure sense of relief overtook me. "I can take him," I thought to myself. Suddenly he motioned me to the piano, still continuing the song. I walked to the stage and slid over the bench attempting not to create a break in the tempo and line of the song. I felt wonderfully relaxed and decided to stick the dagger in. There was a favourite figurative descending run that Marlow had used quite often in his first playing of the tune, and I decided to use that same run while adding a couple of notes of my own. To bruise him even more, I did something with it that he had not done—I turned the corner with it, and played it in an ascending direction, which I was sure he was not expecting. To flatten his ego a little more I ended the chorus by playing it with two hands simultaneously, at which point I heard him yell out "Shit!" as he stomped out of the club, never to be seen again in Montreal. There was untold jubilation amongst the people that had gathered to see this musical gun-battle when Marlow departed, totally deflated.

Typically, my trainer retained his ringside attitude by saying, "You got lucky this time, but that doesn't mean the next time you won't get your head whipped!" Wise words, and I knew that what he said was always going to be possible; but at least I now felt ready for any challenge that Carnegie Hall could throw my way.

Editor's Note: Peterson's debut in New York was one of the most spectacularly successful jazz has known. With characteristic artfulness, Norman Granz announced to the Carnegie audience that he had "just happened" to see the young Canadian pianist sitting in the auditorium, and would now ask him up to play. In truth, of course, Granz had stage-managed the entire affair for weeks: Peterson could not be granted a working visa, so had to be present as a watching guest; if he was then persuaded to "sit in," fine.

Amongst the tunes Peterson played were Fine And Dandy *and the song that would become centrally associated with him,* Tenderly. *Accompanied by Ray Brown on bass, Peterson was rapturously received and shortly afterwards attracted glowing reviews in the jazz press. His American days were off to the most auspicious start.*

AMERICA: THE 1950S

12

EARLY AMERICAN DAYS

During the period following my Carnegie Hall appearance, I returned home to Montreal to regroup and ponder what direction my musical career might take. Upon my return I was toasted, congratulated, and lauded for my New York success by my musical peers and other well-wishers. Beforehand, I had been so engrossed in my own thoughts about the debut that it had escaped me that all these people were interested in the outcome. Canadians have always looked on the acceptance of anyone's endeavours by our southern neighbours as a full endorsement of their worth, even though they may themselves have entertained doubts about that person's talents. On the other hand, there have been those who have been almost ostracized purely out of jealousy of their American success. Happily, this was not the case with me. I was welcomed home with congratulatory abandon. People whom I didn't even know would stop me on the street to heap words of praise and encouragement on me, and I was truly moved by this outpouring of local adulation and pride. But I remained worried by the thought of where to go next, for the world of jazz I had now entered was complex and strange to me.

Norman Granz and I eventually decided that the best way to make a re-entry into the jazz scene at the time was for me to form a trio and accept some of the offers that had come in after my stint at Carnegie. Although I had a ball playing with Ray Brown that one evening at Carnegie, he was unfortunately not available to play with me, being busily engaged with his then wife, Ella Fitzgerald, as her manager and bassist. Ray and Ella were travelling all over the world with a trio completed by Hank Jones and Charlie Smith on drums. I believe that it was on one of these trips, to Scotland, that Ray found the beautiful Amadi fiddle that he used for such a long time.

I accepted an engagement in Bop City in New York, and used Major Holley on bass, and Charlie Smith on drums. I particularly remember negotiating Charlie's salary. When I called him about the gig and stated the sum I was offering as weekly pay, he replied that he would agree to the figure, if I would agree to an additional $1.20 per week. When I inquired what the added $1.20 was for, he calmly replied that he read the *New York Times* nightly and its cost had to be included in his salary! For the two weeks that we appeared in Bop City, I acquiesced, just to keep the gag going. The funniest part of the joke was, he took the money! Regardless of such high finance, this was the first operational Oscar Peterson Trio since my departure from Canada. I very much enjoyed this new group, primarily because Charlie and Major were in effect completely open players. We had few arrangements, so we were obliged to use an "open" library, including lots and lots of standards!

This sort of playing gave me the chance to really get into the "American" type of time interpretation. I have always felt that the interpretation of "time" differs from region to region. In jazz in those days, we referred to this diversity as a "different lope." I suppose an analogy might be the different gaits or type of steps that people use on various terrains. American is the freest of all: it has the most natural gait, allowing players to adopt a laid-back approach. Charlie Smith was a genius with brushes. He, along with Daddy Jo Jones and Ed Thigpen, had a command of the brush stroke that to me was uncanny. Charlie had that unmistakable sense of meter that so few drummers have (as I came to realize later). To him, playing an "up tempo" did not mean getting progressively faster, as seems to be the case with many drummers. Major Holley had an immense sound on bass, and also a firm understanding of what the word "time" truly meant.

This Trio personnel continued off and on for about two years, whereupon Norman asked me why I didn't really settle down and put together a more lasting group, thereby giving me the opportunity to create a more permanent musical library, and also feel much more comfortable. Indeed, Norman Granz was instrumental in the creation of what turned out to be the most famous and musically successful trios in jazz history. Because our relationship meant much more than just an artist and his manager, he was able to fathom my insecurities and discomforts musically speaking, and therefore could address the areas troubling me with instinctive personal understanding and sympathy. He would call me from all over the globe while I was working in order to make certain that all was going as we had planned—something that many managers do not do. It was common-place for my phone to ring at 4.00 a.m. and for me to pick it up, only to find Norman on the other end from Rome. He thought nothing of allowing me to ramble on about any or every thing. This kind of back-up gave me a sense of stability essential to a young player in a totally new environment.

The Trio with Major and Charlie disbanded after a year or so, but not before I'd been able to fulfill my first night-club engagements; I had also had the opportunity of playing to concert audiences throughout the Eastern Seaboard. I returned to JATP in the fall of 1950 and this time completed the full tour. The tours of these early years with JATP were quite long and wearying, starting in September most usually in Hartford, Connecticut, and generally ending in Los Angeles in December. After this first complete tour, Norman came to me with the idea of my forming a duo with Ray Brown, particularly since that format had worked so well on the concerts. He offered to approach Ray with the idea but Ray hesitated, because of his marriage. Nevertheless, he was intrigued with the idea and agreed to try it for awhile; and so the new duo hit the road.

These remain some of the most memorable days of my early musical life. Anyone wanting to become a brother to another man should form a duo and go on the road. There was a special kind of close kinship and camaraderie that built up in a most natural way between us. Not only did we perform together at night; we spent many hours rehearsing and setting up a repertoire during daytime hours. We even roomed together in order to cut our expenses, and I feel that if you can do all that and still be friends, you have something even more meaningful than a friendship; you have brotherly love and understanding. I cannot remember ever having any kind of prolonged harsh feelings towards Ray, or vice versa. We certainly had our disagreements, but we would somehow always solve them, and end up calling each other all kinds of jive you-know-whats, culminating in our jumping on one another while pummelling each other in fun, ending up on the floor in gales of laughter. The ironic part of this, now that I think back, is that I was never able to effect this kind of solution when my marriages suffered upheaval.

We were two guys who were out to play the world into bad health while having as much fun as possible in our free hours. I used to kid Ray about his meticulous dressing habits, and endowed him with such nicknames as "Pretty Willie from the coast," or "Ice-Cream Charlie." During these years we subconsciously learned to think and breathe together musically as second nature—and this continued not only through the years he was in the group, but even to this day. It remains a natural sequence of events for me to sit down to a piano, while Ray picks up his bass, and for us simply to start playing.

In those days we didn't have a lot of money, but we sure had a lot of fun. I remember one gig in Winnipeg, Canada, where we were the featured act in an Italian restaurant. We stayed at the best-known local hotel, and when we returned from our shows, well after midnight, the security staff would be sitting in the lobby having what would be their lunch. The house detectives got to know us quite well and would greet us nightly as we came in from work. One of the men had kiddingly told Ray that he didn't trust him, and said that in his view Ray had the look of a man who was always up to something.

One night as we returned to the hotel, one of the detectives called me over and told me that he had something for us, and with that he produced one of the juiciest-looking apple pies I have ever seen. We thanked him for it and took the elevator up to our floor. We had to make several right turns in the hallway before coming to our room, which was on the other side of the building. We swaggered in a very carefree way down the hall, me guarding the apple pie followed by Ray Brown carrying his bass under his arm, as was his habit, resplendent in a beautiful wrap-around fawn-coloured cashmere coat, tied with a belt.

Arriving at our door, I handed Ray the pie while I proceeded to get the key out and place it in the lock. By now Brown was well into his anticipatory speech about what he was going to do to this apple pie once he got it on the inside. "Hurry up and open the God-damn door!" he said as I now knelt on one knee attempting to peer into the keyhole to see why the door would not release. Somehow during all this, I managed to get the key stuck in such a way that it would neither open the door, nor could I get it back out of the lock. Just as I informed Brown of my dilemma, I heard a female voice on the inside say, "Honey, somebody's trying to get into our room." I looked up in horror upon hearing that voice, only to discover that we had gotten off the elevator one floor early without noticing it—and there I was on my hands and knees with the key jammed in somebody else's door. When Brown noticed the mistake he started to laugh; as he did so, I heard a deep baritone voice say, "Don't worry, Honey, I'll take care of whoever that idiot is!" followed by what sounded like a pair of size eighteen feet hitting the floor.

Just as I was having panic-struck visions of this hulk yanking the door open with me down on one knee with a key in my hand and a stupid look on my face, I somehow managed to get the key out before the monster appeared. As I took off I glanced sideways to say something to Brown—and all I remember seeing was the tail end of a bass fiddle almost suspended in the air going around the corner, trailed by a coat-tail of cashmere, with a hand delicately balancing an apple pie. Somehow Ray managed to accomplish all of this as he went around the corner full tilt. We both arrived at the elevator and leaned against the doors doubled over with laughter while hysterically recounting what might have happened had I not been able to get that key out of the door. We were still hysterical an hour later as we sat in our room laying waste to the apple pie and some cold milk.

Ray and I travelled all over the USA and Canada doing our duo thing, amazing many of the local resident musicians in these cities that came to hear us. They marvelled at the intricacies of our arrangements, and were also overcome by the powerful swing we were able to generate and project to our audiences. Quietly we prided ourselves on these abilities, and relished the reaction that we got, especially when it came from drummers who grumbled about what it was that we were trying to prove playing without drums. It became even more of a challenge when we appeared on a bill with other groups: we set out to prove that we could swing as hard without drums as they could with. Meantime, we continued on our merry way, acting at times like a couple of college kids on the loose, and enjoying the freedom of being a couple of devil-may-care young jazz players.

Some of my happiest memories concern Mom Edwina's Rooming House in Washington, DC, where we automatically stayed when playing that city. Edwina Swope was famous in Washington and well-known in show business everywhere. People like Louis Armstrong, Nat Cole, Fats Waller, Pearl Bailey and Louie Bellson, and Ella Fitzgerald all at one time or the other stayed at Mom Edwina's. Mom was a no-nonsense type of person with a heart bigger than the White House: if she liked you, you were in. Lie to her or cross her, and you would end up with more on your hands than you had bargained for. She was a small, rotund woman of mulatto complexion who could cook you into bad health; she obviously had friends in the Washington police department, because she would sell all kinds of whisky and assorted drinks after hours without any apparent fear of a raid. In fact she was basically under the protection of the police, for no one dared act up or threaten her for fear of retaliation by the law. "Go ahead and do something wrong in here young man, and see how fast they'll have your ass down there in the station booking it!" she would say to some loudmouth youngster feeling his oats. Moreover, any of her guests that committed any wrongdoing on her premises had to buy her a beer to atone for his crime. "Now for that, you just bought Momma a beer!" she would declare en route to her fridge. A can of beer was one of her favourite pleasures; it was indeed the only thing I recall ever seeing Mom drink.

She was a woman who would laugh and joke with anyone, yet there was a deep and serious side to her too. One evening we were alone in the kitchen just rapping about life in general, when for some reason the topic of the South came up. "You really don't understand any of this, do you?" she asked, and before I could respond she continued, "No, where you come from they play a whole different game than they do down here, Honey." She sat quiet for a moment and I waited for her to continue. "These people down here sent my sister to the mental hospital." I asked her what she meant by that and she proceeded to tell me one of the most grisly tales that I have ever heard.

Apparently her sister's husband was employed on a street repair crew. Early one evening, he was working late on a road in front of some bar. Inside were some white men busy getting drunk and rowdy. The story goes on that they somehow coerced her sister's husband into coming into the bar where they proceeded to insult him. It finally ended with them decapitating him and sitting his head up on the bar while they continued to drink and hurl racial invectives at it. By this time, of course, her sister had become worried about her husband being late, and went outside onto the porch to peer into the darkened street awaiting his return. Suddenly a car sped up to her house and the rowdies threw her husband's head up onto the porch while remarking that they thought she might be looking for her old man. Mom became very silent with a grey look on her face, and simply said that her sister was never to be the same, as she put it, "to this day."

When Ray introduced me to Mom, she took a tremendous liking to me, and catered to and fussed over me day and night. She watched over me like a hawk and would allow no one to attempt to lead me into any bad habits. It is only now, having become fully aware of the tremendous drug problem that exists today, that I can appreciate how fortunate I was that she cared this much for me. One night, when Ray went off to visit Ella in nearby Baltimore, I got an invitation to a party at Billie Holiday's apartment and, for the lack of something better to do, I decided to attend. Unbeknownst to me, there was very little that went on in the city of Washington that Mom didn't know or hear about: her intelligence service was flawless. The day after the party and on Ray's return, I was in the midst of a mouthful of sausage when she suddenly put her hands on her hips, looked at me, and said, "And just what kind of excuse are you going to offer me to explain what you were doing at that wild party down the way last night, young man?" My mouth fell open in amazement, and I decided to duck the question as best I could.

"What wild party, Mom?" I asked, feigning confusion.

"Don't give me that look of innocence!" she snapped. "I know exactly what went on there."

And with that, she proceeded to recite some of the names that were at the party and some of the things that had taken place.

Even though I knew very little about what kind of party I was going to, I should really have had some idea of what I was in for as soon as I arrived. As I stepped through the front door I was greeted by a body tumbling down the stairs towards me. Looking up, I saw Billie at the top of the stairs with a Coke bottle in her hand, taking careful aim at the body now lying at my feet. Clearly intending to let fly, she continued screaming at him, observing in no uncertain terms what it was that his mother did for a living. What intrigued me was that the body belonged to the gentleman that was her accompanist at the time! Upon seeing me, her tone mellowed swiftly, for she said, "Oh, just step over that son of a bitch and come right up, Honey." That was when I should have turned and left, "as if I had some sense," as Mom would say.

When I got upstairs into where everyone was really partying, I knew for certain I didn't belong there. People were walking about obviously out of their skulls. At one point, I saw a few guests on their hands and knees searching around for something. Being bored, I decided to join in the hunt for the mysterious bottle they were all looking for. Suddenly, some lady screamed out that she had it, and I felt a strange chill go through me when I realized that the bottle contained cocaine. Yet I remained for a while, too dumb to leave: I didn't want to offend Billie.

When I did escape, I failed to do it gracefully. I agreed to drive a member of the naval forces (a drummer) to the bus terminal, and it panned out that I was also accompanied by a black horn player and some Caucasian lady whom he'd just met at the party. They decided to sit in the back and the drummer sat with me in the front. We said good-bye to him at the bus terminal, and as I started to drive back to the party there was lots of giggling and laughter from the back seat. Embarrassed, I tried to ignore it as best I could when suddenly the woman's leg hit the back of the front seat and the giggling changed to moaning and groaning. It was now about two o'clock in the morning, and having heard stories about the brutality of the then Washington police force towards blacks, I became fearful for my own safety. My worst fears were confirmed when another car pulled up beside me at a red light and the driver of the car did what most drivers waiting on a red light will inevitably do. He was a male Caucasian who sort of half-nodded to me, then glanced into the back of my car. When I saw the look of disbelief on his face, I took off without waiting for the light to change, knowing full well what the scenario on the back seat was.

When I got back to the party, it became a big joke about what had happened in the car. I somehow missed the humour, being too busy wondering what might have happened had the person in the other car been a white policeman instead of a civilian. This, I suppose, is the kind of behaviour that Mom was referring to. I was completely snowed by the fact that only hours before I had been one of the guests at the party, and yet here was Mom recalling some of the events that had occurred just hours earlier. She went on lambasting me, and ended up by saying that she wouldn't cook for anyone who enjoyed that kind of behaviour. Brown of course thoroughly enjoyed seeing me in trouble, and did everything that he could to keep Mom on my case.

Indeed, Brown caused me a fair amount of strife during our various sojourns at Mom's. Once, while she was away shopping, we were more or less looking after the place in her absence. Although Mom was a straightforward woman in her everyday attitudes, she knew how to enjoy herself and live the good life. Her home was relatively simple in many respects, yet there were various articles around the house which anyone could recognize as being abnormally valuable. For instance, on one of the landings going up to the third floor, there was a huge Chinese vase that stood about five feet tall and two-and-a-half feet in circumference—a thing of real beauty that was typical of the many lovely pieces to be found throughout the house.

On this particular day Ray and I were sitting in the kitchen playing cards, when I decided to mess with him. I started betting ridiculously on the different hands that he dealt me. When it was time to show my hand, I suddenly grabbed all of the cards and threw them up in the air, and headed upstairs with Brown in hot pursuit. On the way, as we rounded the third-floor landing, I reached out with my hand to stabilize my turn and unfortunately snagged the large Chinese vase, which immediately started spinning and bouncing its way down the stairs. Nothing much more than that happened—except for the loud explosion as it finally reached the bottom, and smashed into what seemed to be a thousand pieces.

I was mortified, and ran up to Ray's room to ask him what we should do. His door was locked, and from the inside he informed me that it was going to remain that way until Mom came home and kicked my ass out for breaking her beautiful vase. Naturally, I spent the rest of the time until Mom's return in dire fear of her reaction to the news of the loss of one of the more beautiful art pieces in her home, especially as I knew that she had uncanny vibes about anything that went on within her home, always seeming to know that something either had taken place or was about to take place.

This particular day she came into the kitchen, saw me sitting there, and almost immediately asked, "Now what have you and your partner in crime been up to, and why is he hiding?" I hesitantly told her of what had happened to her vase, and she slowly sat down for a moment and said nothing. She rubbed her forehead with her hand and then in a very slow and fatigued voice said, "You know, I've had that vase in this house for nearly forty years, and never thought about it ever being broken, and you tell me it's gone. Is that why Mr Slick [Brown] is nowhere to be found? You better tell him to get his narrow ass down here right now!" I was never happier to deliver a message, and as Ray reluctantly put in an appearance in the kitchen, Mom now stood with her hands on her hips in that familiar stance of hers, and delivered a blistering reading to both of us, after which she directed us to both get our rumps upstairs and wash up because supper was not too far off.

Her statement about supper was of course her way of telling us that we had been forgiven. She was a woman of tremendous human fibre and understanding, and although she went through life with a stern and forbidding exterior in many ways, beneath it lay a warm and sensitive human being. She had seen a lot of life, and many of the idiosyncracies for which show people are famous. She had also seen much of the cruelties of the earlier South, and these too had left their mark on her. Washington at that time was steeped in the traditions of Southern life, including the ban on any Negroes being permitted to stay in any of the palatial white hotels. This is precisely where Mom Edwina's home came into play. It provided comfort and convenience (being located quite near to the Howard Theatre) for the various black big name acts that came to town. The conveniences were all there, from chittlings to champagne; she even had a Lincoln Continental, should you ever desire sophisticated transportation. She honestly tried to make the performers comfortable while they were at her home. Her cooking talents became the talk of the show world, and many artists— even those who were not residents in her home—would often come by to enjoy her culinary talents. She would give total priority to her houseguests, however, and would dismiss requests with a remark such as, "I'm sorry, son, but this man is one of my roomers and he's spending money with me every day. You're a Johnny-come-lately weekender that I only see once in awhile when you get hungry." This kind of statement was not intended as an insult but merely as a fact of life.

I learned a lot from my visits to Mom Edwina's. I grew to love her as I feel she loved me. Hers was a haven to many of us, and it was a most welcome haven in a confused and segregated nation's capital.

13

FROM DUO TO TRIO

Ray and I continued as a duo for nearly two and a half years, and the longer we continued, the more we realized that we were reaching the limits of the duo format. Norman also felt this but for a different reason. He believed the jazz-club owners had by this time developed a mental barrier about the amount of money that they would pay for "just two guys." Once, when we arrived at a club in Los Angeles for a two-week engagement, Ray walked in carrying his bass as usual, and upon passing the owner at the door was asked, "Where's the rest of the group?"

"Right behind me," replied Ray without stopping.

As I came through the door, the owner put his hand out to stop me, and said, "What is this, a joke? Where's the rest of the band?"

"This is it," I answered and headed for the dressing-room. He followed me, ranting and raving about how the booking office was crazy if they thought he was going to pay this kind of money for two guys, regardless of how much music they made. This was precisely the attitude that Norman was referring to when he advised me to consider changing to a trio format.

I finally decided to take the step, and brought in guitarist Barney Kessel. Prior to his stint with us, Barney had been doing a lot of studio work and recording in Los Angeles, and hadn't really planned on coming out on the road. He agreed to join us for the period of one year, which would allow us to establish the Trio as an operational group in our listeners' minds.

I will always remember his entry into the Trio: we were playing a little club in Cincinnati, and he came in "smoking." Our very first tune together was Charlie Christian's *Seven Come Eleven*, which has remained in my group's staple library right up to the present time. We opened up by playing the melody chorus in unison, after which I nodded to Barney to take his solo. Kess proceeded to take control of the solo spot for the rest of the evening. How I abdicated this role is still a mystery to me; the only conclusion I was able to come to was that Kess was looking at playing in the Trio in the same way "that a Great Dane looks at a meat counter," to quote Harry Edison. He continued roasting me on every tune that I called and I could not find any means of opening the door that would allow me back in solo-wise. I have since realized that Kess, constricted in the way that bedevils so many talented studio musicians, was really starving for this kind of jazz improvisation. Brown, of course, enjoyed every moment of my musical consternation, and regularly punctuated the evening by looking over at me with a grin on his face, waiting until Kess had ripped off 12 choruses of something and then asking, "What are you going to do with that?" Or, "This is still your trio, isn't it?" I never did get myself together and as the end of the evening arrived, I gave up trying, fully realizing that I had gotten my ass resoundingly kicked.

The marvellous thing about jazz is that such rude awakenings can pay dividends in your life as an improvising soloist. Thus I went home vowing, as Major Holley would have said, "to open the vast doors of devastation and destruction" upon Kess at my earliest opportunity. Arriving for work the next night I was immediately serenaded by Ray Brown's carping about whom he was working for in the Trio, so struck was he by the difference between the two soloists. I resolved that somehow, somewhere this evening I was going to have to make Barney reckon with me. As we got ready to play, I decided to retrace our steps of the previous night and once again called for *Seven Come Eleven*. Brown chuckled and asked, "Oh? Are we looking for another head-whipping?" Ignoring him, I counted off the tune and we roared into the first chorus, after which I decided to take the first solo. Knowing that Kess was a great Charlie Parker fan and steeped in the bebop era, I geared my solo approach in that direction, quoting segments of Bird's phrases and reshaping others, while linking them to phrases of my own. The strategy worked. Kess took another line of approach, and I realized that he was still subconsciously listening to some of the things that I had played, forcing him to go around them musically and change his linear structures. From then on, it became a virtual head-to-head battle between the two of us, punctuated by Ray's solos which we used to separate the two combatants. At the end of the night, Kess walked up to me and said, "Lord, Oscar, I just came here to play with you, not to make you mad at me. You got terrible on me!" I still remember my reply, which was made with loving antagonism: "It's my trio, Barney."

Having Barney Kessel in the group opened up new avenues of sound for us. His prodigious technique and harmonic sense allowed me to write arrangements which not only facilitated long flowing lines together, but also contrapuntal lines between which Barney would weave in and out, accompanied by Ray's big sound and rock-steady time. To add more impetus, we would sometimes have Ray join us in the linear playing, thereby giving tremendous depth and impact to the already exciting effect of three instruments joining forces. Working with a trio such as this, with Ray's legendary bass foundation and Barney's marvellous harmonic twists, curls, and "shouts" behind me, was something akin to pure heaven. To be in nightly competition with these two great soloists served not only to inspire me but also made me hone my own improvisational efforts. This group accomplished exactly what its original intent was: the initiation and establishment of the first totally integrated—musically and racially—Oscar Peterson Trio.

14

HERBIE'S STORY

"There's a something-else group playing over in Buffalo. Why don't we go over and hear them on the weekend?" These words, uttered by a friend of mine, signalled my first meeting with Herbie Ellis. The group he was playing with, The Soft Winds, was appearing at a hotel in Buffalo and had caused quite a lot of comment amongst the Toronto musicians who had caught their act. Herbie, along with Johnny Frigo on bass and violin, and the sensitive and talented Lou Carter on piano, had built a big following in the Buffalo and Toronto areas that was dedicated to their sound. I managed to get over to listen to them and was immediately impressed by their total togetherness and intuitive playing. I was especially enthralled with Herbie on guitar, who had a very natural, flowing solo style (he was obviously a lover of Charlie Christian), and a rhythmic sound and conception of time the likes of which are hard to come by. We had a great evening listening to them while exchanging musical ideas and stories between sets, but before I knew it, I was headed back to Toronto.

As Barney Kessel's year with the Trio drew to a close, the debate started as to who was going to take his place. Oddly enough, Barney suggested that he thought he had the perfect nominee for the spot: Herb Ellis. I agreed to contact Herb to see if he was interested, and sometime later we met in New York, where we reminisced at once about that fine evening in Buffalo. Herbie was a red-haired, freckle-faced, college-looking type with a Texas accent and—evident from the moment I first met him—a very trusting soul. He had adamant beliefs on many things in life; he also had some pretty strong musical beliefs. He loved Charlie Christian, Lester Young, and Charlie Parker, and made no secret of the fact. He also loved Freddie Green, as was obvious to any listener from the way that he played rhythm guitar in his group. I invited him to join us and he replied, "Oscar, I know you can play the piano, and I've also heard what you and Ray can do. I'm not sure if I can come up with what you want, but I'll sure give it a try." He also said that he was nervous about becoming the newest member of the Trio, because he had heard that Ray and I were heavy kidders and would go to almost any length for a laugh. I assured him that we did like to kid around, but that we had a standing rule that no one should ever get hurt as a result of any of our practical jokes.

It may seem unlikely, but I honestly believe that the question of a single white person between two Negroes in a group on stage never came up amongst us until the subject was broached in a newspaper interview. If I recall correctly, when Herbie was asked how he felt playing in such a group, I believe his answer was something like, "I can't answer that because I really hadn't noticed who I was playing with racially." Herbie's attitude remained this way throughout his entire six years in the group, and it's still true for all of us today.

On his entry into our group Herbie decided to hold a miniature press conference, with only the three of us present, in order to let us know "where he stood." He made us fully aware that he could enjoy a good laugh, but there were certain boundaries beyond which he was not prepared to go. He told us that he would not meddle in our personal business and expected reciprocal treatment. He then made the formidable mistake of saying that he had inquired of Barney Kessel what it was like working in our group. After much deliberation, Kess could apparently only come up with the reply, "Different." When pressed for a more detailed description, Barney told him he would have to wait and see. Upon hearing this, Ray and I glanced at each other: we instinctively knew that Herbie was in for it, and we decided he deserved a proper initiation into the Trio.

One of our first engagements was at a night club in Boston called The Top Hat, and we agreed to share an apartment-like suite in one of the residential hotels. There were two bedrooms, one at each end of the apartment; Ray and I said that we would take the bedroom with the twin beds, and as Herbie was the newest member of the group, he should have the one with the double bed in it until he became more at ease with us as his new confrères. Herbie agreed, and after sitting up talking at some length, we all said good night and adjourned to our separate bedrooms. Ray and I lay in bed keeping an eye on the light in Herbie's room until he apparently finished reading and it went out. Then we both silently crawled down the hall on our hands and knees into Herbie's bedroom, one on either side of the bed. At a given signal we both jumped up and into the bed with him, pulling the covers over us as we grabbed him and started kissing him on the cheek and telling him how much we loved him, and how happy we were that he was one of us. Poor Herbie didn't know what to make of this and when he managed to squirm loose, he careered out of the bed and headed down the hall towards the kitchen, with us in hot pursuit. By the time we caught up with him in the kitchen, we stood there, the three of us in our pyjamas, laughing until tears rolled down our faces and knowing that the bond had been formed. The second Trio was in force.

From our first musical get-together, there was a natural, almost spiritual musical bond within this particular group. Herbie brought an ease to the Trio in his own way that was totally different from the kind of musical impetus that Barney had supplied us with. There was also one other thing that I couldn't help noticing that interested me very much. The Trio took on a very strange split. Not only was it a trio as we had always known it to be as we rehearsed and played, but somewhere along the way, Herbie and Ray splintered off into another group of their own in which I had no place because it was something very private to them in their own musical way. I would go by to hang out with one or the other in the daytime on non-rehearsal days, and would walk smack into a rehearsal. The fascinating thing was that these were most often strictly rhythm rehearsals. Upon listening and asking what they were practising and rehearsing, I came to realize that they were laying out different harmonic road maps of various tunes that we were playing, while memorizing all the varying routes—highways that they would use to get from point A in a tune to point Z as smoothly as possible, as inventively as possible—and yet also creating different directions for my own lines.

They also worked on how, as a rhythm section, to turn up the steam gradually via differing methods. They rehearsed how to give a simple two–four rhythmic time a cooking lope, so that it swung so hard that the listener could anticipate the arrival of the four–four time which always seemed to be lurking in the rhythmic shadows of what they were playing. In addition Herbie and I had our own rehearsals, which we used to meld our lines into one with the same feeling and intent. When all of these elements finally meshed, the Trio blossomed, and we knew that we could go anywhere under almost any circumstance, and swing just as hard—in some cases harder—as many larger groups. There was a tremendous sense of gratification and accomplishment about what this particular group evolved into; I believe that we not only implemented what the Nat Cole and Art Tatum trios had started, but also took it in another direction.

15

TRIO CONTROL AND GROWTH

One of the regular comments that my various trios would elicit from listeners concerned the tightness and driving control we had on our night club and concert hall performances. However, these qualities were hard-earned, and only achieved after much discomfort and dedicated work. We aimed for total cohesion and pulsation, where the three of us thought and played as a single unit. This was an elusive goal at first, particularly as we were operating on what might be termed a split schedule. Part of the year was spent playing various night spots and supper clubs, while the balance was devoted to touring the world, playing assorted concert halls and such-like.

These differing musical environments formed the source of our main problem. I did not feel that we maintained our rhythmic groove or proper depth of pulsation in larger arenas. We eventually sat down at rehearsal and worked at a solution. Ray declared that he was pulling as hard as possible and that the adjustment would have to be made in some other area; Herb Ellis said he too was operating at maximum volume already. After a lengthy discussion we decided that the first people who had to be musically serene were ourselves, and that the overall volume would have to come down to a more comfortable level of playing.

As soon as we took this step, there was an almost instant meld of cohesiveness evident amongst us. Not only could I hear the rhythmic pulsation much more easily, but the harmonic pavement that Ray and Herb laid down for me became much clearer and more distinct. At the same time, I was able to initiate musical directives via my playing that would indicate to Ray and Herb exactly how much rhythmic steam I wanted behind me. This was done in several different ways so that it would not become noticeable to our listeners. First, my articulation on the piano would sometimes deepen, thereby indicating the need for a heavier "walking" type of time behind me. Another enabling device was the repeat of a definitive rhythmic figure that would serve as a gathering point for all of us. Many times, were you to be close enough to the Trio on stage, you would hear Ray say something like "OK Herb, let's tighten him up!" He would many times use what I called his "stutter step" on bass while Herb would lay out some of his well-known guitar shouts. All of this would mean that the Trio was "shifting gears." Then, as the impetus of the group increased, I would go into a deeper articulative bag on piano, and the group would move into high.

The one basic discovery we made was that we first had to make it happen for ourselves before it could possibly happen for the audience. The secret of success, whatever our mode of playing, lay in our control of dynamics: we could communicate in a whisper, a roar, or any of the levels in between. Added to this, both Herb and Ray would practise harmonic movement between themselves separately, so that they could easily operate as one. This gave us an even more significant feeling of tightness, which, in turn, enlivened my playing. As my lines surged higher, the rhythm section would react, and again increase their pulsation. I believe this is how the Trio was able to impart that tremendous sense of cohesiveness during the heat of playing, and sheer power.

Armed with these tools of rhythmic intensity and pulsation, the group was able to retain its shape and sting even in the largest of arenas. We feared no one. We had no apprehension about meeting any other jazz group, even if those groups contained horns.

As a case in point, we were once booked into the Blackhawk in San Francisco, opening on a Friday for two weeks. When we arrived in town, we discovered we had been booked to open while the Dave Brubeck Quartet still had three days to go. The owners, seeing the opportunity of profiting from this booking error (and envisioning one hell of a weekend) insisted that the contracts be honoured as they stood. My guys called for a meeting, and Ray informed me that he had been elected as spokesperson to deliver a specific message—that unless I laid some pianistic lumps on Dave, they would both give their notice. I inquired of them what they were going to do with the rest of Dave's group, and they replied that they would look after the rhythm section if I took care of Dave and Paul Desmond solo-wise. This kind of competitive spirit typified the jazz scene years ago. There was absolutely nothing sinister and vehement about it, but it meant that the audience got to enjoy the musical result of jazz people duelling with one another, locked in a creative war of ideas.

Having no intention of losing my Trio, I responded to the challenge and went for broke: I felt that my Trio had never played better and neither, perhaps, had I. The marvellous part of all of this is that Dave Brubeck and I remain friends to this day. There is no place in the world of true creativity for pettiness and shallow thoughts. The jazz medium is populated by a select group of truly talented people, and talent sustains itself simply by its need for growth and refinement, coupled with an unbiased curiosity to find out who is best of the best.

16

MEMBERSHIP FLOW IN THE TRIO (I): THE 1950S

During the period that Herbie Ellis was battling with his drinking problem, he was sometimes unable to fulfill the Trio's engagements, so I was forced to bring in various substitutes to maintain a working group. Many well-known players were kind enough to come in and help us fill the void: Kenny Burrell, a guitarist of rare talent; Bobby Atchinson, a percussionist out of Philadelphia, whose story in itself is a sad one; Gene Gammage, another percussionist who possessed considerable talent; and lastly Irving Ashby, familiar to many through his stint with the Nat King Cole Trio.

Speaking first of Kenny Burrell, I remember him primarily for his melodic solo lines and introspective inventions. Kenny was not a "cooker" in the sense that I associate with Barney Kessel, Wes Montgomery, or Tal Farlow, being a more pensive and laid-back player. Compared to Barney and Herbie, he chose less intense harmonic structures, but placed them in such a way and in such effective places that they invariably stood out on their own. Kenny was only in the group for a short while before Herbie recovered and returned to us.

Bobby Atchinson joined the Trio under similar circumstances and remained in the group for a few weeks. Normally, of course, we were a guitar trio, so when Bobby came to fill in for Herb, it was a total and sudden change for us. He had a drivingly intense conception of time and I particularly remember his ability to radiate the same rhythmic heat with brushes as he did with sticks—a really difficult feat. This gave our music a seamless, fluent feel that pleased me very much.

I was aware that Bobby had problems, although at first it was only noticeable during intermissions, when he would simply disappear. It was not until he failed to show up for an engagement that we found out he was a prisoner of drugs. Unfortunately we never heard from him again until we were informed of his death from this ailment some years later. I not only mourn the man, as most humans would, but I also mourn a great talent that was never properly heard.

Irving Ashby entered our group as a very well-known player in his own right. Having spent many years with Nat King Cole's group, he came in with a confidence which was fully deserved; intriguingly, however, he was also somewhat apprehensive. He had become accustomed to playing lines with and against Nat's piano, but wasn't entirely sure he could do the same in my group. He cautioned me that Nat and I were obviously two different pianists; he also intimated that latterly Nat was increasingly interested in vocal rather than instrumental development, and that the Trio's work had come to reflect this.

During his tenure in the group I noticed a very interesting thing: here was an unspoken rivalry between Irving and Ray. It was not exactly a war, but it most certainly was a matter of neither one giving way to the other. Ray was always willing to play any lines required of him, no matter how difficult, whereas Irving seemed to feel that we did not need as many linear statements being made by both bass and guitar. Irving's presence meant that the Trio swung in a notably mellow fashion. He never pretended to be a great up-tempo player, but he sure could mellow into a righteous groove if the tempo was put anywhere within his liking. He brought a rich and swinging melodic feel to the group.

Drummer Gene Gammage was added to the group at the request of an establishment that we were going to play in Vegas. The management didn't believe a drumless trio could survive in the room (obviously they had never heard the Trio in concert or in Basin Street opposite the Stan

Kenton Orchestra!). Nevertheless, we acquiesced and brought him in. He was a tall, lanky, good-looking youngster, and multi-talented: he was not only a gifted drummer but also quite a comedian, and a "sleight-of-hand" artist to boot, and would keep us amused during our off moments in Vegas. His most famous remark was made while standing backstage during one of the intermissions. Ray, Herbie, and I were engaged in conversation and in this particular instance Gene was referring to the normal Trio and leaving himself out of it. He suddenly turned to me with a serious and perplexed look on his face, and asked, "Tell me something, Oscar, if you ever have a race riot in your band, whose side are you on?" Needless to say this virtually destroyed the next set, and that remark still lives on and is repeated over and over again—a fitting memorial to the kind of person Gene Gammage was.

Once, on pay night, he pleaded with me to give him only $100 of his pay, and under no circumstances, were he to come back to me for more money before the next pay day, was I to relent and give more to him. I said that if he was serious about this I would do it and would not at any point give him money. The following night the group was off-duty, and as we always did on such evenings, we made the rounds of the other clubs to see some of the musicians we could not normally catch. Almost from the first club we visited, I received the news that Gene Gammage was running around looking for me. I somehow had an idea of what he wanted! At around 3.00 a.m. I was sitting in another club when in walks Gene with a chorus girl on each arm. Upon spying me, he rushed over and said, "Hey, Pete, I'm sure glad I found you, let me have $300 and keep the rest."

I immediately reminded him of his request the night before and told him that I could not give him the money. His request became much more emotional, and he became really aggressive. I calmly kept repeating the instructions that he had given me, which only served to bring on more anger and threats.

As I mentioned earlier, Gene was a tall and very slight youngster, probably weighing in at some 135 pounds, in contrast to my weight then which was around 290 pounds. After realizing that pleading was getting him nowhere, he started bleating in a very angry way that he just had to have the money; by this time we were standing face to face looking like Mutt and Jeff. When I made what was my final reply to his request, I added, "I am afraid that you will have to whip me for your money, Gene!" His reply brought gales of laughter from our party of musicians who had watched this scene from the very beginning: Gene suddenly reared up in my face and shouted, "Well, P, I guess we are going to have to go outside and waltz!" This threw the whole party into pandemonium at the ridiculousness of the two combatants standing nose to nose, and it was only then that we decided to sit down and laugh it off.

That is Gene Gammage as I remember him. A young man with an irrepressible sense of humour, but with an honest love for the music that he made his life. It was a very sad moment years later when I was informed of his passing away.

Editor's Note: By this point in the narrative Peterson's career had undergone a major transformation. Fully established in the United States as a star attraction, he had revealed himself to be an accompanist of remarkable sensitivity and catholic range, and by 1952 he was, in effect, Norman Granz's "house pianist." Moreover, even before Herb Ellis took over from Barney Kessel, the Oscar Peterson Trio had emerged as a nonpareil rhythm section, forming the mainstay of Granz's Jazz At The Philharmonic tours and assisting at a host of recordings for his Clef, Norgran, and (eventually) Verve labels.

Although JATP first saw the light of day on July 2, 1944 at the Philharmonic Auditorium in Hollywood, there are grounds for regarding it as a definitive 1950s phenomenon. During that decade Granz promoted virtually every modern-mainstream musician of note, and many others of a different category too. Furthermore, his adamant refusal to play to segregated audiences and his insistence that every employee be accorded first-class facilities and treatment meant that JATP became important for reasons other than just musical ones.

By 1957, which saw JATP's last tour of the USA, the face of jazz—and of America itself—was changing fast. But in those six years from 1952

Oscar Peterson's life and work described a pattern both regular and sumptuous, taking him all over the world and bringing him into the company of as diverse an array of musicians as could readily be imagined. The chapters which follow reflect Peterson's life on the road and in the studio during this time, and, like JATP itself, they document a significant slice of musical and social history.

17

EARLY TRIO LIFE AND DEALING WITH THE ROAD

T hanks to Norman's expert guidance, the Trio with Ray and Herbie evolved a yearly schedule that was both enjoyable and flexible. In the fall, the annual JATP tour of America took place, usually followed by several weeks of night-club engagements that would bring us close to the Christmas vacation. Towards the end of January, the group would re-unite and resume its night-club schedule, which was usually interspersed with concerts and recordings.

After the fall tour, a lot of record dates would be set up in LA to coincide with the Trio's night-club stay there—in effect we became Norman's "in-house" rhythm section for all the artists he wanted to record. Then, as of 1952, the Trio would be off on the spring JATP tour of Europe. At the beginning of these European tours, the Trio would once again function as three-quarters of the rhythm section for the jam session end of the show, returning after the interval for our own trio performance. On our return home in late spring or early summer, we would then appear at some of the festivals, and eventually break off for summer vacations.

From the outset there were encouraging signs that this trio had the potential to survive for quite some time. Not only did we hit it off musically: we also got on very well personally, which made it even easier to operate as a group. Part of this pleasing normalcy was down to Norman's aforementioned scheduling and our consequent professional serenity; but we were also helped by the fact that each of us had his own individual hobby that took up some of the hours not occupied by working or rehearsing. Ray and Herb were both avid golfers, while I became passionately interested in photography—to the extent of carrying a miniature darkroom around with me, enabling me to develop and print some of my negatives in the early hours of the morning in my hotel room.

I badly missed some of the hobbies that I was able to pursue at home, and it had taken me quite some time to adjust to road life, but photography was an ideal "road hobby," for it could be easily assimilated with all the travel and touring. Indeed, it was not until I began involving myself with various studies and art forms that I wished to know more about that I was able to escape from that notorious road illness: loneliness. At one time I bought myself a very powerful miniature telescope, and would spend hour upon hour at night after work on hotel rooftops, trying to look at distant objects through the haze of the city lights. When you are lonely on the road, your hotel room tends to become your cell, and I found that until I was able to solve those long hours of depression, I couldn't totally enjoy touring.

My efforts even stretched into the sporting field, in that I became a golfer of sorts for a while. This lasted until I developed cysts or ganglions on my wrists, which were not only ugly but extremely painful. Towards the end of a tour of the Far East, while I was preparing to return home to have my wrist operated on, one of the cysts broke in Hong Kong as I was playing, which worried me enormously. But next day I noticed that the cyst was gradually disappearing, and they had all done so completely by the time I returned to the USA, thereby making the operation unnecessary.

At this point I decided to use some of my road-time to learn more about various things I hadn't previously had time for. Once the Trio was fully established and recording successfully, I studied audio and electronics to a point where I could at least converse with studio engineers without feeling uncomfortable, for I intended one day to have my own studio—a dream that has since been realized. My interest in studio gear was both intense and permanent: I remain as fascinated by today's rapid electronic advances. I also took instruction in photography, including a couple of correspondence courses—most of which were mailed to me on the road by my wife.

I have always wanted to be able to fly-fish, and with the aid of a musician friend of mine, Butch Watanabe, and lessons from one of the kind salesmen at Hardy's in London's Pall Mall (Scotty by name, I believe), I became a disciple of the Sir Isaac Walton school. On certain mornings I would rise early and be driven to meet Scotty at a misty body of water on the outskirts of London, in order to stand there shivering in the damp cool of the day while he taught me how to handle a huge salmon fly rod, which he threw with an ease no one would believe. Fishing is a very special part of my life: it brought about a form of tranquillity in me, and also taught me how to enjoy such serenity to the full.

I have long believed that nothing can surpass the beauty of being out on a lake at dusk when nature gradually quietens, coming almost to a standstill before awakening briefly to feed and refresh itself before absolute darkness descends. These are treasured hours: quite apart from the enjoyment of catching the occasional trout, I have sat in my boat and found the answer to key questions that seemed answerless in the continual grind of the city. The province I live in is dotted with many majestic lakes. On the drive from my home in Toronto to my cottage, passing these bodies of water magically festooned in colour and loveliness, I have often wondered how many Ontarians realize how fortunate they are to live in an environment that sits at their very elbow, waiting to enrich their lives. Although I have composed the *Canadiana Suite*, which musically travels from coast to coast, one day I would love to do a specialized composition that evokes the beauty and healing tranquillity of the area known as the Haliburton Highlands. It has afforded me great moments of understanding myself as a human being, supplying nourishment that has sustained me during my more gruelling tours around the world.

18

THE DINNER BATTLES

As soon as we started travelling together, it became apparent that Ray was as much of a put-on addict as I, and as the duo days progressed, the practical jokes abounded. I should stress at once that they were all subject to one rule that was never broken: neither the original joke nor the reprisal was allowed to cause either party any form of hurt or harm. Some of our jokes were too complicated to recount here; however, Ray instigated one that at the time I could see no end to.

We had fallen into the habit of taking turns to host dinner for each other night by night. This worked well for a while, until I noticed two things: my own bills were becoming ever-heftier, and what I was eating as Ray's guest bore no relationship to such expenditure. I decided to bring this to Ray's attention, and also get my own back by giving him a night he would never forget.

We were appearing at the (now defunct) Blue Note Jazz Club in Chicago, and staying at the Palmer House Hotel downtown. Our sets began at 9.20 p.m., so we usually ate dinner at about 5.30. I called Ray, reminded him that it was his turn, and shortly afterwards arrived in his room at about 5.45. I started by ordering the most expensive appetizer I could find on the menu; at this, Ray looked up but said nothing. I then ordered the costliest main course I could find, at which Ray merely nodded and said, "That's okay, Tommy Tucker, but you better eat all that order or you won't live to get to work tonight!" I finished off with the biggest dessert available—a full baked Alaska, which the operator told Ray would take at least an hour to prepare. I insisted on having it, and Ray condescended to confirm the order.

In my mind this did not constitute enough of a bruising for what Ray had been doing to me, so I decided to embarrass him as much as I could. Just before the time when I figured dinner would arrive, I donned the sheet from Ray's bed and put it round my shoulders; as a knock sounded at the door, I quickly reached over, grabbed the living-room lampshade, plonked it on my head, folded my arms, and assumed a regal position at the window. Ray came out of the bathroom and let in the two waiters. They bade him a congenial "Good evening, sir," and pushed the trays into the middle of the room, whereupon they noticed me and my regalia. They uttered a confused "Good evening, sir" to me, to which I did not reply. Ray explained that I was an African chief visiting America and that I spoke no English. The waiters nervously set out the hors d'oeuvres, all the while sneaking the occasional glance at this huge immobile visitor who stood gazing out on Chicago with a lampshade on his head.

By now, Ray was about to burst from restraining his laughter; fortunately, the waiters retreated to the door, nervously informing us they would be back to serve the main course. Once they'd left I turned from the window to find Ray convulsed over the table. He eventually recovered enough to say, "That's all right, you idiot: the joke's on you, because you're going to have to assume that same pose each time they come back in this God-damn room!" At which point we both collapsed in unstoppable fits of laughter.

Oddly enough, I never got invited back to Ray's room for dinner for the rest of that tour.

19

A DIFFERENT KIND OF TAPING

On one of the Trio's visits to Detroit's Rouge Lounge, Ray and Herbie got their revenge for some of the gags I'd laid on them. They arranged for the owner (and normally my good friend!) Ed Sarkesian to take me for a walk during the intermission of our Sunday matinée, and in my absence taped the front side of the keyboard with transparent tape. They were very astute about it: they didn't tape all the keys, but were diabolically selective—three notes here, skip the next four, two notes there, and so on. As a result, I was totally confused when I came to play: there was, obviously, no consistency to the problem, and I had no idea what had gone wrong with my keyboard. The decisive factor was that it was impossible to see the tape under even the closest scrutiny, so I remained unenlightened, sitting there like a dummy with no next move in mind. In the end, the only way out seemed to be to sing—so I did.

20

THE BUS—PART ONE

Touring on Jazz At The Philharmonic was a very special occupation. I might categorize it as a totally separate realm, a unique university with its own very special curriculum. Being a heavy player in the concert halls and arenas bought you no favours in this college-on-wheels: living on a bus had its own specific rules, and you either lived by these or became a non-entity. Luckily, I had experienced some of this "tour-on-a-bus" life in earlier days with the Johnny Holmes Orchestra, which aided me at JATP, although these tours were something else again.

First and foremost, you chose a seat on the bus and it remained yours for the duration of the tour. Second, you did not, under any circumstances, take a seat already chosen by another member of the group. You respected the space around other members' seats, meaning that you did not stand in the aisle to hold a conversation next to a sleeping member's seat; you went to the back of the bus or some equivalent place. Other people's property was definitely off limits to you, and nothing was ever taken for granted. These and many other rules, most of them unspoken, were rigorously enforced, and hardly ever broken. Problems only arose when "foreigners," or people who were guests of the various members, travelled with us. Fortunately, these situations were few. For the most part, the bus rolled along with us enjoying one another's companionship.

One scene that remains etched in my memory is of a particular trip that we had after an afternoon concert at a university in Kansas. We all boarded the bus in good humour and Norman, with his usual sense of caring for his brood, had arranged to have some hot food put on board for us. And not just any old hot food: he would go to great lengths to customize our meals to our individual tastes. For instance, he might have hot BBQ brought in for us, but knowing Ella was a lover of seafood, would provide a hot seafood dish for her. I recall Coleman Hawkins being handed the very special kind of brandy that he had been unable to pick up for the last few days.

It was after one of these great meals that the group settled down into a sort of contented repleteness, and some of the members began reminiscing about other jazz people. As is generally the case in such discussions, certain tunes were almost automatically associated with particular artists. I remember Ella asking Roy Eldridge if he recalled the way that Billie Holiday used to do this or that tune. Upon which Lady Fitz launched into a "Lady Day" version of *What A Little*

Moonlight Will Do. She glanced around at Herbie Ellis, gesturing for him to get his guitar, which he did, supplying her with that beautiful soft-finger strum as only he can do. Out of nowhere, Roy uncased his horn, put in the mute, and commenced playing a beautiful obbligato to her vocal. Our bus driver, Bart, had an intuitive sense about the various members of the troupe, their reactions, and also the situations that developed among us. Sensing this to be one of those "moments," he very quietly slipped the bus into overdrive, slowed down, and relaxed in his seat to enjoy the music.

Try to picture the scene as I saw and heard it, and try to envision what a great cameo it was, both visually and musically. Here was this great big Greyhound bus rolling down the Kansas highway on a picture-perfect evening; inside some of the greatest jazz people that could possibly ever be mustered at any one place and at any given time. There sits Ella in her seat, her eyes closed, totally engrossed in making each word of the lyric count to its fullest. Behind her sits Herbie Ellis, his guitar perched across his knees playing a soft accompaniment, while Roy Eldridge and Lester Young engage in playing soft, sensitive lines behind her. Ray Brown somehow manages to balance himself and his bass in the aisle in order to lend Fitz his support. She sang her heart out, song after song, and we all applauded and grinned in excitement and appreciation, for we all knew that we were a part of a very special "musical moment."

21

THE BUS—PART TWO

P eople seem to develop a different sort of personality when travelling on a bus with others. Perhaps it is a form of self-protection, a character-armour we acquire to hide our true emotions at such close quarters. Some, normally extroverts, become laconic in manner; others, usually laid-back, become more highly strung. And almost everyone becomes an authority on some subject or another: mine was photography.

I had always had a profound interest in this art, and with the opportunity to travel, my passion for it grew. I accumulated more and more expensive gear as the tours progressed, and could often be seen struggling on and off the bus trying to balance copious quantities of photographic equipment. Whenever someone was tempted to purchase some new piece of camera gear, this invariably entailed checking out its operation with yours truly. I must say that I enjoyed the expert status bestowed on me; it also made me pursue my photographic studies even more. There I would sit on some of those long overnight hauls, the bus silence broken only by the occasional hiss of the air brakes or one of Charlie Shavers' punctuating snores, my camera on the seat beside me and various magazines on photography spread out alongside, the tiny overhead lamp forlornly trying to illuminate the words that were bouncing around the page as the bus swayed on its springs. In this way I soaked up whatever camera knowledge I could as the night passed in an endless parade of little towns.

The faith and trust that the JATP guys showed in my photographic know-how was not entirely typical: they tended to be suspicious of claims to expertise. Some member would suddenly volunteer some specialist information, and if he was not challenged would enlarge on the subject, growing more elaborate and profound with every sentence.

One such person was J.C. Heard, also known as Sweetie Dee. JC was renowned for being very nattily attired at all times. As Ray Brown likes to recall, whenever JC decided to take a nap on the bus, he would first carefully arrange the crease in his pants and jacket while standing, and then would descend into his seat ever so carefully so as not to mess anything. On one trip I waited until he had dropped off into a sound sleep, and, borrowing Ella's nail polish, I carefully painted JC's nails, eyebrows, and mustache. When he awoke, he looked around to find everyone, almost to a person, convulsed or snickering in their seats. He asked us what was the matter, and waving his hands in frustration, suddenly saw a flash of red go by his face. He stopped: "Damn, I cut myself!" This fuelled the laughter, which quickly grew into high-octane chaos as he first realized what had been done to his nails, and then took in the facial damage, thanks to a mirror handed him by his regular partner in crime, Charlie Shavers. JC sank to his seat in total defeat, muttering helplessly, "Oh my God, I don't dare get off the bus."

JC's most celebrated debacle, however, was what came to be known as The Borsalino Incident, which took place when the tour reached Milan. JC suddenly jumped up into the aisle and held forth about the famous Borsalino hats for men, declaring them the finest headgear in the world. As usual, Charlie Shavers told him he was full of shit. "You wouldn't know a genuine Borsalino if they were to hit you in the ass with one," he insisted, and the argument went on and on until they agreed to settle it the following day.

The next night, backstage at the concert hall, Charlie Shavers waltzed in and started yelling for JC to show. They both had the now familiar cylinders that Borsalinos came in (I bought one that day also). Charlie made no bones about his hat being a genuine article, while JC's tube did not contain a Borsalino. JC insisted that Charlie prove it. Charlie pulled the hat out of the tube, slapped it on his arm, flicked it into its natural shape, and put it on his head. JC asked just what that proved, and put his own hat on. It looked good to me.

"Means nothing," said Charlie. "Watch this. Only a real Borsalino can stand up to this!" He took off his hat, rolled it up, unrolled it, re-formed it, and put it back on his head.

"Lemme see that jive Borsalino of yours do that!" said Charlie, with full disdain in his voice.

"That ain't no big deal," said JC, as he removed his sky piece. "The problem with you is that you think that you know everything. Dig this!" He then proceeded to twist his hat with true vengeance and then folded it over on itself.

"When I put this lid down, baby, it will go back to its natural self."

He let go of the death grip that he had on the hat and tossed it onto the table. It lay there for a second, looking like a miniature car that had been rescued from a car crusher. It twitched limply once or twice, and then just rested there as if it had passed away. JC reached over as the laughter started and took the hat in his hands.

"What happened to your lid, baby?" taunted Charlie. "What happened to your Borsalino? It's as jive as you are."

JC walked away muttering to himself, "The man said it was a genuine Borsalino. He guaranteed it when he took my bread."

22

KISSING BANDIT

A s in any confined environment, the JATP bus sometimes put a strain on the occupants' tolerance; any kind of upheaval tended to become amplified and people often overreacted. And although it was not often that Norman suffered from this syndrome, when he did become incensed with any one of us, a deathly silence would descend on the crew.

One particular night Norman became enraged with one of the

members who had committed some kind of *faux pas*. He gave tonight's target what I would evaluate, on a scale of 1 to 10, a size 8 "reading" (i.e. dressing down). True to form, upon hearing this fracas, the whole crew fell into silence, quickly mounted the bus, and took their seats to get out of the way. Ray Brown happened to be sitting next to me and the seat in front of us was empty. The people on the bus were, at most, carrying on whispered conversations in order not to draw attention to themselves, though Norman was not even on the bus at this time. He finally boarded with the familiar scowl on his face, and slouched into the seat immediately in front of Ray and myself. The bus took off in almost total silence, with no one wanting to attract Norman's attention. Low profiles prevailed.

Norman had a habit that I am sure he was not aware of: sometimes, when enraged, he would suck in his breath at measured intervals. This mysterious, subconscious tic was well in evidence tonight: as the bus rolled along, practically the only sound you could hear was Señor Granz's intermittent sniff.

As we sat there Norman took off his hat and put it on the seat beside him, thereby exposing his now semi-balding pate. I was in a silly frame of mind, and leaned over to Ray Brown and said, "How much if I kiss Norman right on his bald spot?" At that point Ray broke into barely stifled chuckles, rolling back and forth in his seat as he envisioned what would happen if I actually did this. The devil in me prompted "Go for it!" and I raised myself up, leaned over Señor Granz (who was now into a semi-doze), and planted the loudest resounding kiss right on top of his balding head. There was an ominous half-second of absolute silence in the bus and the next moment the whole crew broke into uproarious fits of laughter. I thought Ray Brown was going to die!

While all this was going on Norman just sat in his seat and nodded his head, as if to say, "That is not the end of this." The laughter became even more uncontrolled until finally Norman himself was forced to break up.

Immediately the tension was released. Illinois Jacquet started a game of crap at the rear of the bus; everyone realized that the squall was really over when Jacquet yelled, "Shoot the 50!" and Norman yelled back, "You're covered!"

Another crisis had passed.

23

ICE-CREAM CHARLIE DOES
IT AGAIN

In the mid-1950s JATP concerts invariably closed with *Perdido*, fronted by Ella and featuring the entire troupe of horns. On one tour the tune's ending not only got longer by the night but funkier too; after a couple of weeks of this, Ray Brown observed, "I can see where this shit is going to have to end. It's going to get so funky that Jo Jones will have to lay one of those four-bar Dixieland drum breaks on us, and we'll all troop off stage playing a real funky Dixie ending!" We all broke up, and Roy Eldridge added to the hilarity by outlining the way he'd leave the stage, employing his famous Thirties strut.

A few nights later Norman Granz was, as usual, standing in the wings, ready to time his walk to the mike so that it ended just as we played the final downbeat to the finale. Ella had really got down into *Perdido* and it was grooving something fierce; Ray slapped the edge of the piano, and on looking up I heard him saying, "This is it, this is it!" He had primed both Jo and Roy for the new Dixieland ending, and tonight was obviously going to be the night.

Norman arrived at the mike in perfect synch with Ella's final "Per—di—do," and Jo came down on his two main cymbals with that inimitable smile radiating through the entire auditorium. Naturally assuming that we were all done, Norman began his thank-you speech—

just as Jo dove into his four-bar Dixie break. Norman's eyebrows shot up and the head came round, an icy stare fixed on Jo. Roy then stuck his trumpet inside his coat and strutted away towards the piano; Jo came down on his final crash all by his lonesome self, with Norman's gaze still locked on him with all the ferocity with which a Great White zeroes in on its prey. The cymbal sound—and Jo's smile—faded away, leaving a deafening silence for what seemed an age. Norman restarted his closing announcement and strode off with imperious fury, with Roy and a worriedly contrite Jo bringing up the rear. Ice-Cream Charlie got off scot-free, naturally.

24

THE SLASHER

Prolonged travel breeds tedium, and tedium can prompt people to do silly or strange things. Once, simply because I had nothing else to do, I decided to buy a straight razor. There was nothing wrong with the razor I was using at the time, nor did I know anything about shaving with a straight razor, apart from its being highly dangerous if not wielded properly; it just seemed like a good idea at the time. So I went ahead and bought it, complete with strop and safety lecture. Perversely, I let it lie idle for several days; then one afternoon in a motel in Kansas, I decided it was time for its momentous debut. I carefully laid everything out, showered, and, finally addressing the mirror, lathered up my face and stood with the razor poised in my hand.

There were two things I wasn't aware of. First, the door to my room was ajar, affording passers-by an almost complete view of my nude state; second—and rather more important—Dizzy Gillespie happened to be out and about and on the prowl for mischief. Just as I made the first pass at my face, something bit me on the ass; I yelped and, of course, striped my face with the razor. Now I'm nude, exposed, *and* bleeding like the proverbial stuck pig, while Dizzy is running away down the path, laughing his head off and only partly aware of the havoc he's caused.

I played that evening's concert with my face adorned by the biggest piece of tape you've ever seen, and later that same night the straight razor went straight into the garbage can.

25

THE RETURN OF THE DALLAS FLASH

This story hinges on three main things. First, Dallas happens to be Illinois Jacquet's home town; second, it does not take anyone long to discover that Illinois is not exactly short on self-confidence; third, whenever he had had a drink or two, he would not have thought it impossible to take the Challenger Shuttle or some other rocket out for what he might term "a spin."

During an early JATP tour, we arrived in Dallas for our annual concert there. As usual, Norman was a bit leery about the concerts in the South; one never knew what might befall the mixed group. He was noticeably edgy this particular night; there was a huge crowd, and the police were having problems getting everyone into the auditorium, eventually calling for a delay. This complicated things further as the hall had a curfew, and the audience was certainly not going to be short-changed.

Illinois arrived regaled in a royal blue satin tuxedo, with the appropriate stripe down the pant done in an even brighter shade of satin. "All right!" he shouted to all of us. "This is my home town! This shit belongs to Illinois tonight!" He strutted around backstage uttering all kinds of pronouncements about the importance of his appearance here this evening. He glanced in my direction and said, "Ah, you big bitch! [his normal greeting to me] You'd better play your big ass off this evening 'cause you're in the King's home town tonight."

He continued to prance around and generally heckle whoever was at hand. Finally, the road manager Tommy Harp called us all on stage with the curtain down, and said that Norman had to go to the box office for a moment, and to wait for him to return and start the show. We stood around and quietly conversed amongst ourselves, when all of a sudden Jacquet strolled on stage and asked what the hold-up was. When Tommy told him what Norman had said, he replied "Shit! You've got a whole house out there waiting to hear me, let's go!" We dissented, and reminded him of what Norman had said. He shrugged his shoulders and said, "Screw that! These people are waiting to hear me. Hit it!" With that he took off by himself on *The Star-Spangled Banner*.

Upon hearing this, the stage-hands figured the show was starting and proceeded to raise the curtain. Just then Norman came rushing backstage and yelled to the stage-hands to lower the curtain, which they did. He strode to centre stage where Jacquet was still playing (by himself) and asked who gave the permission to start the show. Jacquet looked up at him and said, "Hell Norm, these people came to hear their man! They can't wait forever, so I started the anthem."

Norman gave him that now-famous glare, said, "You're fired!" and walked off, pursued by Illinois, who was now pleading with Norman to change his mind. To no avail. A few moments later, Norman had the curtain raised, walked on for the introductions, and made the announcement that Illinois Jacquet would not be playing this evening. He continued by saying that anyone who was disenchanted with that fact could go to the box office and have their money refunded. As he reported to a dejected Illinois later that night, there were no takers.

26

FIVE CAMEOS

Art Tatum to Ray Brown, while they were playing cards and as Ray was attempting to sneak a card from the pack to see if Art would notice:

"Ray Brown, the last man who tried that one on me is still drawing compensation."

Harry Edison to Ray Brown, as they boarded the bus in Chicago on a bitterly cold and windy evening after a concert. Ray was wearing a beautiful new topcoat that in no way suited the kind of weather that Chicago was in the midst of.

"Shit, Brown, you are prettier than a bitch in that coat but if Hawk [the weather] catches your ass out here in the street in that onion skin one more time, I am going to inherit me a new spring coat!"

Lester Young to Bobby Scott, after standing behind Bobby who was deep into a Bud Powell-type solo in which his left hand was not playing that much, but rather skimming over the keys without striking them:

"Say Lady Bobby Sox, those right people [his right hand] are really trying to say something, but how about those left people [his left hand]? Aren't they kind of doing a Silent Night?"

Norman Granz to the JATP troupe at the beginning of the first of two concerts to be held on the same night:

"Horns, do me a favour and keep your solos shorter on the first concert because we have two shows tonight. We must have enough time to empty the first house and refill it for the second show. The stage hands have an eleven o'clock curfew and we must get the two concerts in, so do me a favour and don't make your solos too long."

Dizzy Gillespie, in his normal off-handed way as he stood there with that impish grin on his face: "Don't worry about me, Norm. I can play everything I know in four bars!"

Illinois Jacquet to Ben Webster as Ben prepares to tee off on the first hole (some 240 yards away):

"Go on, Frog, go ahead and lay it up there on the green."

Ben pauses in his stance and glares at Jacquet: "What in the hell do you mean, 'lay it up there on the green'? Shit! There ain't nothing up there but green!"

27
THE KNOWLEDGEABLE MEDIA

"I feel it could be a very interesting album, particularly to the Canadian public because, after all, it isn't as if you're unknown to them, OP. Plus which, all of the tunes in the album were written by Canadian composers, and we're using Canadian musicians on the date and recording it right here in Toronto."

So spoke Norman Granz in McClear Place recording studios as we waited for the musicians to assemble. "We even have the major Toronto newspapers here too, so that it will at least get coverage prior to the release of the album."

At that moment, a man approached me, presenting himself as a photographer from one of the major local newspapers. Informing me that he wanted to get a couple of fast shots before the date started, he led me into the area in which the group would be playing. "Please, Mr Peterson," he pleaded, "would you be good enough to show me exactly where you stand when you're playing your trumpet?"

28

THE SOUTHERN DRAUGHT

"That's a talent like I've never heard before. Somebody's going to bring him Stateside and make a real star out of him."

He was a man of medium height, dark brown hair, wearing a neatly designed business suit. He was addressing our manager at the Alberta Lounge, Joe Woldarsky. "You can't keep that kind of talent up here in Canada and not share it with us."

Joe stood there, rocking back and forth on his heels as was his habit, and nodded assent. He had told me several days ago that this man had been in every night so far, and was overcome with my playing. As I passed by on my way to the bar for refreshment, Joe caught my sleeve and said, "Oscar, meet a gentleman who is a great admirer of your music." The man started to rave about my playing before I could say anything, and continued for what seemed minutes on end. When he finally stopped, I put out my hand and said something like the usual "Please to meet you."

At that moment his facial expression changed abruptly; he recoiled in anger, his hand jerked away behind his back and he said, "I could never shake hands with a nigger! I love your playing, but down home in Georgia we don't allow niggers to even come into a place like this, let alone shake hands with them."

I will never forget the pain and enraged hurt that this incident triggered in me. I went home consumed with anger, vowing never to allow myself to be entrapped in such a situation ever again. To be going through what had been a good evening all round and then to be confronted with such sudden racist hatred is very difficult to cope with. It is disorienting: one wonders who one really is, but trying to establish that involves renewed exposure to all that hurt and disillusionment. You can't stay out there, and you can't come home. And that is the precise aim of bigotry: to reduce people's ability to function properly so as to allow the bigots greater opportunity and initiative for their own private goals.

It would be untrue to say I had not experienced bigotry before: I grew up with it, albeit in milder form. We all did: it is commonplace for Irish and Italian kids to fight, or Jewish kids to be tormented by others of the Christian faith, or—pre-eminently—black kids to be pursued and taunted by white children. But I didn't take that anything like as much to heart as the Alberta Lounge episode.

However, my real "education" in bigotry and racial hatred took place when I first toured the South with JATP in 1950. I really wasn't prepared for the fascist oppression that characterized life south of the Mason–Dixon line. To be insulted, called names, or denied access is one thing, however unacceptable; to live in constant fear of physical harm or even death is quite another. To understand my situation and experience fully, we need to look at how those early tours were arranged.

Norman abhorred bigotry and racial indignity of any kind, needless to say, and had quietly decided to do something to right some of these wrongs. And this meant that, to a degree, the black members of the troupe were guinea-pigs, or at least in the front line when it came to potential conflict. It was remarkable—and almost sinister—how things gradually changed as we travelled southwards. There I was, the wide-eyed Canadian Negro (whose nickname on the tour was Frack) with his Montreal *joie de vivre* cavorting on the bus with my Italian buddy, Flip Phillips (nicknamed Frick), with whom I roomed on the northern end of the tour. The jubilant, easy-come, easy-go northern atmosphere gradually changed to one of subdued conversation, then nervous tension, and finally outright bitterness and revilement. Until Mason–Dixon, everything was done together, as friends; beyond that point, one could see Flip and the other Caucasians growing angry and embarrassed by what they knew was coming. I will never forget the bus pulling up to the great big "white" hotel on the "right" side of town, and all the white members saying "So long" as they disembarked with shamed reluctance. There were ugly cuss words about the unfairness and stupidity of it all; then the bus door closed and the journey began to the "other" side of town.

As the bus slowly crossed Kansas City, I noticed sadly that the real estate was becoming shabbier and shabbier as the night pedestrians' colour darkened. Then we arrived at the Street's Hotel—not exactly AAA accommodation. I saw Negroes from all walks of life going about their business. Some were well-dressed, others not. Some were sober, others weren't. Some were amiable, others angry. Some were curious, others oblivious. And all around were the sounds of various rhythm-&-blues hits emanating from the little eateries and bars that dotted the seamy block. There were women whose occupation was clearly announced by their dress; the same could be said of their men. There were also men whose occupation was telegraphed by a shifty look and hunched posture that you sensed could explode into violence at any moment.

It was into this environment that Frack was catapulted. After registering, I went upstairs to my room, angrily slammed the door, threw myself on the bed, and cried. The room stank foully of stale cigar smoke; two filthy towels hung over a basin that had to be seen to be believed; a single light swayed insolently from the ceiling; and in the corner stood a sand pail that had been used as a urinal. I lay there, wondering why I was allowing this to happen to me, knowing that once you are denied human comforts and amenities that you know you need and can afford, your spirit starts to crack and your confidence caves in. That is the harvest of bigotry. Our bodies cannot interpret written signs that denote segregation in restaurants and restrooms: they only know that they need food at certain times and must be relieved at other times. And, of course, it puts a severe strain on otherwise solid friendships, and on the white members too, in its own way. When we re-assembled on the bus after such enforced separation, tempers were a lot shorter, and things that would have been laughed at as jokes a few weeks earlier up north were now grounds for suspicion and prickliness.

Fortunately, this did not last. As the Southern end of the tour progressed, the white members would often sacrifice the hot meal that we all needed, since Negroes weren't allowed to sit down to such fare, and share with us sandwiches and pop away from the premises. They went out of their way to alleviate the strains as best they could, and this helped to heal most of the nervous suspicions that might otherwise have contaminated relationships permanently.

There was another, fearsome side to Southern life in the 1950s: violence-breeding anger. One day I was walking down Peach Street, which I had heard so much about, and stopped to look in a window that had various articles of jewellery in it. Suddenly over my shoulder I heard a voice with that notorious accent: "Why are you looking in that window, boy? Ain't nothing in there you can afford." I turned round to face the ruddy complexion of a man whose eyes blazed with anger and hatred. He asked me why I didn't get on my way like I had some sense; I directed him to plant a kiss on a particular part of my anatomy. At this point he reached for me and I instinctively hit him, knocking him down. Immediately realizing where I was and what might happen if I stayed around, I hailed the nearest cab. The driver was black, which I thought lucky; but when he saw the man lying in the street he took off at full tilt. Thereafter, none of the black cabs would stop; I had more sense than to waste time flagging white cabs, so ran around the corner and managed to find an unsuspecting black taxi driver who took me back to the house I was staying in. (Norman had taken to putting us up in private homes rather than futilely attempt to get us into any of the major hotels.)

Within a few years Norman had managed to open a crack in various hotels' attitudes towards blacks, and we should remember that this was a full decade before the flowering of the Civil Rights movement. Even so, we Negroes had to endure another set of bigoted practices once we gained admittance to these establishments, and they were just as demeaning and hurtful, albeit subtler. The desk clerks that would never speak directly to you, firing the registration card at you with a sneer; the bell-men who would walk away to the front door to pick up someone else's luggage after you'd patiently waited your turn; the head waiter who made sure that the only seat available to you was next to the swinging door by the kitchen or else up against the outer wall of the room; and the waiter who destroyed your appetite and all enjoyment by deliberately spilling your soup and never once looking at you from the moment he grudgingly took your order to when he thrust the bill at you.

As I think back on all this, I wonder how and where Norman found the continued will, akin to a resistance fighter, to battle against and finally break down this huge wall of bigotry and ignorant nastiness. Quite apart from his immense contribution to jazz in specifically musical terms, he holds a special place in my heart for the courage, tenacity, and sensitive understanding he displayed throughout those volatile and debilitating days in America's South.

NORMAN GRANZ

29

NORMAN GRANZ:
RELUCTANT GENIUS

For some people, to know Norman Granz is to hate him. This is something that I can accept: I do not expect everyone around me to agree with me about any individual. I try to take into consideration the possibility that other people certainly may not have been exposed to the person in question in the same circumstances as I have, thus not giving them the same insight into the subject. And so I have generally shrugged off the various innuendoes about Norman that have raged so virulently. Long ago I took a good look at these stories, and soon found them to be suspiciously rehearsed, almost learned to a formula. I took a good look, too, at the people spreading them, and found they shared a telling characteristic: they had all in some way attempted to cheat or hornswoggle either Norman himself or someone associated with him. Obviously, they did not succeed and have since sought to cloak their lack of intelligence and mental agility in dealing with him.

We've been close friends for 50 years, and the "real" Norman Granz is very different from the persona such tawdry rumour-mongering suggests.

Like any interesting and successful person, there are two parts to Norman's make-up: the outer shell and the inner core. His outer shell has evolved through years of dealing with people in the music and show-business world; almost from the start he found it necessary to develop a kind of armour in order to cope with the charlatans and pimps of the industry. Those may seem harsh words; they are actually very mild when one thinks of the raw deals and sleazy situations to which these people have subjected their clients. When they've encountered Norman Granz, they've run up against this outer covering, which serves primarily to let them know he'll go to any lengths to protect his artists from them.

Accordingly, he's absolute hell to deal with when he sincerely believes he is right. There is virtually no possibility of dissuading him when he's decided his way is the right way. Someone once asked me just what it would take to make him reverse a judgement on which they disagreed. After giving it some thought, the only thing I could suggest was possibly the Second Coming. Please note, I said "possibly"! Those are the odds you take on when you tie in to a battle royal with Norman.

He abhors dishonesty. He refuses even to talk to anyone who qualifies as a liar in his book. He is repelled by anyone and anything that smacks of bigotry or racism. He scorns pseudo-liberals, believing them to be greater bigots and zealots than the persons they profess to disdain. From artists he will accept nothing less than the best they have to offer each night, and if anyone falls short, Norman will make his feelings vigorously clear. He is an ardent and immovable fan of the blues, holding it to be the fundamental strain and backbone of jazz; indeed, he looks with suspicion on any jazz players who refuse to revert to a blues performance, believing that such reluctance calls into question the true value of their creative impulse. He is totally intolerant of injustices, regardless of where they occur, and has many times put himself into what could have been a no-win situation—by which I mean putting his life on the line.

So much for the outer shell. If one now focuses on the inner core (and few have had the opportunity), one finds a gentle, sensitive human being who cringes at the thought of hurting, even in a minute way, the feelings of someone he cares for. His hard-nosed exterior is deceptive: in many ways he is vulnerable, and he faces his insecurities daily, spending most of his waking hours attempting to deal with them. He is a lover of great art, whether it be music, painting, or literature. He has a voracious appetite for certain great members of the literary world, and avidly devours almost everything that his favourite writers put into print. He is a man who, despite his exterior calm, worships at the heels of his various idols, whether they be Bjorn Borg, Coleman Hawkins, Pablo Picasso, or Roy Eldridge, finding time each day to pay homage to their individual talents. He is a worshipper of children and a sensitive father.

Norman can in the course of a moment be reduced to uncontrollable laughter, his head buried in his handkerchief, tears streaming from his eyes. He is also a man who, when hurt, used to recoil into himself and attempt to blot out the pain by getting stoned. He has an astonishing memory, and even now can recall things that his apparently more sprightly and mentally vigorous juniors have forgotten. He is generous to a fault, and asks nothing in return. He is the man who has quietly footed the bill for burying various penniless jazz musicians, and has continued to contribute in a low-key way to the support of their widows left behind, while this fact remained unknown to some relatives whose only purpose seemed to be to bad-mouth him.

These are all ingredients of the inner core of Norman Granz. Few people have managed to penetrate it, but the ones who have are immovably loyal friends of his: people such as the late Benny Green, Benny Carter, Roy Eldridge, and, of course, myself.

From very early on in our relationship I felt that I had made a lifelong friend simply because there was a mutual concern and respect from the outset. When I asked Norman to be my personal manager the agreement was sealed with a handshake rather than a contract. To this day many people find it hard to believe that our association has lasted over five decades with no need for that ever-famous piece of paper. I've always felt comfortable about Norman's handling of my income: he's overseen it (and Ella Fitzgerald's) all these years, and I've never even contemplated questioning him on the matter.

I have known Norman Granz as the young promoter striving to put his idea of jazz concerts in classical halls into existence. He was the first to initiate this concert and touring procedure—an achievement I have hardly ever seen properly recognized in the jazz press. Being a part-time music educator myself, I can appreciate now the major educational significance that Norman's tours had. By bringing Jazz At The Philharmonic, with its raft of soloists and players and rhythm sections and vocalists, to a host of cities (not just New York, Chicago, and LA) Norman immediately made it possible for players, students, and interested listeners to hear some of the great solo innovators in the history of jazz improvising at full tilt, riffing behind one another, and bringing to magical life music that we had only heard on records. These concerts had the same status in jazz of the 1940s and 1950s as did the classical concerts with Oistrakh, Menuhin, and Horowitz, and it is surely high time that he got full and proper credit for this profound and lasting breakthrough.

From an early stage Norman established himself as not only an outstanding and original impresario but also an arresting figure sartorially. His white saddle shoes and his famous porkpie, aided by his now well-known eyebrows, became his own personal logos, further distinguished in later years with the advent of success by tweedy suits and vicuna overcoats fashioned in Savile Row. Out on the road with JATP Norman was "one of the guys." Comfortably riding the bus as did Lester Young, J.C. Heard, Ella, myself, and many others, Norman threw himself into being simply another member of the JATP fraternity, joining in the crap games, aiding in the put-ons, joining in the reminiscing about earlier jazz groups and jazz people—even down to chasing chicks. He somehow managed to juggle this carefree "member of the tour" personality with the totally different and authoritarian persona of Norman Granz, the impresario.

I remember one instance on the bus, when he had been dissatisfied with the deportment of some of the members of the troupe on stage during the show and immediately afterwards laid out one of his famous "readings." There were definitive signs that all hell was going to break loose, which I for one became very expert at predicting. The eyes would take on a concerted glare into space, the colour would rise in his cheeks, the eyebrows would elevate like slow-moving theatre curtains, the head would cock to one side, and the gaze would be fixed on his intended subject. He also had a habit when angered of inhaling very quick snatches of breath through his nose in a measured fashion. Then the hand would come out with the famous forefinger extended and he would call the person in question "into his office," which could be anywhere from a dressing-room, to the stagehands' room, to a corner behind a pile of equipment backstage.

This particular night he had read out the concerned parties *en masse* and stomped off to the box office, only to return sometime later as the last person to get on the bus. The conversation came to an abrupt halt and we were off into the night, headed for our next destination. For some reason Norman took a seat immediately in front of Ray Brown and me, turned the overhead light off and pulled his porkpie down over his eyes. Various members now carried on conversations in very low whispered tones; even the crap game was suspended for fear of irritating Normie.

After about 45 minutes of silent travel, Lester Young, who was a dedicated advocate of the galloping cubes at any time of the day or night, decided to go into his "Dr Willis" act. We all looked on Lester as more or less the travelling philosopher who could heal the many hurts and alienations that might occur. Off he went down the aisle with that famous swinging gait and came to a halt immediately in front of his resonating pulpit, Buddy's drum. He looked up at it, a look of frustration on his face, and identified himself to it by simply saying, "Dr Willis" (much as I might say in the opening of a phone conversation, "Oscar here"). "We would like to know how to straighten this thing out. Here we are on the bus and everything with everybody acting like Shirley Temple and things like that and people trying to act so refined, and nothing out here on this whole big bus but silent night! Lady Granz has got her feelings torn up and is acting like she's got her period and things. When we had those dotted boys [the dice] out, Dr Willis was in the process of dropping Lady Jacquet and Lady Roy to their knees, 'cause they didn't think I was going to make my point, but I was."

By now, almost everyone is sitting trying his or her best not to be the one to break out laughing for fear of making Norman think that we had taken his anger lightly, but Dr Willis is on a roll and senses it. He glances down and catches Ella holding her hand over her mouth in an attempt to silence an inevitable laugh, and pounces on the opportunity. Once more, he addresses the drum.

"You know some shit must have gone down for real if Lady Fitz is silent night too," he says, with his eyes closed and his head tipped back. "However! Since none of you refined people can't hear that, see if you can hear this! Dr Willis fades your ass whoever you are! See if you can hear that! [faint, smothered giggles from various spots in the bus] "What?" he continues, "Faint hearts? [more laughter now] Wait. Lester has to get a taste from his Red Boy.* [a swig is taken and then, a loud "ARGHHHH!" as he swallows] Now Pres is ready for all asses! Will you join me in my parlour?"

With that the bus breaks into immediate laughter, and Norman jumps out of his seat and says, "All right, shoot, Lester! You're faded!"

Pres' answer to that is "Come on and give me some help, Roy! Lester can't take on the whole box office by himself!"

By that one single shouted statement, "Shoot, Lester, you're faded," Norman had immediately reinstalled the figure of Norman the member of the tour bus. This is how quickly he was able to solve what could have been a difficult situation and shift it to one of comedy rather than tension.

Norman has an uncanny racial understanding. It's not just that he is totally without bias: he is one of the few people I have met who is aware that any race has specific weaknesses. As a Negro I know these inner frailties all too well, and that we not only feign ignorance of them but do everything in our power to keep them invisible to whites (and indeed all other racial groups). And it is very difficult to have a really penetrating conversation with whites, however unprejudiced they may be, unless they have the breadth and toughness of mind to recognize that fear, inhibition, and even intolerance are common to all blacks.

---

*See page 154, Chapter 33.

Earlier I wrote about colour differentiation—and consequent segregation—within the black community (see pages 25–26). Norman and I have often talked about the frailty of almost-white Negroes who are never secure about their status within either race and whose lives are seriously fragmented as a result. I found his instinctive understanding of this remarkable; indeed, he was more attuned to it than most blacks.

By the same token we have had long conversations about his own people, the Jews, and in the same freeswinging, truthful manner he has been able to condemn where condemnation was needed, yet also extend love and sympathy for them when appropriate. On our trip to Israel, as we were walking together down the main street in Tel Aviv early after our arrival there, I had been kidding Norman about his inability ever to score with a member of his race here. He laughed half-heartedly for a second and then his expression changed: "You know, OP, all kidding aside, you can virtually see some of the hurt and pain that has been inflicted on my people on their faces as they pass by." I never forgot that remark, for it shows his deep awareness of people's hurt and his love of humanity.

As I rounded the last few bars of the second to last chorus of *Perdido* in Tokyo at the Nichigeiki Theatre with the full troupe on stage, I glanced back into the wings and saw Norman standing there with an angered look on his face. It puzzled me and yet I had to finish the tune. I did so and as Norman walked out, he leaned over and said, "When I come off, follow me immediately without fail." As the piece finished, Norman walked by the horn section, said something to Benny Carter, which I couldn't hear, and closed the concert. He stepped back from the mike as the curtain descended and we all held our places; the moment the curtain hit stage level, he sprinted off stage-right, followed by myself and Benny Carter. Still wondering what this was all about, I nevertheless raced upstairs with him, breathlessly wondering when these endless stairs would terminate.

As he headed for the balcony, the picture came into focus. Several times during Ella's part of the concert she had been interrupted and visibly upset by some very crude and uncouth language from the balcony. This occurred two or three times, at which point Norman had threatened to stop the concert. The remarks were definitely in English—or, rather, foul-mouthed American. We raced out into the foyer adjacent to the balcony and I saw four marines, who obviously had had one too many, raucously exiting the balcony. Without the slightest hesitation, Norman marched over to them and bluntly asked who was the wise guy with the foul mouth. Benny Carter and I stole over and took positions close to the marine that Norman ended up talking to. The marine asked what all the God-damn fuss was about; Norman insisted that all he wanted to know was who was the wise guy who had been yelling all of the foul words, at which point the marine unleashed a new tirade of verbal bile on Norman, immediately identifying himself as being the original culprit. Like a shot in the dark, Norman uncoiled a left hook and knocked the marine back into the curtains behind him. His buddy to his right took off into the crowd and Benny and I stepped between the last two and Norman, just to keep it equal. The marine got up and Norman knocked him down again, delivering a short sentence of advice to him about human diplomacy.

Just then one of the two marines that I was standing in front of started screaming that it wasn't fair, indicating that he wanted to get into the fray. I extended my arm in front of him and quietly exhorted him to let well enough alone before he got hurt. Suddenly from out of nowhere an arm with a clenched fist at the end of it shot out from over my right shoulder and landed square on the protesting marine's jaw. I saw his eyes twirl and he hit the deck as I heard Benny Carter's voice behind my ear, saying, "Oh, shut up." There was applause in the foyer from the Japanese audience, which not only witnessed this fracas, but certainly must also have heard the obscenities shouted at Ella during the concert. The three of us went back down the numerous stairs we had come up and returned backstage to tell Ella, who was in tears, that the unasked-for favour had been paid back. This is Norman Granz, the reactionary.

In my early days with JATP I was always struggling to keep my monetary affairs afloat, but year to year they seemed to end up the same way—in danger of drowning. I was still liable for a huge tax debt incurred before I left Canada, and I was never able to get clear and start afresh, owing nothing. When tax time came, the cry for help would go out to Norman's office, and he would provide the necessary funds. The eventual result was that I paid off the Canadian tax debt, but now owed Norman a comparably enormous sum.

My expensive enthusiasms hardly helped—especially one that he inspired in me, for I was learning an awful lot about life from him. He was passionate about art, and I remember countless traipses through the world's galleries as he viewed, and sometimes bid for, paintings that stirred his fancy. Sometimes, in order to disguise Norman's interest and thus keep the price down, I would bid on his behalf. I used to lie awake at nights wondering what I'd do if "my" offer was accepted: I didn't have that kind of money! Norman—"Don't worry about a thing"—blithely stuck to this practice, which had the valuable side-effect of teaching me a great deal about many artists' work. Indeed, I soon started to buy some smaller pieces myself.

That made three new crazes to satisfy, for around the same time I became passionately interested in both photography and audio. Anyone who has fooled with such equipment knows how costly it can be; typically, I made things worse by constantly changing equipment in order to keep up with the latest hi-tech trends. And while all this was going down, I was also attempting to pay alimony and child support (little did I know that within a few years that would triple) and incurring major expenses on the road, where I refused to live like a second-class citizen. All in all, my debt to Norman was increasing ominously; furthermore, I was falling behind on the commissions I owed him as my manager.

After a while he called in his tax lawyer at the time, Gary Hendler, with whom I became friendly, and we reset our strategic plan to bring all of these things into line. During all of this I must say that not once did Norman ever taunt or badger me in an unfair way. He did, however, from time to time ask me how things were going, and he even insisted on getting statements from the accountants as to where I stood financially. He would express his concern for my well-being should anything happen to my hands; he pleaded with me to bring myself level at least so that my life could take on a different meaning. He felt that having this continual overhanging debt to him was unhealthy for me.

All of this was to no avail. I agreed with him airily but continued on my merry, uncontrollable way. Finally, one day he told me that he wanted to have a talk with me; he did not want to meet in a restaurant, but would rather have it in his office. I agreed to it without a second thought and we set a time. Upon my arrival he instructed me to close the door as usual, and to have a seat; then he told me he wanted to say some things uninterrupted and at the conclusion of his remarks I could say anything I wanted. The gist of what he said was roughly as follows. He wanted to make it unequivocally clear that he loved me as his best friend and revered me as a genius in what I did musically. He felt, however, that I had taken advantage of him. I recoiled at these words but he stared me down and continued on his way. He said that perhaps in trying to be my best friend he had probably done me more harm than my worst enemy. He went on to itemize the various backups that he had made available to me over the years and continued by saying he didn't care about interest factors, which never entered into it. But the thing that was hurting him the most was that I was not making any financial progress at all, and in fact was digging a deeper hole for myself year by year. He then said baldly that he wanted his money and he wanted his commissions paid, and that he didn't care what I did with the rest of the money from there on.

I was stunned; nevertheless, being a fairly rational person and one that can be honest with himself I responded, with tears in my eyes, that I now realized that I had used him in a manner in which I had never intended—indeed, in a manner that I had abhorred seeing other people try on him. I told him unceremoniously that I would put things right regardless of time and cost.

That might possibly have been one of the hardest days in Norman Granz's life; from the end result, now that my operational status is the way it is, it turned out one of the happiest. He had done something that only a true friend could have done. He somehow reached down inside of himself and pushed the emotional stop button which had been allowing me to run rampant over him as a friend. The miraculous thing is that he managed to do this in such an honest way that he never touched the stop button to our friendship.

He and I have had some very deep moments together, some with fond emotion and some with very deep anguish. I recall a phone call one night in Montreal many years ago that I received from him while he was still in Europe, where he had been hurt in an emotional affair with a lady and had picked up the phone and called me. I knew from the outset that he had been drinking, and I also knew that when a woman hurts a man, there really isn't anything that another man can say to heal the wound. All he can do is be there to listen and to be leaned on. I have done the same thing to him during a couple of my emotional and bizarre marital upsets. This kind of closeness isn't something that is easy to speak about, for we have fought with the same emotional drive.

Once on an early tour with JATP Norman had gone ahead of us to do some publicity. The group had been driving and, unfortunately, coming into this city in the South, Coleman Hawkins' automobile had been involved in an accident. None of us at the time knew exactly where Norman was for those were the days in which he sometimes covered three or four cities in one day, not even bothering to check into a hotel until his final stop that night. I had had a bad experience with one of the members of the group and a disagreement that had almost reached the physical stage, so I was not exactly in the most conciliatory of moods. We sat around that night, all in bad spirits for various reasons, and bitched about everything we could think of bitching about, including Norman. With him being the only person absent, I guess he became the recipient of all the ill will, and his name was bandied about back and forth at various times during the evening in the most negative of ways, although I don't believe that any one of the troupe was serious in the remarks. We all finally went to bed and I awoke feeling a lot better the next morning, as I'm sure everyone else did.

At about 10.30 in the morning Norman came on the line. He had obviously returned from his trip and asked me if I would meet him in the lounge for a talk. Without thinking anything, I agreed and set to getting myself prepared to go downstairs. We said hello and I noticed right away, to coin a Lester Young phrase, that "I felt a draught." He casually looked at me and said, "I thought you and I were friends." I immediately tried to reassure him of this and he retorted in a laconic tone, "That isn't the way I heard it. You apparently had a lot to say about me last night in my absence." I couldn't believe my ears and immediately became enraged at the fact that someone had opted to dump on me to Norman, when in fact I had primarily been a listener the night before. During my years with the group, having entered as the junior member, I was careful to distance myself from any controversies; Norman's manner told me that on this occasion I had failed. No matter how I denied being involved, I could not convince him, and I finally gave up, asking him what he suggest I do. He very calmly said that he thought that since I no longer had faith in him as a manager and certainly not as a friend, I should leave the tour and go back home, and perhaps think of getting someone else not only to record me but also to manage me.

I was totally demolished by Norman choosing to walk away from our association, regardless of my denials of involvement, and the fact that I knew I was innocent. I finally agreed and he said that my ticket would be in my room box in the afternoon and said so long, and I went to my room. After much painful deliberation, I fell off to sleep because the trauma of that confrontation had worn me down. I must have fallen into a deep sleep because the phone ring seemed to be miles away in the distance. I reached over in the darkened room and finally found the receiver, and managed to say hello.

"I just thought I'd better let you know that it's now 7.15 and you're due on stage at 8.30. I figured you were sleeping and I didn't want you to blow your gig." It was Norman's voice and in those two short sentences I relived the whole mental experience that had transpired earlier and realized almost at once that he was telling me that he, too, must have rethought the whole situation, and that he believed me as a friend.

I didn't miss the concert, but when I finished the Trio segment and Gene Krupa's group went on, I called Norman into my dressing-room and told him how happy I was that he believed me and tried to make him understand that from here onwards in our association, if I ever was disenchanted over anything he had said or done, he could count on hearing it from me directly. He apologized for approaching me the way he had and told me that he too did not want to lose a friend and that he had realized what had in fact really transpired the night before.

I cannot forget such moments in our friendship: they stand out like landmarks along the highway. Perhaps it was in these times of tension and dissension that our friendship was actually formed. Whatever it was, it has stood up for all of these years.

Norman approaches a recording date in much the same way as he does a meal in a three-star restaurant. He usually starts with a phone call in which he tells me that he just had a wild idea flash past in his mind. What if he were to pit this player against that player? Would it not be one hell of a record date, assuming he could line up the proper rhythm section, should they all be free at the same time? Norman has always thought in a competitive manner when it came to recording. I know that he has believed that in exerting a little pressure on a soloist by having another soloist standing in the wings waiting to play, it would effect a record session of higher quality. He has continually frowned on sessions where he has sensed any kind of patented comfort and lethargic submissiveness, primarily caused by overdone repertoire and uninterested personnel.

He carried this same outlook into the various dates that he has done with Ella. I can recall him coming into the studio and going over the selection of different lyrics with her, evaluating the impact it would have on the performance of the song, much in the same way as he did with Astaire. You don't fool around on one of his dates, unless your goofing has some musical value or focus. I've often seen him stand in the background while Hawk and Roy were engrossed in reminiscences about other players or other jazz times; but if the musicians began chasing each other around or comparing stock reports, he would instantly lurch into the studio with a "Come on, let's stop screwing around and get this thing together."

Norman's record date is never really completed in the studio. He takes home a set of cassettes from each date and meticulously replays them day to day, even in his car as he's driving to and fro on various errands and appointments. Suddenly I'll get a call. "You know, I've got to make so-and-so the leading tune in this album because Sonny [Stitt] turned that tune out. I mean, he played some shit on there that you're not going to believe when you hear it." Sure enough, I'll get a copy of the cassette in the mail a few days later and, just as he indicated on the phone, the solo that he referred to will turn out to be one of outstanding virtuosity and merit, which during the studio playbacks had been dismissed as a "good take."

Norman seldom had a lot to say during record dates, preferring to let the musicians sort out their musical problems on their own. He would only involve himself when he felt that their staging could have been better, for instance, or that from a listener's standpoint the tempo might have sounded uncomfortable, or even when the key for Ella should be lowered to give her a little more ease in what she wanted to do. On the larger dates with orchestras he would leave most of that up to the soloists and the conductor, preferring only to interject his opinion about the "feel" of each take, or the placement of the solo segments.

It boggles my mind when I think of the legacy of historical jazz that Norman has left the world. At a time when everyone was busy nodding in assent about the virtuosity and the genius of Art Tatum, it was Norman who decided to chronicle it all into one huge musical ledger.

His continued recording of the Basie Orchestra right down to Basie's demise, interspersed with some intriguing musical confrontations between Bill Basie and myself, leaves a legacy for jazz aficionados to treasure for ever. The same can be said about artists like Ella, Coleman Hawkins, Charlie Parker, Tal Farlow, Dizzy, myself, and on and on and on. His undying belief in "American music" is eloquently enshrined in his record companies' catalogues.

In 1953 Norman agreed to have JATP come to London and perform a benefit concert for the victims of a recent flood disaster. He was really enthusiastic about bringing the group to England for two reasons: to tender some financial aid to the hapless people caught in this unfortunate circumstance, and to be able to present JATP for the first time to the British public. Prior to this, due to disagreement between the American Musicians' Union and its British counterpart, it had been an impossibility.

Upon our arrival in Great Britain, the first thing that miscued was at customs. For whatever the reason, they decided to subject us to one of their famous search and destroy inspections. By that I mean that film that some members had shot on tour was exposed in order to search the containers, medication of any kind came under the greatest suspicion, including some laxative powder (under a brand name), and on and on. Norman called a halt to the proceedings when a body search of Ella and her road secretary was contemplated as the next move. "Cancel the concerts!" he yelled in frustration. "If this is what we have to be subjected to in order to do these benefit concerts, forget it! We'll just go back to the continent, take the days off, and continue our tour. We don't need this!" At this juncture all the searching came to an abrupt halt, and the group was ushered out of the customs hall and into the arms of the waiting press. This turned out to be mistake number two.

We sat through the press conference and endeavoured to answer all questions. Unfortunately, though we attempted to be patient and answer the battery of inquiries tendered by the reporters, the printed result in some newspapers did not match the answers given by the various members of JATP. This enraged and hurt many of us who had tried to be as co-operative as possible. Perhaps the most glaring misquote that day involved Ella, who was reported to have remarked, as she disembarked down the plane's ramp, something like, "Ah sho' can't wait to wrap mah chops around a chicken leg." In all of the years that I knew Ella Fitzgerald, she never spoke with as much of a Southern accent as even Lena Horne. For her to have said anything remotely like what that particular paper quoted her as saying is unimaginable.

Norman seemed more upset over this episode than anyone else, and said that he was sorry that he had asked everyone to give up their time to come to England to be insulted in this way. One afternoon he called me and said that he was calling a press conference. I winced inwardly because I know just about what to expect when he gets like this. He is a person who carefully plans his every move and will leave no stone unturned in order to complete his strategy.

He made arrangements with the hotel and rented a large suite for the afternoon. He ordered tomato and cucumber sandwiches (which we all know get soggy as hell), and augmented this with warm beer (ugh!), and sat back and awaited the arrival of his guests: the writers from the various journals.

I sat quietly to one side as the invitees sat, stood, and chatted awaiting the start of the press conference. Norman finally called them to order and proceeded to explain his reasons for having called them here at this time. He informed them that he had always tried to believe that the people who wrote for the newspapers did so with some integrity and honesty, but that after having read the various quotes from the last press conference, he now found their integrity to be in question, let alone their honesty. He then produced a dossier of clippings and proceeded, one by one, to take each journalist to task. He began with the gent who supposedly quoted Ella, and asked him how and when he could have heard her make such a remark while disembarking since there were no press members allowed at the plane. There was an almost inaudible reply, to which Norman responded, "I don't care what you write as long as it is the truth!" He immediately took on another writer and continued in the same vein. He finally fixed his gaze on the group and announced that he was finding this boring and that he had provided refreshments for everyone. "There are sandwiches on the sideboard and also some warm beer; please help yourselves. As for me, I'm flying to Paris for a decent meal." With that, he strolled out of the room, leaving behind a group of bewildered newsmen. They had just been treated to a medium dose of an enraged Norman. Judging from the more professional way they dealt with his concerts from then on, they obviously did not want to undergo any return consultations with Dr Granz.

In my view Norman Granz still does not fully recognize the extent of his massive achievement in the staging of American music. He doesn't see with the luminosity that the followers of his records do the historic importance of the music catalogues he has left the world. I see my dearest friend now in the autumn of his life, his sight failing him and his health making him at times a frail person, as a man that the jazz world has taken for granted: in its usual blindness and rush towards commerciality, it has failed to bestow on him the honours he so signally deserves. Norman Granz, the reluctant genius, is in shameful danger of becoming Norman Granz, the forgotten genius.

30

NORMAN THE GOURMAND

All Norman's friends are aware of his dedication to the great foods of the world. I first discovered this on our early trips to Europe. As with all he does, he adopts a very meticulous approach to learning about a subject. First, he rids himself of all shyness and reluctance to admit his lack of knowledge of the particular matter at issue (the sign of a good student). Second, he has invariably done some prior research. Third, he then immerses himself in the subject completely, allowing the people that do know about it to be as informative and helpful as possible.

In the case of gourmet food, he decided that I should be a student as well and accompany him on his various gastronomic tours. The city where much of this education took place was of course Paris, although we later branched out to other places on the continent renowned for their cuisine. Many fellow-promoters and friends in these cities were also able to recommend outstanding bistros that were not so well known.

Over the years Norman made friends with various world-famous chefs, and they in turn took him under their wing, teaching him things that are not normally available to the average gourmet diner. Amongst these were François Bise, who used to take Norman along on his morning shopping treks to the marketplace; Paul Bocuse, who would cook for Norman every time he visited him in Lyons; and Fredy Girardet, Antoine of Chez Amis Louis, and the late Monsieur Allard of the celebrated Chez Allard.

Thanks to Norman, I also became friendly with these people and certainly benefited from knowing them. The striking thing about Norman is that he was not just content to know these giants of *le monde de Haute Cuisine*: he enrolled in cooking schools to enhance his ability in the kitchen and today is a gifted creator in his own right. On various occasions when I've visited him in his London flat, I have dined royally with Norman the Chef Supreme. His knowledge of rare and great wines is prodigious, and his ability to search out little-known bistros featuring marvellous cuisine is still a source of wonderment to his friends.

31

LIFETIME ACHIEVEMENT
GRAMMY

In 1997 I was awarded the Lifetime Achievement Grammy by the National Academy of Recording Arts and Sciences, an award I consider to be the ultimate kudos for my recording endeavours over the years. I also consider it a *dual* award: although I was the performer on the albums, Norman Granz was the creator and overseer throughout my career, and the honour is his as much as mine. It was through his belief in me and the talent that he detected that I can now proudly look back on my recorded achievement. So many of the ideas for the various albums were his: not only would they not have occurred to me on my own, but in several instances I did not understand them until the recording sessions were well under way. Only then, when the exhilaration and sheer joy of the emergent music came through to me, was I able to understand and fully appreciate his musical foresight.

I have recently helped John Gittins and Lance Anderson to compile an interactive CD-Rom listing virtually my entire discography, and that project has brought home even more decisively how extensive my recording career has been and how much that is due to Norman. I am very proud of it, and he should be equally so.

THE IMPRESARIO

"Get the best from an artist," is a phrase often used.
Sad to say more than not, it is usually abused
By the very people who believe they know best
For performers who in reality are suffering stress.

Stress from the standpoint of creative duress,
Brought on by the stigma of just who knows best
In areas that surely should reside with the person
Who walks out on stage, feeling freedom, not coercion.

What the artist needs is more a musical parent
With sensitivity and love, someone who is coherent
In a musical sense, much like *savoir faire*
Who is intelligent and honest and warm enough to care.

Who by the same token is strong and not frantic
Regardless of the ego, and no matter how pedantic
The artist becomes, if the subject is vital,
He should stand his ground, leaving the artist to his recital.

Such a man in the forties walked onto the Jazz scene
With a temperament that, true, was not entirely serene,
But the mood of the times more or less dictated
The manner in which Norman Granz operated.

Civil rights was a thing virtually non-existent
Only serving to make Norman all the more persistent
In his ardor to present his mixed concerts as he chose,
And from this, racial tension and upheaval arose.

He faced it as he seems to face most altercations,
Realizing the fact that this encompassed race relations.
Facing the bigots with uncompromising will,
He fought them with words, legal footwork and skill.

Up to this time, in the south when concerts took place,
The halls were divided according to race.
The main floor being relegated to Caucasians you see,
Whilst Blacks inherited the balcony.

When confronted with auditoriums that had segregated seating,
He decided to solve it, and yet still be meeting
Their requirements, without leaving them room to quibble,
He simply divided the hall down the middle.

These trying days were not at all aided
By the various hotels that blatantly paraded
Their Jim Crow rules for all to see
Adding anger and frustration to this tyranny.

To circumvent this bias, Norman oftimes would
Use fictitious names whenever he could.
This many times worked, but sad to say,
On others, it just didn't work that way.

Racism was rampant from airport to hotel
Putting pressure not just on Norman, but the players as well.
It was difficult to stand by and watch as though disabled,
As a redneck cop stuck his gun in Norm's navel.

The reason for this tenuous and heated confab
All centered around an airport cab.
The reason that precipitated this venomous attack
Was that Ella was seated in the aforementioned hack.

"I hate you worse than I hate those niggers!"
Was the reason for his anger, yet all of this figures
When one stops and considers the mentality,
Measuring this against Ella's ability.

All of these scenes and others even more cynical,
Dot the history that made JATP such a pinnacle
Of musical success, in note and in deed
Thus allowing Norman to sow the seed
That has burst forth today and given birth
To Jazz concerts and festivals taking place round the earth.

In the field of recording he has managed to trace
A history of Jazz that certainly embraced
Special moments in the making, that might have been lost,
But were salvaged by Norman regardless of cost.

A history of piano in itself most complete,
For the recordings of Tatum will never be effete.
The library on Ella from Gershwin to Duke,
With unlimited blues from Joe Turner to boot.
The Jammin' the Blues album, its contents so rare,
The tasty documentary on the late Fred Astaire.
And in contrast to the small groups and big bands like Herman,
Caustic humor from Mort Sahl, Lenny Bruce and Shelley Berman.

All of the derivations serving to enhance
An unusual gift, which is by no means happenstance.
The gift of being able to guide as overseer
Varied artists so immersed in developing their careers
They leave themselves open to the frustrations and fears
That plague them, thereby diminishing their productive years.

It indeed takes a person of special ilk
To understand and be able to carefully milk
The creative juices, without scaring the being
And leaving a carcass uncared for and lean.

Norman Granz has fulfilled this need for years,
While in return he can show the many scars he bears
From the hurts inflicted by egos and guile
Yet he somehow manages to recover and smile
Understanding seems to be his rule of thumb
Prompting us to believe, his best is yet to come.

JAZZ PEOPLE

32

COLEMAN HAWKINS:
THE ENIGMA

I knew Coleman Hawkins both as a musician and as a man, and elegance pervaded everything about him: most certainly the way he played his horn, but also his mannerisms, carriage, dress, speech, and overall appearance. He had the kind of commanding voice that would bring you to attention immediately, and a way of laughing while looking at you with an impish look in his eye that could certainly make you wonder what his next move would be. Whenever delighted with a saying or event, he would let loose with a guttural, "Aha!" He walked with an authoritative gait that seemed to make people automatically open up a pathway for him.

He appeared to consider his fedora as essential to his attire at all times, wearing it most of the time backstage in his dressing-room right up until the last moment before going on stage. His suits were usually of the dark charcoal grey or brown variety, with a very subtle English stripe that we all came to know. His shoes were from London, and seemed never in need of a shine, and his shirts and ties were similarly impeccable. He had a way of letting people know what kind of haberdashery he wore. He'd choose one of the more carefree dressers on the tour (and certainly a lesser earner) and direct a very penetrating question to him that, to answer, required a knowledge of the better makers and stylists of men's clothing. "Say, man!" he would bellow, "Have you noticed that they're not putting those good collars on those Sulka shirts anymore?" His intended victim would of course be caught flat-footed, realizing that he knew nothing about Sulka shirts, while at the same time not wanting to be embarrassed by Coleman's question; as a result, he'd be forced into immediate agreement—"Yeah, yeah"—searching for the closest and nearest exit.

Coleman would not permit escape to be made that easily and would immediately reply with something like, "I bought a dozen of those fellows last week while I was in Chicago and didn't get a chance to try one on until a few nights ago, and do you know, they didn't feel at all like the last ones I bought. You know what I mean?" "Yeah, yeah," would be the weak reply from his now petrified subject as he slid quickly out of the doorway. Coleman would close his eyes and return to his sax case while emitting low chortling sounds of satisfaction, knowing that he had scared the daylights out of his prey—which, of course, was the whole intent of the exchange. He would stand there rocking back and forth on his heels; then, slowly opening his eyes a little, he would give me that look with a half-grin while muttering something like, "Do you believe that? He wouldn't know a Sulka shirt if you hit him in the ass with it with the pins still in it."

Coleman enjoyed not only the cutting edge of competition but also the chance to stand around and watch other players as they were confronted by the intensity of competition from their peers. Jazz history tells us that, in his earlier years, he had to learn to cope with the pretenders to his crown in the saxophone world, and that experience informed every performance that I witnessed. Coleman almost always retained a distant, quasi-uninterested attitude when confronted with challenges of any sort. He would take on the half-closed eyes, head-supported-by-the-hand posture, and at times would even feign sleep. The one thing that remained almost constant throughout, however, was that devilish half-smile. Using all of these predetermined methods he would immediately put his opponents on the defensive and so gain the upper hand. His opponents would find themselves straining from the outset in order to prove their point, and would continually run into a wall-like pose of uninterest in them.

Another ploy used by Hawk at the outset of the challenge was his refusal to really open up his creative floodgates, all the while cagily watching his opponent submerge himself in complacency, thinking that he had indeed instilled some sort of fear in Coleman's mind. At precisely the right moment of lassitude on his opponent's part, Coleman would appear, saxophone in hand, and commence his dreaded walk to the bandstand. The famous gait; the beautiful horn with its filigree embellishments (a gift from a famous saxophone maker); the fedora, worn at a jaunty angle when relaxing, now pushed back on his head as if not to impede the flow of musical ideas that he was about to unleash; all of these things, I am sure, contributed to the discomfort and apprehension of his intended victim.

These are some of the attributes of Coleman that I learned during our times together. I also realized that he maintained a fierce pride in people once they had won his respect. He would choose to reinforce this in various ways. Sometimes he would walk up to you, assuming that you rated as a friend of his, and suddenly ask you to loan him some unlikely and ungodly sum of money. I am sure that this was done to reassure him that all was well with his friends; if they were not able to meet his demand, he would deliver a lecture about coming out on the road while anxious about money, enumerating the many things that could—and did—go wrong.

The same attitude characterized his musical endeavours. I felt an unbridled pride as he took me around from place to place, showing me off to his musical buddies and insisting that they take me on, while revelling in their responses to my playing with that ever-present smile, which expanded into a full guffaw if someone really felt overwhelmed.

I was totally unaware of what "Bean" (Hawkins) had in mind for me one night in Chicago in 1952, when he invited a group of the guys to join him at the Blue Note after the concert. It wasn't until Flip Phillips asked me if I had ever heard Phineas Newborn play that I realized what Hawk was up to: it was obviously my turn on the skillet! Bean was unusually solicitous to me all evening as he delighted in what he believed would be forthcoming. Phineas Newborn had burst onto the jazz scene with well-deserved praise from his player-peers, along with the usual banal and boring criticism from many jazz critics, who found his talents much too perfect and uninspired. (Par for the course with such people, who believe that *they* are the star makers, and that the general listening public is incapable of recognizing talent, even though audiences are many times made up of players, music students, and similarly literate listeners.) Phineas was appearing at what was then the Blue Note, a listening room that specialized in bringing in the big names of jazz, while introducing new names and talents as well. As it happened I was already aware of Phineas' work prior to this meeting, thanks to Ralph Watkins, who ran the Basin Street club in New York. Unbeknownst to Hawk, Phineas and I had earlier become friends, and had a mutual-admiration thing going.

This was during the bebop era and the reign of Bud Powell, Bird, and players of that ilk. Although I admired Bud's playing from a creative standpoint, I was not a total devotee of his from a pianistic point of view. I was enamoured of people such as Art Tatum, Hank Jones, and Teddy Wilson, whom I felt had a much more beautiful approach to the instrument than did Bud, whose primary intent seemed to be to run various groupings of sax or trumpet phrases while rather neglecting some of the necessary pianistic left-hand nuances that characterize the complete player. But Phineas encompassed all of these attributes and then some. His lithe, flowing ideas were based on complementary left-hand harmonic phrases that sometimes served not only to augment but even supplant the right-hand phrases. His keyboard fleetness was marvellous and must have seemed awesome to many other pianists. The thing about his playing that seemed to undo a lot of pianists was his ability to play double-handed phrases with ease. As it happens, this particular feature of his talent did not unnerve me, simply because it had been a vital part of my own development. Consequently, I was attuned to its use and considered myself to be the originator of this particular technique.

Returning to that night in Chicago, I can still see Coleman seated at the table in his familiar instigator's pose as we listened to Phineas. As the set proceeded, Bean punctuated various things that Phineas played with the occasional "Ummm! Uh-uh," and every once in awhile, "Oh my goodness!" You can't possibly hang out with Coleman Hawkins without learning from the experience. I registered no reaction whatsoever. Finally, as Phineas wheeled into a left-hand only version of *Body And Soul*, Bean turned to me and said, "What are you going to do with that, Oscar?"

"Nothing, Bean," I replied in my calmest of voices. "I've heard Phineas before, and not only that, we've been friends for quite a while."

"You mean he doesn't bother you at all?" he queried.

"Not in the least," I responded, retaining the same coolness in my voice.

Bean sat quietly for a few seconds, and then broke out into unrestrained laughter. He patted me on the shoulder, and I realized that I had passed the acid test. I hadn't cracked under the pressure of his little charade. He also knew that I believed in myself, and perhaps that meant more to him than anything else.

Coleman did everything with measured perseverance. I remember once when he found out there was a newlywed on the tour, he came into the room and started a general conversation about how much it takes in the way of attention from the groom in order to make a marriage work. "You just can't get married and take it for granted that it's all going to work out, you know what I mean, man?" He did not address his remarks to anyone in particular: they were just sort of tossed into the air and more or less left there to be caught by whoever he had elected as his next victim. "You better show your new wife a lot of attention. Things like flowers and candy and all that crap, and regularly at that!" he would admonish. Next came the fateful pause as he prepared to deliver the wipeout line: "And whatever you do, don't be getting married in any hurry and be having to leave town shortly after that!"

Pause. "Why? What would happen, Bean?" Sweets Edison would ask, the perfect stooge.

"Are you kidding?" Hawk would reply incredulously. "Aha! That's when Shorty moves in!"

"What are you talking about, Bean?" Sweets would ask innocently, while stealing a quick glance at the now totally flustered newlywed sitting nervously on his chair.

"Who the hell is Shorty?"

"Shorty is the guy that goes around fixing all that shit in these new marriages, you understand," Coleman would reply. "He's the man that you never see but he's also the reason that if you came off the road suddenly and went home and put on your house slippers they'd still be warm."

By this time Coleman would be chuckling all over the place, and the new groom would be nervously walking up and down. Bean would continue this dialogue with the aid of Sweets and other members until they figured they had accomplished their purpose. It must have worked, because the following night the newlywed was missing from the tour. I recall Coleman coming in the following night with a contrived look of disbelief on his face, and asking whatever happened to the newlywed. Upon hearing about his absence, he immediately broke into his legendary deep, guttural giggle.

Coleman and I met for the first time in 1948 when he came to Montreal with JATP. He came to the Alberta Lounge and listened to two of my sets, and after someone introduced us he casually said, "Why don't you come down to that other club after you finish work and have a drink with me?" I thanked him and went back to finish the evening. After work I was off to the Cafe St Michel where Louis Metcalf was leading the house band. As I walked in, Coleman spied me right away, and signalled me over to his table. He was sitting with Roy Eldridge, Ray Brown, and some other members of JATP, along with some ladies who had joined the party.

"Come on and have a taste," he said as he motioned me to a chair beside him. "Roy, this is the piano player I was telling you about. He can sure play, man, and guess what—he's West Indian." With that, he gave one of his famous hearty laughs and threw his head back in enjoyment. He was quite a presence; and just how influential his elegant strength could be suddenly came to me in the form of a weird flashback.

In the Metcalf Orchestra at that time was a tenor saxophonist by the name of Herb Johnson. Herb was a good-looking mulatto-skinned

Negro who had become a sort of special figure in the jazz world in Montreal, not only because of his musical talents, but also from his carriage and deportment around town. Herb sounded a lot like Hawk when he played, mainly because he used the same type of big sound. Herb was also known for his neat, immaculate appearance. His clothes favoured the very tweedy English look. His shoes glinted and gleamed nightly on the bandstand as he stood taking his solos. His voice was a deep mellow sound and his choice of vocabulary had an unmistakable British tone to it. When he agreed with something that you had said, he would reply by uttering his most famous expression: "Indeed, indeed." Almost at once the light went on. I had been standing looking at a ghost created by Coleman Hawkins' influence.

It was then and only then that I realized how deeply true geniuses can affect their admirers, that this sort of reverence could so mould their lives. Yet as I sat with Coleman Hawkins in person, I felt no diminution in my respect for Herb: if the role model is as good as Coleman, such love and admiration are to be honoured.

"You know, Roy," Coleman said, "you gotta hear this kid play. Why don't you go up and play something for us?" he asked with such a note of insistence in his voice that I immediately went over to the pianist in the band, Steep Wade. It had become commonplace for me to sit in for him whenever he wanted a break, so he automatically slid off the stool on one side, while continuing to comp with his right hand as I slid in from the other side and took over for him. I played a couple of tunes with the band, and gave way to Steep once more. During the time I was playing, Herb Johnson sat there with a look of satisfaction on his face, along with that same wry half-smile that I learned to expect from Coleman after getting to know him. The evening ended with various questions about why I didn't come to the States, which I parried and answered in some form, and finally I said good night and left.

I didn't see Coleman Hawkins again until my debut concert at Carnegie Hall when he walked into Roy's room and bellowed, "Aha! I see you made it, huh." Because he was featured as a soloist on the early tours that I did with Norman, we would sit together in his dressing-room many nights and talk while the others were performing. I came to realize that "class" mattered very much to Hawk, both as a racial phenomenon (about which he was passionate but stoical) and as an artistic one. He spoke many times of the differences between Americans and Europeans. He reflected on the understanding of jazz that he felt Europeans exhibited more readily than Americans. He ached over the barriers that he felt racially in America, which would prevent Negroes from reaching the possible heights they might have achieved had they been located elsewhere. He spoke also with deep hurt in his voice of his belief that jazz would never be accepted in America the way that classical music, or, as he called it, "the white man's music," was being accepted.

I frequently wondered if what he said was valid or not, because if he was right, I realized that all my earlier years of classical training, study, experimentation, and self-prodding, and all the disciplined exercises that I was still putting myself through, might all be for naught. I argued with him from time to time that it was not all in vain, citing such names as Art Tatum and Duke Ellington. He would merely laugh. "Do you think for one minute that Tatum will ever receive the plaudits and acceptance that Rubinstein has? Do you think Duke Ellington is going to be remembered over George Gershwin, regardless of the fact that Ellington's music is true jazz and Gershwin's isn't?" He would speak these words with a profound and fiery pain. "If you believe all that," he would add, "then you're going to be the next president of the White Citizens' League or the KKK!"

I vividly remember the way Hawk intimidated all of us when it came to driving on the tour. He was known to be a formidable speedster on the highway, and revelled in the fact that we regarded him that way.

Once, when driving with him overnight to some lower Midwestern town, we came up over this hill, and I began peering down into what seemed to be an unusually dark part of the road ahead of us. Hawk sat at the wheel in his normal position, one hand on the steering wheel, the other arm propped up on the armrest holding a cigarette, with his eyes at half-mast. Suddenly I became frighteningly aware of why the roadway up ahead was so dark. There were two horses standing across the highway with their butts together directly in our path. I looked at him and said, "Hawk, Hawk! Look out! There are horses on the road!" His only reaction was to utter, "Hmmmm," and open his eyes perhaps an eighth of an inch more. I gazed down at the speedometer and realized it was registering 110 miles an hour. I sucked in my breath expecting the worst, when for some unknown reason, and at what seemed like the very last instant, the horses decided to walk opposite ways, and as the gate opened up, we careened through with Hawk still at the wheel with his eyes at half-mast, totally unperturbed. I had visions of the headlines on the cover of *Down Beat* magazine had those horses not moved when they did.

It was common practice for Coleman to hang out with us until all hours of the morning and almost certainly be the last one to return to the hotel. We would all request the appropriate wake-up calls in preparation for an early start in the morning. On one particular journey of some four hundred miles, as we were exiting our rooms I heard this deep voice saying, "What's happening? Where's everybody going?" It was Coleman, standing in his silk bathrobe in the doorway to his room with a quizzical look on his face.

"We have a long drive ahead of us, Bean," Flip Phillips explained in his calm, tired voice. "Knowing you, I suppose you're not going to leave for another hour or so, right?" he asked.

"Hell, man, it ain't but four hundred and sixty-odd miles. That sounds like a five-hour drive to me," Coleman taunted.

"Well, you do it your way, Hawk, and we'll do it ours," Flip retorted as he headed for the elevator.

We now cut to our arrival in Topeka, Kansas. The elevator door opens on the tenth floor; Flip and I and two other members of the troupe start the trek down the hall towards our rooms, the fatigue of the road visibly etched in our faces. "Where the hell you guys been?" booms a voice from out of nowhere, and as we look up we see the figure of Coleman Hawkins in that same silk dressing gown, leaning on his door frame, cigarette in hand, with that half-grin on his face. "You guys must have gone via Seattle. How long did you stop to eat?" taunted Hawk, knowing full well that he had managed that four-hundred-and-some-mile drive in just under six hours by himself. That was Coleman Hawkins: a special man. He had to do things this way, for he knew no other way of dealing with life.

Once in Columbus, Ohio, when we had three days off, Coleman decided to take me with him and informed Norman that he would look out for me. We ended up going to a house owned by a woman who was obviously running a bordello. She welcomed Hawk warmly, and he introduced me, telling her that he was responsible for my well-being, and that he wanted nothing to go wrong. For three days we ate and slept there and I watched Hawk as he ate, drank, and kibitzed and joked with the working girls, trading stories with them, and putting them on with his glib remarks and razor-sharp humour. I learned a very vivid lesson on that trip: there wasn't a person that came in or out of that house who failed to address him as "Mr Hawkins." Many have accused Hawk of being frugal; well, he picked up the tab for the three days and told me to say nothing about it to anyone on the tour or else he would "come after me with his pistol." His elegant sensitivity was exemplified by the way he could one minute be talking with the cats in full and unbridled street jargon, and next moment discussing the subtle difference between several types of brandies that he had enjoyed while travelling in Europe.

Hawk played his horn with this same versatility and scope. I don't believe that Coleman Hawkins ever saw a tune as one whole song. I believe that every bar represented a microcosm of harmonic deviation and perusal to him. Long before such post-modernists as John Coltrane, he found all sorts of ways to re-fashion and transcend a composer's original harmonies. He also loved to play with time, tinkering around with how far into this musical maze he could venture while still retaining his hold on the open doorway to the next segment of the tune. He spawned a whole rash of followers—people like Herb Johnson of Montreal, and, more globally, Don Byas and Paul

Gonsalves. To play for him was a joy, and he would thrive on you laying down the musical cobblestones that took him down these pathways. His reactions to your shifting harmonic and rhythmic deviations resulted in an excitement that seemed to prod him even more vigorously into harmonic depths of his own and even more daringly into metronomical experiments.

For various reasons, I didn't see Coleman or work with him for a few years; it wasn't until 1966 that we once again crossed paths. Several things had changed drastically in that time frame. He had grown an immense grey beard; mentally he had become acutely withdrawn and caustic; physically he had become frail and was now heavily relying on spirits. He said that he had not been playing that much, and complained that he was having difficulty finding good players to accompany him. Even though I doubted this, my heart went out to him, and after discussing it with Norman, invited him to join my trio and me on an upcoming European tour.

That was one of the most difficult and certainly one of the saddest of all the tours I had made up to this time. It was a daily fight, attempting to get Coleman to take in some food in order to maintain his strength. At night, he was oft-times too weak to go up one flight of stairs to his dressing-room. In sum, he was a distressing shadow of his former self, but we somehow managed to finish the tour and return him safely to America.

Unfortunately I didn't meet him again until a JATP tour in 1967. Our musical relationship came to an abrupt end at a concert in San Diego when Hawk walked out to the mike to play his first solo, acknowledged the standing ovation which he got from the audience, put his horn to his lips, and blew into it, only to be rewarded with a rush of wind and no sound. He muttered his familiar "Hmmm," and made a second attempt at starting his cadenza, only to have it end with the same result. Absolutely no sound came out of the horn. Hawk's shoulders hunched together, and I heard a muffled, "Oh my God!" at which point he began to shake and reached out to grab hold of the microphone stand for support. There he stood, this behemoth of the tenor saxophone, a shaky, aged man with this huge beard, immaculate suit, and embellished horn trembling at the mike. The audience moaned in dismay, as they watched this unbelievably sad vignette. When I managed to reach him after leaving the piano, I attempted to remove his hand from the mike in order to assist him off stage. It became almost impossible to do so, for he had a death grip on it. As Norman came on to assist me, I remember Hawk repeatedly murmuring over and over again in dazed dismay, "Oh my God! Oh my God!"

That was the last time I saw Coleman Hawkins alive; but my inner memories of this great man will not allow me to remember him in such a way. I prefer to commemorate the immensity of his sound, the swagger of his gait, his elegant taste, and the unqualified love that he had for the creative spirit within him and others.

33

MEET THE PRESIDENT:
LESTER YOUNG

He scans you with that puzzled look that only he had. Chin cupped in his hands, head tilted to one side, his gaze riveted to your face. "Canadian! Right? Right! [confirming a fact he already knew] A big Canadian, too! Right, Pres?" [now waiting for your response to his foray] "Right," you concur, finding this ritual rather strange. "Me Lester." The hand comes out, topped by that bracelet I became so accustomed to seeing. The strength of the grip amazes you. "We'll talk later," and he saunters off with that ever-familiar sidewinder shuffle of his. A tall figure in a dark blue suit and slim tie. "Neat, neat," you mutter to yourself, and then you suddenly notice the blue canvas shoes that you know do not belong with the rest of the attire, and yet—somehow they don't seem out of place. Why? I know better than this. Why ask why? If the President is wearing those scampers (as we called them at home in Montreal), that's okay, and if he chose to wear slippers with a tux, that would be okay too.

Lester Young was basically a reserved and shy man. Yet he was very strong-willed: entering a room, he tended to dominate the space. That unique dress sense, his personal trademark, was actually quite sombre—the midnight-blue porkpie hat, the dark-blue topcoat worn exceedingly long, the array of dark suits. However, his personality belied his dress, for he was a man with a remarkably original sense of humour who regarded people as essentially comic. His closest companion on the road was his "baby doll," his tenor sax in its soft brown leather case. Many was the time during off-hours while we were sharing a laugh and a drink with friends, when he would suddenly look at me and ask, "Lady P, where's my baby doll?" It became a natural habit for me whenever we were out together to ride shotgun over it, so to speak, in order to ease his mind of any worry about "her."

Looking back over my days with Lester, his linear solos reflected his inner person. He was a very plain man, preferring to have non-complicated people and non-complicated things about him. He was forever coming to me with something in his hand, saying "Lady P, please show me how this bitch works. She won't talk to me at all." He would then stand there in amazement while I attempted to solve his problem for him, punctuating my efforts from time to time with challenging goadings such as "See? This bitch has got you too!" or words of admiration if I was successful: "Lady P, you sure kicked that bitch in the ass, didn't you? Doom!!" That was Pres' equivalent for the word "boom!"

As is well known, Lester had a vocabulary all of his own. He clearly felt that some ordinary expressions did not fully dramatize certain situations, so he would substitute his unique idioms wherever necessary. I recall once running down a tune for him with the rhythm section, and he wanted to go back over the middle section, or, as musicians call it, the bridge. As we approached the end of the chorus, he took the horn from his lips and said, "May I please have my George Washington one more time?" On another occasion, he looked at Gene Krupa, who was playing a press roll on his snare drum behind Pres, and said, "Lady Krupa, could I please have some Tinkty-Boom behind Lester?" "Tinkty-Boom" was an exact onomatopoeic simulation of the cymbal beat many drummers employed at the time. And an "onion skin" was a raincoat* much too thin for inclement weather, known as "Hawk" in Pres-speak. If he spied someone heading outside with improper clothing on, it would invoke a warning on the lines of "You better not let Hawk catch you out there with that onion skin on, 'cause he's kicking ass!"

Pres had a habit of calling for advice on "Dr Willis," a mysterious (and fictional) psychologist. He would always allow members of JATP to be present for these consultations: indeed, they invariably took place backstage or on the group bus. He would often use Dr Willis to clear the air if there was any undue tension present, which was inevitable from time to time on a long tour. Once, Norman had asked all the soloists to be brief because we had what was termed a "double-header," i.e. two concerts in one night. He explained that there'd be a traffic problem if the two crowds overlapped; in addition, the management wanted the concerts over by a specific time and threatened to turn the lights off if this was not adhered to. On this tour we had three tenor saxophonists—Flip Phillips, Illinois Jacquet, and Pres—and two trumpeters—Roy Eldridge and Charlie Shavers ("The Midgets," as we called them). Everything went well on the first concert until Flip and Jacquet suddenly decided to get it on, ending up in one of their famous tenor duels. When the show finally ended, Norman was livid. The theatre manager was screaming at him, and Norman was screaming back. Cut. The second show started and went smoothly

---

*In normal parlance "onion skin" is an almost transparent paper used for scoring music.

enough until Roy and Charlie decided to lock horns. This threw the whole evening into bedlam. Charlie blamed Roy, but Roy said he hadn't started it; he was merely defending himself, and so on. And on and on.

Eventually it was time to board the bus. This was done with whispers and hushed responses, for we all knew that Norman was not in a playful mood. When he appeared, he enacted the routine that he invariably used when feeling really salty at us: topcoat pulled up around his face and both hands jammed tight into his pockets, he slunk to the rear seat that had been nervously relinquished to him, and pulled his hat down over his eyes. The bus got under way, and as it weaved out of town, the silence was deafening.

Suddenly a tall figure in a dark-blue coat emerged, proceeded to the middle of the bus, turned to the coatrack overhead, and quietly said, "Do I feel a draught? Huh? I'm going to ask one more time. Does Lester feel a draught?" He paused measuredly. "Say what?" Louder: "Say what?!! The Midgets fucked up? What?! And Lady Granz is about to kick their asses?" Snickers now from various seats. He senses a gathering momentum and pushes home his advantage. "What's that, Dr Willis? You say that Lady Flip and Lady Jacquet are 'bout to get their buns kicked too? My, my; and Lady Granz has got her feelings all hurt and everything. Ugh!"

By this time, Ella is in convulsions, Norman's hat is bobbing up and down with laughter, along with everyone else, and Pres has accomplished what he set out to do. With Dr Willis' unseen help, he has kneaded everything back into a single happy unit. Take a bow, Pres—and Dr Willis too, of course.

PRES PLAYS THE LIGHT DOZENS

The term "the dozens" needs explaining. Amongst jazz musicians, if two people got into a vitriolic argument, and if one of the parties really wanted to hurt the other (short of inflicting grievous bodily harm), they would put their opponent into "the dozens," that is, say something most unkind and degrading about the other party's mother or father. Thereafter one would expect the argument to escalate into physical violence.

During the JATP tours of the late 1950s we all became aware and, obviously, concerned about Lester's continued drinking. He started out by consuming a bottle of gin a day, and later at least doubled that. Somewhere along the way several of us, myself included, became alarmed and as a result attempted, in one way or another, to dissuade him from drinking at this worrisome rate. One thing bothered us in particular: he was eating less and less. And on the rare occasions when we persuaded him to eat something, he would order the weirdest combinations imaginable. I recall that in San Francisco Roy Eldridge and I once badgered him relentlessly and finally managed to get him to a lunch counter and order some food. His order? Sardines and ice cream! Hard to envision but true. Nevertheless, we all continued our efforts to get him to eat more and, of course, drink less.

One night after one of the concerts, Ray Brown, Illinois Jacquet, and I decided as a gag to hide his "Red Boy." (The Red Boy was the red plastic zippered case in which Lester carried his beloved bottle of gin.) We hid it in the underneath compartment of the bus where the baggage is stored. I should mention here that Pres usually kept his Red Boy in the rack immediately above his seat. This was a nightly routine for him. Just before he would alight from the bus for a concert, he would take one "taste for the place," as he often said, after which he would stow away the gin in the hat rack.

Everyone was aware of what had taken place and most of the troupe was sitting, silently expectant. Pres entered the bus laughing while making some aside to Roy Eldridge as he passed Roy's seat. He continued down the aisle to his seat and after settling his "baby doll" (his saxophone) in a safe position he reached up for his bottle. He felt around in the area above for a few moments and then enlarged his search to a bigger area as he moved towards the front of the bus. Someone asked him what he was looking for, and he replied that he had lost his Red Boy. The search now extended to the other side of the bus, and by now had taken on an air of mildly controlled frenzy. He next proceeded to ask various members if they had seen his flask, and after receiving countless denials slumped into his seat with a look of total frustration and disbelief. He sat there half-audibly rationalizing what could have possibly happened, while intermittently asking various members if they had taken his flask. Finally, his voice took on a more determined timbre and he started to philosophize on how rotten a person would have to be in order to mess with him by viciously infringing on his "good feelings" and hiding his beloved Red Boy. His dissertation became ever more impassioned and inflamed as he progressed with his dialogue until, in anger, he stopped short and said that he would wait for a moment in order to give the culprit a chance to return his flask. After several moments that hung like heavy humidity, he got up out of his seat and said, "Well, whoever the dirty motherfucker is that's taken Lester's Red Boy" (pause and in a very lightened tone), "I want him to know that I am his mother's *very* best friend."

34

THE LEGEND IS REAL: LADY FITZ

She loved to walk up to you and ask what you thought about a certain song. If you asked her why, she'd shyly say that she thought that she would like to include it in her repertoire, and that it more than likely would sound good with a big band. It wasn't hard to work out the proper key for her, mainly because she would often make herself stretch rather than saying it's either too high or too low for her. I never understood this quirk within her. Perhaps it was some sort of test that she felt that she had to run on herself.

There were many parts to Lady Fitz (as I affectionately named her in 1951) that I still don't claim to know, although I knew her for over 40 years and worked with her on and off throughout. She was innately shy and insecure, a very private person who remained somewhat enigmatic to even her closest friends.

After we'd met in 1950, I got to know her fairly well. I used to stand in the wings almost every night not only to listen to her sing, but also to hear how Hank Jones played for her. The early trio on JATP was Hank on piano, Ray on bass, and Buddy Rich on drums. These were dream nights for me. Here was Ella doing at least a one-hour show, accompanied by these three masters of their instruments. Were someone to ask me to choose my favourite Ella period, I would have to name the early 1950s as one of the strongest contenders. Those nights of awed listening are as fresh in my memory as yesterday—and remember that Ella in the early 1950s was not even close to being the worldwide international star that she was to become. She was just beginning to enjoy the musical challenge of Jazz At The Philharmonic.

At the outset, Ella's set would follow the intermission; but later developments—my trio's slot and guest appearances by other groups (e.g. the Gene Krupa Quartet and the Modern Jazz Quartet)—led to her batting in the "clean-up spot." If one thinks about all the heavy traffic that preceded her on stage, one begins to realize how much music Ella and her group had to produce to survive, never mind break it up (which she did almost nightly). It always amazed me how this woman could sit in her dressing-room from the start of the concert— she was invariably one of the first to arrive—joke and chat with the guys, the press, and the hangers-on who didn't know when to leave, and then when the moment arrived, go out on stage and rip up the concert!

What was it she had that earned not only the love, but also the musical respect of these heavy players around her? Lester Young used to sidle up to me in the wings with his taste in one hand, the other holding his bottom lip with an aghast stare on his face, listen for a couple of choruses, take my arm, grunt, and say, "Sis is kicking ass out there tonight, ain't she, Lady P? Lester better go get his horn and get ready for the finale and things." No one could have put it better.

When Ella reached her own cruising speed or comfort zone, she would make it awfully hard for you to be out there with her, regardless of the instrument that you played. Hank would feed her just enough to cause her to react to his phrasing and harmonic lead. Ella would respond to this and instinctively tack on her own linear answer while retaining the shape and cadence of the particular song. Ray would intercede with a bass figure, and Fitz would come across him, almost pre-thinking him with her response. Buddy would lay in some kind of drum figure that was still appropriate, and she would knead and mould the lyric and line within the same rhythmic structure that Buddy used. They would then often take off on flights of almost impossible key changes, which Fitz would sail through like a Ferrari going through a simple S-curve.

All through those days I had the feeling that Fitz was musically happier than at any other time before or since. She had an unbridled zest for musical investigation and exploration; at times, some pre-arranged things would go out of whack, and Fitz would take over and lead the group out of its confusion via a totally transformed version that vied for inclusion in the books as a new arrangement. "What about that, fellas?" Fitz would laughingly ask as she walked to her dressing-room. "I kinda like it like that. Shall I leave it that way? What do you think, OP?" Everyone would usually nod assent because to us Lady Fitz could do no wrong. It wasn't a case of giving in to the great lady: it was simply that we all sensed that she was on an undeniable musical roll, and none of us even cared to guess when it would come to an end.

Fitz continued on her merry way unperturbed by anything or anyone. She sauntered through her show each evening with that same imperturbable musical confidence. On the finale each night, she courageously took on the front line horns, regardless of who they were—Pres, Roy, Coleman, Benny Carter, Ben Webster, and so on. Ella traded fours, eights, sixteens, or whatever they wanted with them and never got hurt. As a matter of fact, on various nights when some of the horns got a smidgen careless, Fitz would run up over them and keep right on going.

"I told you about getting too sporty out there with Lady Fitz," Pres reminded Flip Phillips one night when he decided to stay at the mike and "fairground" as Pres put it.

"Geez," muttered Flip in disbelief, "I didn't think she'd get that rough!"

"Rough?" repeated Pres in sarcasm. "You stay out there long enough and Lady Fitz will really lay waste to your ass! Lester knows better. Lester lets Lady Fitz sing her little four-bar song, then Lester plays his four-bar song, and then Goodnight Irene. Lester's through!"

None of this was said with any vehemence: Pres was merely stating an honest musical credo—that he never played games on the challenges with Ella. Wise man.

I got the opportunity to play for Ella quite unexpectedly. It was in 1952 and Norman was taking JATP to Europe for its debut over there. We were all assembled excitedly at the New York airport, chattering away, when someone suddenly asked, "Say, where's Hank?" The whole atmosphere immediately changed from one of excited clamour to one of anxious curiosity. Norman remained placid and carried on his business at the counter as before. Finally, departure time arrived, and we all boarded the plane for Stockholm. It took some time for the group to realize that Hank had in fact missed the plane, but after it struck home, everyone settled down to enjoy our first European jaunt.

After our arrival and reception in Stockholm, I asked Norman what was going to happen. He calmly looked at me and said, "You'll have to play for her, that's all." After delivering his bombshell, he left as was normal for him, and I sat there much like a condemned man, wondering exactly how I had managed to come to grief at such an early stage of the tour, considering the fact that we hadn't even struck a single note as yet. I had subbed for Hank on a couple of earlier tours in America, but that was different. Those occasions simply meant substituting for him for one single night, not a whole tour, let alone the first European tour. I knew that Ella would naturally want to do some of her arrangements, and that would normally have meant some quick rehearsals and memorizing on my part; however, with opening night staring us all in the face, there would be no time for any of that.

Daniel Peterson, Oscar's father, and Oscar Peterson. © Canadian Pacific Railroad.

The original trio: Austin Roberts (bass), Clarence Jones (drums), and Oscar Peterson (piano) at the Alberta Lounge. Photo: Salmon Studios, Montreal; © Canadian Broadcasting Corporation.

Oscar Peterson and Roy Eldridge in London.

(left to right) Norman Granz, Fred Astaire, and Oscar Peterson preparing for *The Astaire Story* album. Photo: Howard Morehead.

Art Tatum and Oscar Peterson.

The genius of the jazz world, Norman Granz. Photo: Oscar Peterson.

The Trio of the 1950s and 1960s: Oscar Peterson with Ray Brown and Herbie Ellis. Photo: Bob Streeter.

Ella Fitzgerald and Oscar Peterson in London. Photo: Bernard Long.

Joe Pass and Oscar Peterson. Photo: Carlsen & Co., Oslo.

Best friends: Count Basie and Oscar Peterson.
© Canadian Broadcasting Corporation.

The present Quartet, affectionately known as the NATO Group. Photo: Celine

I searched out Ray Brown, whom I did not know well at this stage: he was working with Ella and I was using Major Holley, and we had not yet teamed up as a duo. I told him what Norman had said, and he was very nonchalant about the whole thing, tossing it off with a "Just listen to and watch me, and everything will be OK." Given that he had not only been playing Ella's arrangements nightly, but had also been responsible for some of them, in part at least, I considered his response to my concern rather cavalier.

Opening night arrived as opening nights must, and throughout the first half of the concert I could only focus on that impending set with Lady Fitz. Finally, the intermission arrived and I nervously followed Ray into Ella's dressing-room along with Norman to discuss her set. They chucked out and installed songs one after the other; it didn't really matter much to me what they called, for I knew that I was in foreign territory whichever way they went. Then, as I nervously stood in the wings with Ella, Norman, and Ray, I said to myself, "Peterson, you screw this one up, and they're going to hear this one all the way back to Montreal, including Pop!" It's strange how we tend to relate to someone in particular whenever we find ourselves in any kind of jeopardy. At this moment, it was Dad who came to mind—not out of fear, but more out of what I imagined would be his total disappointment at my failure. I can remember straightening myself up, and deciding that I wasn't going to quit before I was beaten, which would have been Dad's philosophy.

As Ella walked on to thunderous applause and cheers, Ray set the first tempo with the snap of his fingers and by slapping the inside shell of the piano (a trademark of his). It was an easy loping tempo, and I found it to be quite easy to cope with once the primary flush of apprehension had passed. In fact, it felt good, and I decided to make the most of it. Fortunately, the magic worked and the night was a success. Ella came off smiling and happy, and I thanked the powers-that-be for getting me through that first important concert. I felt that if we succeeded in having a good first shot, things would roll from then on. I am still grateful to Ray for virtually conducting me through the various tempi that were needed in order to make Fitz's set work: he hadn't been so cavalier after all!

I grew to know practically all the little signs and mannerisms that telegraphed exactly what Ella was feeling.

1. The first slight side glance accompanied by a sort of half-laugh.
   Meaning: "What was that change or that line that you played behind me?"
2. The left hand cupped to her ear.
   Meaning: "Something is out of tune. Is it me or the piano?" (Note: Bet on it being the piano!)
3. The head tilts slightly to the side; the left hand starts snapping with a vengeance.
   Meaning: The time pulsation is not reaching her the way she wants it to. Tighten up the time, fellas!
4. The left foot is tapping the time along with a natural snap of the left hand.
   Meaning: All's well up front, guys. She's cruising with it.
5. The handkerchief is nervously being switched from hand to hand:
   Meaning: She's not comfortable. The dynamic level is too high or the tempo is not what she wanted from the outset.
6. The left hand is slapping the hip.
   Meaning: This reaction is gauged by the intensity of the slap, or what accompanies it. If it is a normal tap, she is perhaps trying to raise or lower the tempo. Experiment. If the intensity is much deeper, look out, she's getting ready to go for it and wants to make sure that you go with her.

These are but a few of the vital signs that I learned to use as a guide when playing for Ella. There were of course many other factors that governed accompanying her. One of the most important things that I found out was that Fitz had to feel good about her relationship with her group, or else she couldn't function with the normalcy and flow that we all became accustomed to hearing from her. What she did was an emotional thing, and should some personal strife intervene, certainly between Ella and the group, the flow was broken.

This was the case a little later on into the same tour. It was perhaps the beginning of the end of her marriage to Ray, and of course there were times when things did not go too well for them. It is difficult enough to make any marriage work; add to it the rigours of touring and you have a near-impossible situation. Nevertheless, it reached a stage where Ella seemed to think that I wasn't in her corner anymore as a friend, and became insecure about our relationship; because of her attitude I became alienated from her, and the situation rapidly deteriorated. It came to a head one night in Sweden when I deliberately walked by her table in the restaurant without acknowledging her, and continued on to my own table farther into the room.

I didn't have to wait long for someone at my table to say, "Oh-oh, look out! Here comes Ella with blood in her eye." I timed it perfectly so that just as she arrived at my table with her accusing finger raised, I intercepted her and said, "If you want to have this out, let's take it outside." She agreed, and we stomped out to the amazed and confused glances of the patrons. When we got out into the hallway, I asked Ella what was wrong; she retorted, "That's exactly what I was going to ask you! You embarrass me by walking by me as if you don't even recognize me, and it's been like that for days." I replied that I thought that she was upset with me and perhaps displeased with my playing for her. She was really upset by this, saying that she was not only grateful for my sitting in for Hank, but that she was enjoying working with me. The most revealing part of it all was when she went on, "Why, I even went out and picked out something real nice that I wanted to give you in order to say thanks."

It was the way it sounded that got to me. Here was Ella like a little girl, dumbfounded by my earlier snub, telling me that she thought enough of me to have gone out and done what she had. I was overwhelmed by the ridiculousness of two people who really cared for each other being at odds, and my only reaction was to reach out for her and hug her. A few passers-by stared at us as we stood there telling each other we cared, both of us crying. We returned to our respective tables holding hands, and there were smiles of satisfaction on many of the faces at this reconciliation between two good friends.

Playing for Lady Fitz on the various concerts around the world gave me the opportunity of seeing her in different musical spotlights. She sang in most of the major cities and countries of the globe, and was acclaimed and revered in each. If for no other reason than that, I felt an overwhelming responsibility to give her the best pianistic support that I was capable of.

One other significant factor should be mentioned here. I have, over a period of years, listened to many of the other groups who have supported Ella, and feel that some of them suffered from an ailment that you might term "The Backgrounders' Blues." This affliction was usually found in the groups where the pianist was a viable musical performer in his own right, but felt sidelined, relegated to being a musical "third-class citizen" entrapped behind the huge talent of Lady Fitz. That could be dangerous, producing an underlying resentment of Ella which led to her being denied the musical assistance that she deserved.

The other sandtrap lay in the "comfort zone" that went with landing the gig with Ella. This is one of the oldest ailments in show business. A pianist or group lands the treasured gig with a world-renowned vocalist such as Ella, and over a period of time the rust and decay start to set in. This is quite natural. It stems first from the huge receptions by audiences, then from the repeated replays of the great and glossy night spots worldwide, and the inflated rate of pay (Ella was over-generous to my mind).

I was fortunately never affected by any of this: I had my own group and spot on JATP, and even though I was accompanying Fitz, I was being paid by Norman as a member of JATP, so I was never her employee. As a result, I was able to dedicate myself serenely and freely to supporting her. Our free-wheeling relationship inevitably had its ups and downs; we did, however, have the spontaneity to try things out unrehearsed, even on stage. Sometimes, I would suddenly lay out on a tune, letting the bass and drums carry the tune with her. She might hesitate for a fleeting second, purely out of surprise, and then would take things in hand, sensing the new density in the group, and react to it. The result on my return would be the thickening of the rhythmic impulse and a new impetus would be created to which she would react. When done with the horns, we call this effect "strollers."

Doing record dates with Fitz, I learned the true meaning of the word patience. Ella needed the comfort of knowing not only that her contribution was musically correct, but also that everything was free from strain and any artificiality. When we recorded the *Ella And Oscar* album, I found Fitz to be much more relaxed than I had seen her in many years. She sailed through the various tunes with a confidence that surprised me. The intriguing thing about that album was that it came about as a result of a casual conversation. We were sitting about in Ella's dressing-room one night on tour, when she asked me about some tune or other. There was a piano in her room; I sat to it and laid out some background as she lightly ran through the song. Before we knew it, we had gone through several tunes and Norman, who had been sitting listening, remarked, "I don't know why you two don't do this in a studio! You just about have an album right here."

This impromptu session spawned further conversations and careful encouragement from Norman, and *voilà*! We did indeed end up in the studio! The only tune on the date that caused us any kind of problem was Billy Strayhorn's *Lush Life* (shades of Ronnie Scott's in London*). Perhaps the hex was put on it when Fitz looked at me and said, "You know that Billy told me that very few people do his tune right, OP, so let's make sure that we're not wrong." I nodded assent and we started into it. Before I knew what was up, we were into take # 6. We were taking turns goofing. I would blow one of the chord sequences, and next, Ella would then blow a part of the lyric. Finally, we got to the

---

*See "Carmen McRae: The Special One" (Chapter 43) for this story.

stage where we started each take sort of expecting a goof, and sure enough, we'd goof, and then burst into laughter.

At this point, Norman came over the talk-back mike and said in his calmest tone, "Take your time, you're only up to take # 16." Ella and I both jumped and screamed, "*What?!!* What did you say, Smedley?" Norman, sensing that he really had our attention, took full advantage of the moment to inject some of his famous goading humour. "I said not to worry about it being your 16th take. Actually, you have nothing to worry about. I've just sent out for some more reels." Ella and I looked at each other, and although we were both laughing, we both knew that we would be making the next take our final one on this tune. We settled, waited for Norman's taped ID no. "Master no. ___; *Lush Life* ___; Speed!"

I launched into the intro with a musical determination that perhaps was lacking on the other takes. I released and Fitz entered as I held the harmonic door open for her. "I used to wander all the ___." Her voice held each word firmly as she followed my harmonic leads. Before we knew it, Norman was holding up his hand for silence, and we were through! Strayhorn's *Lush Life* had been documented flawlessly.

I once attempted to pay a television tribute to Ella when she was a guest on a series I did in England during the 1970s. I told her that playing for her was not only a pleasure: the astonishing tonal quality and range of her voice increased our musical taste, and the intrinsic mastery of her phrasing guaranteed our sense of good time. Any pianist, I concluded, fortunate enough to have worked with her had learned immeasurably in terms of timing and overall musical perception.

Many musicians went on to fill the slots in Ella's group once occupied by Hank Jones, Ray Brown, Charlie Smith, Buddy Rich, and myself. I hope my own reminiscences are representative, and also properly discerning, as befits a genius of Ella's calibre. Time finally took its toll of her skills, as it does with any great performer, and then it took her away altogether. But nothing will ever erase the many great memories that Lady Fitz gave me, from that very first night at Carnegie.

ELLA

To touch a cloud, to live a dream
To have life flow like a silvery stream
To ride the wind or grow like a leaf
To sing with a voice quite beyond belief
To use time like a magic wand
Echoing things of which we are fond
To invoke anew memories of old past
Creating new visions that will ever last
To sing of love and its hurtful pangs
To paint a picture that forever hangs
In our hearts, in our souls, in our very beings.
This is what Ella Fitzgerald means.

35

BILLIE HOLIDAY: THE MYSTERIOUS LADY DAY

first met Billie Holiday in 1950 when I was invited to a party in the place she was staying. She lived on the second floor of a building which had a porch and a flight of stairs leading to her apartment. As I rang the bell downstairs I was aware of some commotion taking place inside. The door opened and I nervously stepped inside the foyer, only to be greeted by her accompanist at the time falling down the stairs and ending up at my feet. During his fall Billie was at the top of the stairs hurling invectives at him, and she ended this scene by throwing a couple of Coke bottles after him as he landed at my feet.

Without missing a beat, as I stood there transfixed, she said, "Oh honey, don't pay him any mind. Just step over him and come on up." I started up the stairs with apprehension and was greeted at the top by a hug and a kiss from this beautiful lady. Billie seemed very enraptured by me that particular evening as I seem to remember, for she continually seemed to fuss and fidget over me the whole time that I was in her presence. She shouted at various times to various people around her to get me a drink immediately, and made a project out of this. Also, it seemed that almost every time she passed me, she would make reference to my citizenship, with sayings like, "So you come from that cold country up there, do you?" or, "What kind of jazz do they play up there in Canada?" She was totally preoccupied with my place of origin and seemed unable to connect it to the jazz world.

At some point during the evening she suddenly came over to me, took me by the hand and led me to the upright piano that graced the living-room. This particular instance remains lodged in my memory simply because I received a shock upon feeling her hand in mine. Billie Holiday had a very soft countenance and radiance about her, yet her hand was rough and abrasive, which took me aback; indeed, it is still embedded in my memory. Nevertheless, we headed for the piano. She sat me down on the bench and settled herself on the other half, then looked around at me with that under-glance that was a natural habit of hers. It was then, so close to her, that I fully realized what a breathtakingly beautiful woman she was. Her skin was exquisite in texture and her full, well-formed lips barely moved when she spoke, the words emanating from the side of her mouth. Her pretty lips seemed to curl and roll out the words, which now I think about it probably accounts for her almost slurred singing delivery at times. She sat motionless as I played my version of some ballad for her, and seemed almost hypnotized by my hand movement. Her head swivelled from side to side as my hands moved; the tuft of hair that she had tied at the back of her head swung back and forth like a puppy's tail as she watched me play.

"Say, Leonard!" she shouted suddenly to someone in the other room, "Come and hear what this young man from Canada is doing." Then turning to me she said, "Play that chorus again for me." I replayed the chorus as closely as I could, but she stopped me part of the way through and said, "No, no, you left out that little curlie cue that you played the last time. Play that for me." I tried to reconstruct the chorus in the way she wanted; however, I obviously missed because she came back with, "No, that's not it, that's not it. That's different again. You've got so much music in you, you just can't remember what it is you played." Then out of nowhere, "Play *Body And Soul* for me." As I got into the chorus of the tune, she suddenly started to hum and then said to me, "Play it in my key," obviously assuming that I knew what her key was. I switched to the key of G hoping this would be somewhere within her range, and she began singing the lyrics, which happily suggested I was at least close.

I ought to say that prior to this time I had not been a committed Billie Holiday fan. Perhaps it was not until this direct contact that I was able to appreciate the full impact of her unique phrasing and voice quality. Previously I had heard only some very bad early recordings, which did not do her justice. Seated next to me now was a woman with a voice of pure velvet, and a style absolutely her own; she had an interpretative way with a lyric that was so personal it was almost hard to believe that she was not making up the words as she sang.

To play for her was so easy that it was almost ludicrous. When I play for someone who is capable of stringing together the melodic line and lyric with such a sensitive musical delivery there is very little, I feel, that is needed short of an understatement of the lower harmonic structures that can round out her vocal talents without being obstructive or destructive in any way. Her voice was so smooth and almost hesitant that most of my piano fills, if any, were held back until the absolute completion of her phrases. I crafted my answers to her lines with a shifting base of harmonic figures much as the late Jimmy Jones used to do. I called on this pattern to retain the elongated effect which she had created with her voice. We finished the tune and she turned to me with that innocent girlish laugh and asked, "So when are we going to make a record?" In my awed haze at what she had just done vocally, I mumbled something to the effect of whenever she felt like it, or some such insipid remark. Given that I had just met her accompanist after he had been physically ejected by her, I had a flash of panic, wondering what she might have done to me had she not liked the way I played for her!

Over the next couple of years I only saw Billie Holiday by chance: we occasionally bumped into each other in a New York night club, embraced and exchanged greetings and small talk. It wasn't until 1952, when Norman decided he wanted to record Billie with my trio, augmented with a couple of horns, that I got the opportunity to play for her once more. She came into the studio exuding that same aura of feminine softique that she was so capable of projecting. She took a few moments to greet everyone with kisses and embraces, then sat down in a chair and had a drink. She conducted the record session under Norman's gentle guidance with a directness and musical under-standing that caused me to wonder about all the rumours of her inconsistency, unpredictability, and the like. She asked for certain things from Herb Ellis and myself that made total musical sense, and she knew exactly what she wanted. We finished the date; we were all happy with it, and Billie herself was ecstatic.

My questions about unpredictability were answered for me in what turned out to be a horrible experience at Carnegie Hall in 1955. Norman had decided that Billie should do the JATP concert strictly as a surprise guest artist, due to the fact that she had not appeared in New York in perhaps four to five years. This was because she had no "police card"—issued by the NYC Police Department and mandatory for any performer wishing to play the city's night clubs; I am told that no one with any kind of criminal record (including narcotics usage) could get one. In Norman's mind, her appearance on the JATP concert was a way of circumventing her night-club plight, and would serve to reintroduce her to the many fans in New York who loved her. He did everything possible to ensure that nothing would impede her having a fair shot that evening; he even kept the backstage area clear of anyone who might mislead her or tempt her with alcohol or narcotics. He then went over the selection of each tune with Billie and me in order to make sure there would be no misunderstanding about the routine.

I admired all the effort he put into paving the way for Billie to have a great return concert; the part that confounded me was how he was going to justify it to Ella. I thought she would find it inexplicable that he had put another vocalist on the show, and I still don't know how he did it. He refused to discuss it with me, brushing my queries aside with a "Don't worry about it." The concert started with Norman's usual opening announcement, during which he informed the audience that he had a surprise guest artist for them. The concert went on through to the trio segment, after which Norman reiterated what he had said about the guest artist, and announced, "the great Billie Holiday." The audience went berserk and gave her a standing ovation. I laid out the intro to the first tune and Lady sailed through her portion of the show with the same self-assurance that she had exhibited at the record session. She came off after an encore to another standing ovation, and we all revelled in what to us was a great moment in jazz: the return of Billie Holiday.

That particular night in Carnegie was what we used to call a "double-header"—two concerts in one evening. There was an intermission of about one hour, allowing the hall to be emptied and refilled, then the second concert started. I was busy saying hello to various friends that had come backstage and didn't see Norman until the Trio was standing in the wings waiting to be introduced. I couldn't help noticing that he seemed upset about something; however, before I could query him, I was on stage. At the end of the Trio set Norman reappeared through the curtain and headed for the mike. He had the most horrible look of frustration and anger that I think I have ever seen on his face. He stood at the mike for a moment, seeming to take a deep breath, with his shoulders slightly sagged. He made a similar announcement about Billie, much as he had done in the first concert, then walked to the back curtain and escorted her to the mike with a slight shrug of his shoulders.

I was curious as to what was going on; nevertheless, I played the intro that we had decided on for her for the tune *I Only Have Eyes For You*. As we gave her the break for the pickup, I somehow knew at that exact moment that she was not going to respond. There was a seemingly lifelong silence as she stood there, teeter-tottering back and forth with a blank look on her face. On stage at moments like this, time seems to lapse into unrealistic segments, whereby a minute takes on the dimensions of an hour. I sat there embarrassed, maybe even stunned, then decided on the spur of the moment to lay out another piano intro for her. I used a much more pronounced attack, and simplified my lines so as not to create any chance of a misunderstanding in her mind of where the break was to come. We took the break, and once again there was an oceanic silence during which I sat there totally panicked. All I could think of was, "Where is she? How do I reach her? Does she know we're here? How do I get her into this without totally embarrassing her in front of this huge audience?"

By this time the audience had sensed that there was a malfunction of some sort on stage and commenced squirming in their seats and whispering to one another. I ignored this and once again laid out a very deliberate and decisive intro for her. We again took the break, and there was a moment of complete fear mixed with sadness, as through the almost silent hall there came this mournful, tired, toneless, half-cry of a voice. The lyrics became so stretched out that the cadence of the song was completely lost in this senselessly elongated phrasing: "Ar___e t___he s___ta___rs." At this moment Norman appeared from the back curtain and escorted Billie off stage. I sat there stupefied and saddened, for although I didn't really want to admit that I understood what had taken place, in reality I certainly knew. Norman returned and brought on the next segment of the show.

When I finally came off stage, I looked around in the darkness of backstage and finally saw Billie sitting stooped over in a chair. I started over towards her to offer words of consolation, but before I reached her she saw me, with half-filled eyes and that pretty mouth now distorted into a grimace. "There he is," she shouted. "There's Oscar Peterson.

He's the one that fucked up my music." I stopped in my tracks. What moments ago was honest chagrin and sorrow for what Billie had done to herself suddenly turned to anger within me, until I realized that it was the narcotics talking, not her. I also realized that much of this would be forgotten in her mind and lost deep in the stupor of drugs.

I now saw why Norman had been upset. Apparently someone had gotten to her and managed to slip the protection that Norman had set up, and helped her to get high during the intermission between concerts. Norman had hoped against hope that she could still overcome this and do her second show without failing herself; but it was not to be. Billie Holiday had once again taken a huge gouge out of what could have been a more than magnificent and even more meaningful career in jazz. I have always since felt that Billie, due to her unfortunate affliction to drugs, not unlike many others of this era, was simply just another part of the harvest that she had sung about: *Strange Fruit.*

LADY DAY

Languid is a word that I have always felt
Went with limpid ponds and the steamy veldt
It conjures up visions of soft moving streams
And of sensuous women that inhabit men's dreams.

To think that one day I would make the choice
Of attributing that meaning to a human voice,
And yet as I sit here reminiscing in kind,
A vision of Billie slowly forms in my mind.

In truth she was languid in music and speech,
For she phrased with a cadence that could easily reach
Each listener who savored her every line
With a hunger that only true fans could define.

To reshape a phrase was to not take a break
In places where other singers would hesitate.

In reading a lyric as if it were her own,
She would reshape the notes to let it be known
That she knew full well exactly what they meant
As they continued to flow long after her voice was spent.

Her torture was in life, for it held many downers
Which was in no way aided by the viperous downtowners
Who plagued her relentlessly, while she struggled in vain
To throw off her habit, and once again reign
Like the true Lady Day, as we all knew her then
With the voice that slowed traffic and silenced Big Ben.

But time would have none of this, its prophecy was due
And it called upon Billie, with its message so terse
That she barely had time to finish the verse
To "More Than You Know," which we all loved to hear
Yet before we knew it, she was taken from here
To a place far distant and viper-free
Where she lives now and sings just as soulfully.

36

THE LADY DAY SESSIONS

O ne of the most memorable of all my recording sessions was the first date I cut with Billie Holiday. Although I had met her a year or so before, that had been a totally different and much more personal experience. Today it was all about music and how to go about making the album.

When I arrived at the studio, there was a slight air of apprehension: nobody knew what kind of mood Billie would be in. Any fears were soon allayed, for she came through the door with Norman in just about the happiest mood I ever saw her in, making the rounds of all the players, embracing us with that catching smile of hers and planting a kiss on our cheeks.

I was still nervous, however, as I knew how difficult things could get with her at times. On this occasion, though, she was almost submissive, agreeing instantaneously with Norman's suggestions about tunes; curiously, that increased my nerves—I had never seen her like this before. She even deferred to Norman's request that the pieces' arrangements be changed. Billie had been very precise about which soloists she wanted to follow her vocals, but Norman felt the sequences were becoming too samey, and she happily agreed to his adjustments.

Best of all, so far as I was concerned, she seemed to bask in my accompaniments, several times insisting that I repeat a couple of nuances that I had played behind her earlier. We got along fabulously, and during Charlie Shavers' various solos, she would get a certain light in her eyes and raise her right hand in the air, rhythmically accompanying him. I tried to stay out of her way as much as possible, allowing her interpretation and unique timbre to come through. As a rhythm section we looked to enhance and encourage rather than stomp.

At the conclusion of the date she made the rounds once again, kissing all of us, and before I knew it she was gone from the studio. Within only a few years, to everyone's sorrow, she would be gone from the jazz world forever.

37

BUDDY RICH

"Hey kid, how'ya doing?" That was how Buddy Rich greeted me on our very first meeting backstage at Carnegie. He stood there with a towel thrown around his neck, stripped down to a simple T-shirt and pants. He immediately impressed me with his off-hand air of self-confidence. He seemed to thrive on the bustling buzz of the numerous people who had managed to invade the backstage area. This compact, slight man moved easily among them, seeming to feed on their adulation and awe.

As I lay in bed later that night, I thought about the powerhouse drumming I had heard. During the jam session he, Ray Brown, and pianist Hank Jones had handled each of the alternating soloists with unsurpassable ease and fire, and I hoped that one day I would get the opportunity to kindle some similar heat with them. About four weeks later, I got my shot. Hank Jones could not appear one night and Norman called on me.

It is odd that when something we've been hoping for actually comes about, we are at once apprehensive rather than joyful! This happened now: I became leery of what was about to take place. Fortunately, Ray Brown came to my rescue, talking to me at some length about a variety of things in order to reassure me. Finally we were off, and I was out on stage into what in effect was the start of my days as part of the JATP rhythm section. I laid out the intro for the first tune (a blues) and we were into it. Just as my four bars were about to come to a close, I felt this rhythmic hook reach out and snare the last three beats of the fourth bar and carry us over into the tune. Ray entered with that inimitable big-sounding bass stride of his and from that moment on, it became a piece of cake. The rhythm section soared from there on. Buddy sat there behind his drums and propelled the horns through the blues with unerring confidence and relentless drive. As we drove and drove, I inevitably looked up from time to time and was confronted by a red-faced tyrant with the fixed look of pressure in his eyes. His left hand danced on the time, feeding the horns with whip-crack figures on the snare drum; his right hand controlled the time lock-down with Ray and myself, while also occasionally punctuating the choruses on the ride cymbal.

That was the first of innumerable performances with Buddy. He was prodigiously gifted; his talent had its temperamental and wilfull side, however, as this next anecdote illustrates.

Back in the early 1950s, we were both appearing at Basin Street when it was situated just off of Broadway. One night, Buddy came to work and forgot his cuff links. I volunteered to loan him a pair of mine—a pair that happened to be of special meaning to me, and I told him so. He wore the links for the show and somehow got away before I could corral him to get them back. The following night I asked him for them, and he casually told me that he had forgotten them, but that he would bring them for certain the next night.

This went on for the rest of the week until the Sunday matinée. I arrived at the club, and upon reaching the backstage area, I saw Buddy standing talking with some friends. I walked over to him and asked if he had remembered to bring the links. Due perhaps to the fact that he had a captive audience, he brushed me off with some smart-assed reply—at which I put my face directly in front of his and, in no uncertain terms, told him not to come to work that night if he didn't have the cuff links, and walked away. About 15 minutes later, one of his friends came to my dressing-room and put the links in my hand. He had obviously sent someone back to the hotel to fetch them.

I was sitting with some friends at ringside later that evening just off from where Buddy's drums were set. He came out and proceeded to burn up the club, as was his act. During one number he happened to look down and saw me. He leaned over my way and said, "You hate me, don't you?" When I nodded, he replied, "Yeah, but I can play these God-damn drums!"

That summed up his whole philosophy of life. Our hostility then was not the only time when we were not on easy terms: there were also occasions when Buddy and I did not see eye to eye musically. But I always had the utmost respect for him. Whenever one comes across his kind of talent, one must honour it in full—and Buddy Rich belonged to that very select group of people that I would label "genius."

38

ROY (SPEEDY GONZALES) ELDRIDGE

To sit in a dressing-room at Carnegie Hall waiting to make your musical debut is the essence of fear itself. To sit in a dressing-room at Carnegie Hall waiting to make your musical debut on a bill featuring musical legends such as Ella, Coleman Hawkins, Charlie Parker, Buddy Rich, and Roy Eldridge is a masochistic form of suicide.

This is the exact situation that I found myself in on a fateful night in September 1949. I had arrived at Carnegie at around half past six and of course was the only musician in the hall at that time. I managed to navigate my way to what I believed to be one of the dressing-rooms and found it to be replete with a piano. In an attempt to relax myself, I sat down and proceeded to wander around the keyboard in a slow harmonic form of playing. This must have gone on for some time, because I glanced up at the clock while becoming aware of another presence in the room. Standing to my right, slightly behind me, was a leprechaunian man in a trench coat and hat. As I looked around I saw him nodding his head slightly up and down in a form of assent.

"Uh huh," he said as I turned. "You must be that young cat from Canada that Bean's told me about. I'm Roy. What's your name?"

"Peterson," I answered in near-stunned reply.

"Yeah, yeah," he continued while at the same time sizing me up with that sort of impish gaze that I came to know so well. "They say you're pretty mean at that box, and it sure sounds to me like you know what you're doing. Go ahead and play something for me."

I slid back down on the piano stool and nervously set out a chorus of *The Man I Love.*

"Well," he said with a smile creeping across his face, "I guess Coleman didn't lie to me after all." Now a full roaring laugh followed, then he said, "Man! I can think of a whole bunch of cats that ain't goin' to want to know about you. I sure would like to take you around to some of my after-hours joints and turn you loose on some of those studs! Come on over to my room while I warm up."

I followed obediently and thankfully, because I felt I had made a friend; even more of a gas, my new friend was also one of my big idols in the world of jazz.

During the next while, Roy engaged himself with some "warm-up" notes and phrases, pausing every so often to ask me about various people and situations in Montreal that he remembered from his many visits to that city. These questions were often preceded by an askance look at me, followed by a "So you're one of those Canadian people!" and then a chuckle and once in a while a nip from his glass. (Speedy was very meticulous about using a proper glass for his Scotch. He would allow almost any of the guys to come in and have a "taste"; however, the stipulation was that you had to use a proper glass.) My own opinion was that, hygienic reasons apart, with this method Speedy was better able to control the outlay of his spirits. Many dressing-rooms seldom, if ever, had a drinking glass.

As it drew closer to concert time, the backstage activity naturally increased and Roy had a slew of visitors. Everyone from close friends to awed backstage visitors dropped by to say hello and good luck. I sat there realizing how revered this happy and spunky leprechaun was, and how much he enjoyed the love and appreciation of these honest admirers. This was his own special group of worshippers, coming to pay tribute to their own musical guru. All of this, I came to realize, is part and parcel of the total performance: it goes hand in hand with the musical side of the evening. Many players and performers seem to prefer the solitude of total isolation before a concert (as I do); however, I sensed that this was not the case with Roy Eldridge. He somehow seemed to charge himself up on this, never neglecting to refer back to his horn intermittently in order to put his "chops," as he put it, "in shape." I marvelled at the ridiculous power that this man could muster in a split second in order to rend the room and hallway with an F above high C, followed by the comment, "Here they come, uh huh!"

As many times as I was privileged to see and hear that same sequence of events take place on tour, it never ceased to fill me with awe; the same went for the way he strolled onto the stage with that quick little gait that ended with a miniature hop. All of this was part of the prelude to his taking up any musical challenge by any of his confrères out there. Roy thrived on challenge: it served as a form of adrenaline for him in order to catapult himself into musical top gear. If any soloist that he was to follow burned it up on his solo, I can still see Speedy with his horn tucked under his arm in that familiar stance, nodding his head in understanding and yet readying himself for his rounds.

Roy always had a remarkable sense of pacing. Many times he would simply cruise right into the thick of the tune, and commence "cooking," but if he really wanted to separate himself from the earlier player, he would slide over to me and quietly ask, in his best Lester Young inflection, "Can I get my strollers, please?" By this he meant that he intended to start simply with a mute aided by Ray Brown's huge bass notes in the lower register. He trusted the remaining members of the rhythm section not only to sit out and allow the excitement to build between him and Ray, but, more importantly, to anticipate exactly where to re-enter and move him up a few notches emotionally. I can remember Speedy and Ray swinging so hard on the "strollers" choruses that it became almost a sexual strain to wait out our turn in what was becoming a rhythmic orgy. If all went to his liking he would take his bow with that fantastic grin of his and then dance his way back towards the rhythm section smiling. He would then tilt his head to the time-count and say, once again in his best Lester Young voice, "Would you bitches like to come on the road with my band?"

I have referred to Speedy's mimicking of Lester Young's spoken phrases but Roy was actually a very independent person. He learned to survive by himself mainly from the lonely days that he spent travelling as the only Negro in all-white orchestras. Although at times he could be very removed, if he so chose he was always a caring person. If he loved you, as he did Pres, he remained fiercely loyal to you. I can still recall Roy remaining ever so close to Pres at times when he felt Pres needed this kind of support. He rode next to Pres on the bus, sat backstage with him, took him out to eat (against Lester's will many times), and, above all, played for Pres when he could in order to aid the ailing soloist in his waning years.

Although Roy had come to feel that he wasn't wanted in American music circles, he believed in Norman Granz when he met him in Paris, and Norman was able to persuade him to return to the United States. He was forever grateful, and would later say of Norman, "They should put up a statue to that cat, and there's no one else at the business end of our business I'd say that about." He has always impressed me as being a highly emotional man capable of happy highs and painful lows. That little shimmer or vibrato that we hear on the end of many of his notes, especially on ballads, is merely a small glimpse of the flood of pulsating emotion that he is capable of. I truly miss the excitement of hearing the muted sounds of this all-powerful musical leprechaun, who was always capable of becoming at will an awesome swinging jazz behemoth.

39

HARRY EDISON

Harry Edison's fame in jazz circles seems to rest as much on his caustic tongue and repartee as on his music. This is unfortunate: "Sweets" epitomized the great Swing era, a period many young players seem to have forgotten about, and his reputation as a visiting "sage" should not obscure his central contribution to some of jazz's most influential and significant developments. I am happy that I never musically played Harry Edison cheap, for I consider him a permanent landmark in jazz; and while I have often been the butt of his jokes—for example, "When I first met this big-ass Canadian he wasn't wearing any shoes and didn't have his wig together"—he remains to my mind a major force.

The Swing era permeated everything about Sweets. His attire exemplified the convention of those days—viz. "If you show on the scene, your ass better be clean"—and to say he was a "spiffy" dresser would understate the case. His stride and glib hip-talk were also straight out of the 1930s. Yet underneath all the acrid humour lies a great understanding of what jazz really stands for.

Sweets befriended me on one of his visits to Canada and although he would die before admitting it, I would guess inwardly that part of our friendship was due to the polite respect that I offered him from the moment that we met. This was heartfelt, for in my mind he has always been a giant. He plays the trumpet in a plaintive fashion—not unlike Nat Cole's style on the piano, for he too was an openly expressive player: it is no accident that Nat elected to record with Sweets many years ago, using his broad swinging lines to take the Trio into a deeper groove level after his vocals.

Sweets made a rhythm section walk. Once he was at the mike, if the groove was not entirely to his liking, he quietly made use of various repetitive phrases: while these may have sounded as if he was leaning on the rhythm section, they were in fact a fool-proof device for establishing exactly where he wanted the groove to be (another trick he learned from Nat Cole). His approach to more complex tunes was disarmingly simple. He didn't approach them chord by chord, but assessed the sequence as a whole, picking out only the segments that appealed to him; the remainder were taken care of via a series of slurred notes, pauses, and the odd trill or two. That was in no way an escape on his part, for he knew precisely where he was going at all times. The swinging impetus that he generated with these techniques was prodigious; rhythm sections delighted in responding to the swells and ebbs of his lines, for his kind of pulsation is given to very few players. He also knew how devastating simplicity can be—an awareness that no longer graces all too many "schools" in the jazz world.

Sweets' humour was legendary, and had much in common with Lester Young's idiosyncratic version of the English language. When Ray Brown left the Trio and became very successful in the Hollywood music studios, Sweets remarked, "Ray Brown's so rich now that he's got enough money to air-condition a cotton field." On a gloomier note, he said of a fellow musician who had fallen on bad luck: "Him? Why, he's poorer than a crab on a skeleton." But my own favourite Edisonism was delivered on tour during one of the many crap games held backstage.

Ray decided to have some fun and unbeknownst to anyone introduced a pair of loaded dice into the game as a gag. He casually made about six successful passes of 7 or 11, as these dice were set up to do; all of a sudden, when he raised his hand to throw them again, Sweets reached up, grabbed Ray's hand, and took the dice from him. He gave them very close scrutiny, then walked over to a corner and threw the dice several times: 7 came up each time. Cocking his head to one side, he looked at Ray and, with his customarily nasal delivery, said, "Ray Brown, I ought to give you a Wassermann for this," meaning that he ought to take out his knife and cut him.

Ray looked at Sweets with humorous astonishment and said,

"Sweets, I'm your main man. You wouldn't really cut me, would you?"

Sweets' reply was swift and curt. "Would I cut you?? Shit!! Quicker than a crow can piss, and he flies with his dick out!"

Such humour mirrors exactly the direct no-nonsense approach that Harry Edison brought to his music. His credo was as dynamic as simple: if it's meant to swing, swing!

40

BILL HARRIS

H e looked uncannily like a college math professor: tall and balding with rimless glasses, and apparently as serious as could be imagined. Bill Harris, or "The Sheriff" as I nicknamed him, walked with a loping gait reminiscent of Gary Cooper. But this stern demeanour evaporated when anything amused him: he simply giggled. If you can visualize a six-foot-four ambling scholar with a child-like giggle, you've got Bill Harris.

When I first joined JATP I roomed with Lester Young. He believed in staying high on pot, and this transferred itself in a secondary manner: although I didn't realize it, for quite a while I was walking around with a permanent "buzz" on, which I attributed merely to the excitement of my new life. Ray Brown spoke to Norman about it, and I found myself rooming with the sedate Bill Harris. He was entirely without prejudice of any kind, and a natural freewheeling spirit; but I was initially fooled by his bookish exterior, and it never occurred to me he might be a kidder. Then, after I'd gone for one of his put-ons hook, line, and sinker, he stared in appalled disbelief at my naïveté, and voiced a prolonged "WHAAAT?"

What Bill didn't realize, however, was that his nice new Canadian room-mate had quite a devious put-on mind of his own, and was determined to even the score. At that time I had discovered that my face was not taking kindly to being shaved with any kind of blade. I came across a depilatory powder that, when mixed with water and allowed to dry, would remove any beard without the need for a razor. There was one drawback: this hair-removant left the foulest odour in the room after use, not unlike an over-patronized public toilet.

One evening before a concert I had finished shaving, if you want to call it that, and was sitting on my bed, ostensibly reading a magazine but casting regular furtive glances at Bill as he puttered around on his side of the room. Suddenly it hit him with full force: he stopped dead in his tracks, sniffed a couple of times, and then begged me hoarsely, "Pete, whatever went in there with you died, and whatever it was, get it the fuck out of the room now!" Struggling not to laugh, I asked him what he was talking about. "What do you mean, what's the matter? If you can't smell that shit then you're dead as well, and you can get the fuck out of here too!" By now I could contain myself no longer and burst out laughing, only to notice Bill going to the phone: he said he was going to call Norman to tell him the arrangement wasn't working at all. I at last confessed what I'd done, showed him the powder can, and promised that I'd never use it again while he was in the room. His anger quite over, Bill immediately began to wonder aloud what other uses during the tour this powder could be put to, his giggling getting louder and higher as his notions became more outlandish.

He had a taste for the absurd and the studiedly infantile, which he was able to carry off through meticulous planning and straight-faced solemnity. He would get in the hotel elevator with that collegiate look on his face and a whoopee cushion hidden under his coat. At the most opportune moment he would give it a couple of good squeezes; naturally, everyone would turn round, just in time to see him looking at me in horror and disgust. By the time the elevator reached the main floor, especially after another squeeze or two, I was about as popular as a sissy in the Oakland Raiders' dressing-room.

On one European tour, for reasons no one could fathom, the

rhythm section was not serving Bill very well, especially on the ballad medley. We'd either provide the wrong tempo or the wrong key, or we'd have the intro to the tune wrong. This can happen—but I ought to have realized that Bill was taking it much too easily: he'd just walk off, dragging his horn dejectedly and saying nothing. Anyway, one night in Rome, the Trio seemed to be able to do no wrong and was getting a marvellous reception. At the end the ovation was so tumultuous that Norman excitedly suggested "a switch," i.e. that I should sing. I liked the idea and quickly briefed the Trio: I would be singing *Tenderly*—a tune long associated with us, and which also happened to be one of Bill's favourite themes for his own playing.

What I didn't know was that throughout our set Bill had been backstage collecting every glass, bottle, cup, saucer, and spoon that he could lay his hands on, had carefully piled them up on one of those huge aluminium waiters' trays, and balanced it perfectly on the stagehands' ladder. I crooned my way into *Tenderly*'s opening words: "The evening breeze . . . [muffled "oohs" and "ahs" of surprise from the audience] . . . caress the trees . . . tenderly." CRASSHHH! It sounded as if a dump truck had unloaded the entire Steuben glass collection backstage.* Norman came running from the front of the theatre, by which time a little Italian waiter was standing by the wreckage, a stupefied look on his face and his hand to his mouth. "What happened?" screamed Norman. "What the hell happened back here?" All at once there stood Bill Harris, looking surprised. "Gee, Norm, I can't imagine what happened. I came running out of the john as soon as I heard it." Somehow Norman was prevented from drawing and quartering the hapless waiter and the concert got under way again. Bill Harris had avenged himself.

Musically speaking, Bill Harris had no peers on his instrument. His approach to the trombone was astonishingly innovative, and he remains unique to this day. Even before we played together on JATP

---

*Steuben is a branch of Corning Glass Works (Corning, NY) and makers of fine-blown crystal art pieces and serving pieces.

I was a Harris devotee: his *Bijou* with Woody Herman is a classic I shall never tire of. The word "lyrical" can be over-used and misapplied, but not in Bill's case. He was as delicate and sensitive as could be, fashioning his ballad lines with exquisite continuity; in faster mode, few have ever swung more savagely.

I miss Bill Harris: he brought something special into my life. We would sit after concerts, drink Scotch, and talk—conversations that taught me a great deal. He believed in fairness, was remarkably well-informed, and had a deep unspoken anger about racism. His tastes in music ran to uncomplicated, swinging, and, as he would put it, "happy" lines that chonk along with no apparent effort. I can still see those size 12 shoes infallibly tapping the time for all the marvellous melodic inventions he would supply as our section pulsed behind him. When it all really worked and we gave him a "Yeah, Bill" as he stepped away from the mike, he'd stop dead in his stride, give us that deadpan glare and simply say, "Whaaat?"

41

STUFF SMITH

D jango Reinhardt has been immortalized as the great gypsy jazzman, but I would say that Stuff Smith was in every way his black equivalent. Django lived his life with supreme nonchalance, blithely indifferent to the pitfalls and dangers that worry "normal" human beings, and Stuff was exactly the same. And I'd be the last to say he was wrong: if Stuff believed something should happen somehow, it invariably fell out that way.

Take, for instance, the perennial nightmare of shipping musical equipment as airline baggage. Both Barney Kessel and Herbie Ellis used to go to immense trouble, commissioning specially designed cases with extra cushioning for their amps, and meticulously protecting every last item, only to grow old before their time when confronted with the damage sustained in transit. Even if their amps arrived apparently intact, they would plug them in and find that they no longer would work. This raw treatment at the airlines' hands didn't stop Barney and Herb from giving Stuff lecture after lecture on looking after things properly, especially when they saw him putting his amplifier up on the baggage cart with not so much as a plastic cover over it. "I can see that coming back like 30 pounds of minced meat, Stuff," Barney would intone. "No way, no way, Stuff," Herbie would preach. "Those baggage cats are going to chew that up like it was foie gras." "Oh, yeah?" Stuff would reply, completely unperturbed—as he would be at the other end, picking his amp off the baggage ramp as though he had just bought it at the music store, and ambling along to his waiting transportation. And when they arrived at the hall and plugged in their amps, Barney's would immediately do a "silent night," Herbie's would usually give a feeble cough and roll over for dead—and Stuff would stroll onto the stage (ignoring or affecting not to notice the others' woe-begone faces), plug in his amp, strike a few test chords, look around, and ask, "What are we playing?"

Beneath this casual exterior, Stuff Smith was a musician of great breadth and ferocious rhythmic drive. Deeply rooted in the Swing culture, he managed somehow to make the violin roar in the same manner as Eddie "Lockjaw" Davis' tenor sax. His lines had the strength that simplicity can bring, while his rhythmic approach was both joyous and angry, full of savage sneering power. At times he seemed almost to accompany himself, playing linear lines which he'd then answer with pugnacious octaves, much like Duke's brass section. He was a man that walked in time, for it guided his every move, both human and musical.

42

STAN GETZ AND ZOOT SIMS

P laying for two independently creative and innovative saxophone stylists proved to be a very interesting and revealing
experience. Although many listeners tend to lump these two players
together, merely because they sound similar in some superficial
respects, this is an incorrect assumption, for they are two distinctly
original, creative musical forces who should be discussed separately.

I was a listener to and a collector of Stan's records long before I had
the opportunity of playing for and with him. I admired his fluid and
lyrical ballad lines, and marvelled at the way that he could retain this
particular approach and make it work for him on up tempos. Stan
accomplished this through unusual means. Unlike many players who
would seek to increase the articulative definition within the line, Stan
managed to out-distance all of them by intuitively and intellectually
using the direction of his line coupled to a very deep harmonic
involvement. On up-tempo numbers, in order to highlight the rhythmic
impetus behind him, he would commence his solo on the lower end of
the horn, launching an ascending spiral of linear inventions. This
upward cascade of melody and implied harmony allowed him both to
soar over the rhythm section and to spur it on. When he had created a
plateau of pulsation with which he was content, he would then resort
to a more orthodox, figure-like approach, giving the rhythm section an
opportunity to punctuate his phrasing.

Stan did not always employ this technique; he was essentially a
linear inventor of the highest order and took it for granted that the
rhythm section was going to supply him with his full harmonic needs.
You didn't lead Stan Getz through a solo: he led you, and became
uncomfortable if you stepped on his toes either rhythmically or
harmonically. The same thing applied to his ballad playing. He had an

innate sense of harmonies and often seemed to prefer starting his line on odd starting notes, which he immediately made "right" by his unerring sense of linear invention.

The quickest and best way to apprise oneself of Stan's instinctive harmonic mastery is to listen to his various duets with people like Gerry Mulligan and Bob Brookmeyer. Though he was primarily an up-front performing artist, he had that unusual ability of sublimating his role and taking the second part with such ease and ability that, coupled with his crystalline sound, he often drew the listener's attention to his lines rather than the primary melodic line being taken by the other player. He had a very special haunting sound to his ballad playing: it was almost a cry of anguish. He also had an impeccable sense of melodic delay, which allowed him to draw the listener to him by that delicate, almost (apparently) faltering delivery of the melody.

Zoot Sims differed from Stan Getz in many ways. The first is that he used a much different sound and attack on his instrument. Zoot was a master of time. His metronomic feel was one that few players other than people like Lester Young and Roy Eldridge manage to achieve. There is a grace to this type of playing that lets members of the rhythm section know that they are out of step; just the manner of his lines would tell us whenever we got out of synch. It was not relayed to us as an angry reaction, more a subtle hint that the two metronomic conceptions were minutely at odds. It gave us a very uncomfortable feeling, and would cause us to renegotiate at once and re-think the perceptive value—not of each bar but of each *beat*.

Zoot Sims was one of the most plaintive creators of jazz lines. Unlike Stan Getz, who revelled in harmonic complexities and movement, Zoot found his metier in pursuing the journeyman's uncluttered and plain expression of linear development. This proved totally valid over the years because his playing not only survived, but also comfortably absorbed the various changes in jazz style and fashion. "I don't know that tune, Oscar, that's too hard for me," he would say on various occasions, with the modesty that was always part of his personality. On the other hand, the lyrical simplicity that he brought to the reading of a tune was beyond many other great players, who lacked the depth and sensitivity of his understanding.

Some years ago JATP made a tour of Japan (in 1983) and, as usual, various ballad sets were played and recorded. Zoot's playing of Johnny Mandel's *Emily* was a perfect example of what I have been trying to describe in his playing. Several years later, Norman Granz decided to issue the albums of these concerts and asked me to check over the music which he had forwarded to me on cassettes. When I heard *Emily* I was overwhelmed: I freely admit that I sat in my hotel room and cried profusely as I replayed that rendition over and over. Zoot only played one chorus on it, but that was really all he had to play: there was nothing else left to say.

43

CARMEN MCRAE: THE SPECIAL ONE

"Well! I'm not much to look at." That was the opening lyric that Carmen was singing at the Blue Note in Chicago. I leaned over to Ray Brown who was sitting down front with me and whispered in his ear, "I'll buy that!" Ray collapsed over the table, convulsed at my remark. Actually, I was being really smart-assed because Carmen McRae is one of the prettiest women I've ever known. We had been kibitzing with Carmen from our opening night and I just couldn't resist crunching Ray. That whole engagement had been filled with all kinds of mutual put-ons by Carmen and my group—a humour that underscored and enriched our friendship. For Carmen McRae was always a special person in my life, both musically and personally. I was a devoted fan of her vocal talents, and for years, I carried the proverbial torch for her.

When I first met her, I was struck by her unusual countenance: it is almost Indian-like. She had a powerful effect on me for a long time: I found it difficult not to hit on her outright! I had also heard that she was feared by many accompanists. She was credited with causing panic amongst bass players, but this was understandable to me, for I knew of her addiction to Ray's playing.

Carmen McRae had an extraordinary concept of time. She was one of the few people—people, not just vocalists—who had the ability to float freely within the dimension of time, to go against it, and to know subconsciously where she was at any given moment. Many try it, but few succeed. That's why she insisted on authentic swinging time behind her. She wanted to be able to float in space without the mother ship moving from its orbit (immediate trouble for any rhythm section that isn't pulsing together). She was an accomplished pianist in her own right, and she'd soon make life tough for any keyboard accompanist who "shucked" the harmonies, or indeed anyone unwise enough to goof in her presence, as I found out to my cost.

I was appearing at Ronnie Scott's in London several years ago and suddenly decided to play *Lush Life*. For some unknown reason, I momentarily lost concentration, and if that happens on that tune, you'll find yourself in the outhouse! No passing Go, no collecting $200. Suddenly from out of nowhere, I heard this rich deep female voice from somewhere in the back of the room say, "Uh-uh, OP, close—but not quite close enough." Without even looking I knew it was Carmen and immediately kicked myself mentally for tearing it in front of her, of all people!

I played for her on numerous occasions and found that the best way to handle things was to be harmonically faultless at all times, period. Rhythmically, she had to feel completely at ease in order to compress or expand her phrases within various segments of the tune. Carmen didn't fear harmonic movement so long as it was intelligently and sensitively done. I used to let the rhythm section supply the unerring pulsation that she needed, which then allowed me freedom to move harmonically with or against her as the case demanded. I would make the voicings fairly wide, so that she could employ her full vocal range in her lines. And because her voice had such a special timbre and richness, especially in the middle register, I would usually situate my voicings slightly above her vocal area, so as not to distract from her linear movement.

These are merely a few of the things that I employed playing for this great singer. Carmen was one of the few vocalists I have known who could really play intelligently for themselves. (Jeri Southern is another.) This is not an easy thing to do, and I therefore always felt especially gratified when I played for her and accomplished what she wanted. She was a notably creative person, and a very special lady.

44

THE OTHER LADY DAY: ANITA O'DAY

B illie Holiday inspired emulation in many other female vocalists, be it in their chosen musical style, their phrasing, or their everyday attitudes. This influence was so great that it led in some cases to the termination of their careers—even, on occasion, their lives. Anita O'Day was one such vocalist who had a great *sympatico* for Billie; however, she managed to create a style all her own. Many would argue that her totally ad lib phrasing and husky voice were fundamentally derivative of Lady Day, but I disagree. I hear Anita as more of an outgrowth of Lester Young and Roy Eldridge. Her sense of time is strongly akin to the relaxed, almost lazy lines of Pres, while her punchy, aggressive scat-singing is very reminiscent of Roy's instinctive fierce drive.

I played for Anita on many occasions. She seemed almost always to want to challenge the instrumentalists (she would invariably call for fours, no matter what the tempo) and do battle with them. This could make life difficult, but I admired her tenacity and musical courage. She would take on anyone, any time, and try to lay waste to them. This was her way of seeking growth as a vocalist and a wholly independent style: she wanted the elasticity of operating in a group as if her voice were a horn, a distinctive instrument of equal status to the others.

She could be extraordinarily obstinate. On one occasion, Norman Granz was unable to oversee her record date and asked me to act as A&R man, giving me a list of the tunes they had agreed on. He made it clear that this was precisely the album he wanted from her, and entrusted me with the project's fruition.

At the studio, Anita breezed in and kissed everyone hello in a very happy frame of mind. I greeted her, explained Norman's absence and his instructions, and she gave me a "Solid, OP—let's get to it," taking off her jacket and readying herself at the mike. I called off the list of tunes that I had on my sheet; she nodded faint assent and immediately called for a tune that wasn't anywhere on the list! I objected, reminding her that I had spoken to Norman only the evening before. Ignoring this, she started clicking the time of the tune she intended to do. Finally, in frustration, I gave in to her and we did the tune she had called. She seemed content with the first take on most of the songs, and as I was looking on it as her record date, I did not suggest a retake if she was happy with it.

John Poole (her husband at the time) and Ray Brown suggested she did some slow tunes to balance the up-tempo things we had already done, but she was having no part of this and continued with the "roasters," finally calling for one at a really stratospheric tempo, insisting I play against her in the challenge. By this time I was really angry, knowing how displeased Norman was going to be, and I have to say that I adopted a pianistic approach I would usually eschew. In normal circumstances, when a human voice is pitted against the full resources of the piano, I try to sculpture my lines to support the vocalist's continuity and phrasing. On this occasion, however, I gave no quarter and fashioned my responses as I would when replying to other instrumental virtuosi. Oddly enough, Anita seemed exhilarated by the experience, and left the studio snapping her fingers and re-stating some of the lines that had occurred during that last, comet-like tune.

I learned that day that Anita would never fade away in fear of any musical challenge. Indeed, she thrives on it: whatever its outcome, challenge seems to resuscitate her musically, nourishing further her desire to be something more than just another jazz vocalist.

45

A GLANCE AT MY CONFRÈRES
IN THE PIANO WORLD

There's a consensus amongst the general public that jazz players are all cut from the same swath, that though they may take somewhat different stylistic paths, they all view jazz in basically the same way. This is far from the truth: there are very distinct differences of opinion between jazz players—particularly pianists. Whereas guitarists seem to treat each other with adoration, and bass players are similarly prone to mutual worship, pianists respond to each other in a much more competitive fashion. This seems to be the case whatever the level: it is as intense amongst average local pianists as with the performing giants of whatever era.

I first became aware of this phenomenon when I made my inaugural cross-Canada tour. As soon as I landed in Toronto I was trucked over to hear a pianist by the name of Alan McLeod. Greenhorn as I was (the year was 1943 and I was 18), I fell in with the plan happily enough, having no idea of what was coming. We were ushered into a studio, where I was introduced to a young man with glasses. The others insisted that he play something for me, and he went into *The Man I Love*. It was instantly obvious: straight Tatum. After he had cloned Art's recording of the tune, they asked him to play another selection; he agreed and went straight into *Yesterdays*. Same thing: Tatum once again.

During the performance, I noticed that most of the people present had their attention fixed on me rather than on the pianist, and I suddenly realized that they were expecting me to be intimidated by his playing. I rather resented this, and eventually asked the young man if he would play something of my choice. Nervously pushing his glasses back onto the bridge of his nose (his constant habit), he replied, "If I know, if I know it." "Oh, I'm sure you do," I said, and asked him to play *I Got Rhythm*, knowing full well that Tatum had at that time not recorded that song. He proceeded to play it, but clearly struggled: in effect, he was telling me that he could not make a musical statement on that tune until he'd heard what his idol had to say first.

I felt sorry for him: the harsh truth was that his unbridled admiration for Art Tatum was turning him into a puppet rather than a creative pianist. Although we remained friends for quite some time, he eventually faded from the music scene altogether. I often cite his case to some of my students who I feel are in danger of becoming far too influenced by me, or by any other pianist whom they idolize.

The next time this kind of thing occurred was in Winnipeg, Manitoba, on the western leg of a tour I was doing about a year later. Once I'd arrived I was asked by various people if I had heard a young pianist called Chris Gage. I hadn't, but the next evening some acquaintance from the concert bureau took me to a dance pavilion, and the house band's pianist turned out to be one Chris Gage. I was impressed but not intimidated: his ideas were fresh and intuitive, his technique was admirable, and his delivery sparklingly articulate. He was still very young, so had not fully developed his style; nevertheless, I made a mental note that he was very likely to be someone to reckon with in my attempts to establish myself on the Canadian music scene. This was sadly not to be: a few years later I was told of his passing away, but I shall always remember Chris Gage as one of the bright lights that never made it to the front end of Canada's jazz marquee.

Those two incidents were polite, manageable, low-key encounters with "the competition." As my US career progressed, such meetings became much more vehement, even violent on occasion. The first instance occurred in 1950 after my "launch" with Jazz At The Philharmonic at Carnegie Hall, when I went over to hear Bud Powell at Birdland. By then Bud was in the grip of narcotic addiction, and when introduced to me he curled his lips and through gritted teeth, spat out, "Yeah! Yeah! You're down here to try and squeeze me out!" And he took a half-swing at me. Not surprisingly, we never became friends, mainly because he continued to see me as some sort of direct threat to his musical existence. I never hated him: I pitied him for the way he was caught up in the doomed world of drugs and the predatory leeches that constantly surrounded him.

Moreover, I never thought him a pianistic threat. Granted, he could swing; but I never regarded him as a member of the central dynasty of piano defined by such great players as Tatum, Wilson, and Hank Jones. Bud was a linear group player, who could comp like mad for bebop horns and could certainly produce cooking lines that had tremendous articulation, but for my taste there was too much that he *didn't* do with the instrument. He lacked Hank's broad, spacious touch on ballads, and he failed to finish his ideas too often for comfort and satisfaction. Despite his strength of linear invention, in fact, he had a technique problem: although other musicians and I could intuit where those unfinished lines were going, an unschooled audience was left to play a guessing game, having to make do with grunts of tension in place of delivered ideas. Unfortunately, the Powell school spawned many young followers who thought it hip to adopt this uneven and unfinished approach. It took a long time for players like Hank Jones, Bill Evans,

Herbie Hancock, and me to get pupils to realize that the linear approach is not enough on its own. Bud may have symbolized an era, but not true piano mastery.

The city that made me most aware of "piano duelling" was Chicago. The Trio would arrive for what had become our regular stint at the London House, and opening night was invariably "pianists' night." The pianist who normally shared the bill with us was Eddie Higgins—a tall, slim, good-looking young man whose playing I quite enjoyed. He had his own viewpoint about tunes, and his treatment of certain standards was unusual and intriguing. He was also a great fan of the Trio, and made no bones about it; very early in our London House career, he sounded a warning about my being under surveillance: "You've got 'em all out in force," he said once, pointing out the local pianists to me one by one.

These were the days before Ramsey Lewis had his first hit, and he was a regular visitor. I recall being almost taken aback by his boyish charm and charismatic nature; he came at you with a very open, happy manner that I found refreshing. "How come you get to be able to play that much piano?" he asked, feigning irritation. With similarly bogus anger, I borrowed one of Charlie Shavers' famous bus lines to answer, "'Cause I'm evil!" Then Ramsey suddenly became almost sombre. "Seriously, OP, I have to get with you one of these days and find out how you control your group the way you do. Sometimes my group seems to run over me, and that's a drag—especially if that isn't what you want to have happening!" I sensed he was voicing a real concern; we spent most of that intermission talking about it, and agreed to meet in the afternoon to work on it. Ramsey and I remain friends to this day, and I still feel the same way about him as I did then.

From my very first Chicago stint I kept hearing a name bandied about again and again. It wasn't just the frequency that intrigued me, but the *way* the name would come up. It tended to arise after we'd completed a particularly steaming set, one where I'd had the chance to really stretch out pianistically. I would be resting in one of the booths when a local player would come by, congratulate me on my performance, and then casually ask, "Has Larry Novak been by?" Or "By the way, OP, have you had the chance to catch Larry Novak yet?" I was forced into the conclusion that this Larry Novak was a real bad dude whom I'd have to check out; I even asked one of my friends who lived in Chicago, and got a very positive answer about Larry's piano talents. However, it has never been my nature to panic prematurely, due to my Dad's influence. I had learned to try and take things in my stride; in addition, I had learned very early to avoid taking sides when it came to competition between locals, and to remain friends with them if I possibly could. So I temporarily dismissed the Novak mystery as something I would deal with whenever it became necessary to do so.

This came to a head much sooner than I anticipated. Eddie Higgins came up to me one night and said, "You'd better turn it on for real tonight, 'cause the boy genius is sitting right down front." Knowing instinctively that he was referring to Larry, I also sensed that there was a rivalry between Eddie and him; I decided to let things take their natural course. Larry sat through our performance, along with a lady whom I later learned was his wife, Carol, a jazz pianist in her own right. After the set was over, Larry introduced himself and Carol to me. "Phew! You were into it up there, OP," he said with a naturalness I liked. "You guys are something else!" I thanked him and we all started chatting. Then Carol leaned over, took my arm, and with her huge, doleful eyes fixed on me said, "Oscar, Larry is really excited about what you did up there. I've seldom seen him this revved up about someone's playing." I sensed inevitable wifely concern and love when she went on, "You must hear Larry play sometime, Oscar. He really is a great player." My curiosity was now really tweaked, and I decided I must get to hear him.

I got my chance the next week, for Larry's group played opposite us, as Eddie was off on a family visit somewhere. As soon as he started playing I recognized with pleasure a man who radiated a knowledge and respect for the piano. His lines were crisp and inventive, his sense of harmonic movement inventive and he didn't seem timid about tempos, projecting an aura of total confidence and command. I was sufficiently impressed, in fact, to begin plotting how to cope musically with his talent and, indeed, overcome it—a competitive response that I believe *any* creative artist experiences at some time or another. There is nothing vicious about such trains of thought: on the contrary, it is a tribute to the rival's talents and a heightening incentive for the plotter. At the end of his set Larry came over to me at the back of the room, and I sincerely congratulated him, praising his talent on the instrument. When he attempted to shrug off my remarks (perhaps out of embarrassment), I told him that when it came to music I never idly threw compliments around, for music is the one thing I refused to compromise about.

Our musical rivalry continued during the Trio's London House engagements over the next few years. The culmination occurred one night when Larry chose to play four tunes we considered "ours," tunes closely associated with us. I am sure it was done with no malice, but even so I decided to throw the piano battle into full gear, additionally spurred by the fact that some mutual friends had a ringside table to which Larry had been invited. I launched the Trio into a set that exactly paralleled Larry's, tune for tune. The London House had always had a reputation for being a noisy room, but as I increased pressure and output it grew quieter and quieter. As our "burn-time" grew fiercer, I went for broke, and at the end, as we took our bows, Larry looked up at me, shook his head, and laughingly said, "Okay, OP, I get the message."

If all that sounds merely like an ego trip for the musicians concerned, I cannot possibly agree: audiences invariably benefit from this kind of one-on-one competition. Maybe not all such encounters are particularly friendly, but the results always favour the listener, simply because the players are striving their utmost. And in the case of Larry Novak, he was and remains a dear friend—an abundantly gifted pianist whose decision to stay put in Chicago was that city's gain and the jazz world's loss.

I shall always hold a treasured place in my heart for another dear friend—Erroll Garner, or, as I called him, "Oooh-chi-cooo!" He initiated this nickname himself, in fact, during his unobtrusive, almost clandestine visits to hear the Trio in various clubs. Once, playing the

London House (a room that he also worked many times), I elected to play his now-historic *Misty*, unaware that Erroll was at the bar having a bite to eat. I'd been stretching out on ballads during that set, and when I came to *Misty* I lavished special care on my improvisation in honour of a doctor friend who'd asked me to do my "long version" of it. As I came down into the quiet ending, letting some rich harmonic clusters hang out, from out of nowhere came this appreciative exclamation, "Oooh-chi-cooo-chi-cooo!" The audience cracked up, and I knew immediately that my man was somewhere in the house.

I always enjoyed Erroll both as a person and as a player. He is one of the true stylists; a pianist who added something unique to the jazz spectrum. Moreover, his immense popularity was itself a very important contribution: he attracted many new young listeners to jazz, and his sell-out concerts in colleges and halls, not to mention his huge record sales and the colossal success of *Misty*, helped revive interest in jazz piano as a whole. His congenial, happy-go-lucky manner bolstered the public's love of the man, for his happy disposition shone through everything that he did.

As a pianist, Erroll was a one-off. So many pianists tried to copy him, but hardly any succeeded.* His gift was God-given, wholly individual; without becoming too analytical, I would say that the key to his genius was his sense of timing, which was above that of virtually any musician, regardless of instrument. In addition, his technical command of octaves and octave clusters was matched by only a few classical players. He could run off some frighteningly intense figures using that harmonic configuration, cooking like mad while still maintaining the left-hand harmonic drone, as I termed it. It was this drone that was the downfall of those many would-be Garner clones. In their rush to emulate his style, they failed to realize that his left hand was the time-controller, which seldom varied its rhythmic impetus, thus allowing his right hand enormous freedom to play "against" the

---

*An exception was Collie Ramsey. See Chapter 9.

bass and create exhilaratingly retarded lines and a host of cross-rhythmic effects. His lush approach to ballad playing was similarly inimitable, another reason for his huge success.

Erroll Garner was a very special player and also a very special friend.

46

WYNTON KELLY: BRIMSHA MAN

"Mrs Peterson's boy-child! You too boomba-rass, man!" meant that I was being greeted by one of my favourite piano people: Wynton Kelly. Wynton and I made several tours together when Miles Davis' group worked on JATP,* and that was roughly the way that we would greet each other every morning upon boarding the bus, prompting a warning from Lady Fitz, who wasn't sure she could stand the laughter she knew our "act" would inspire. She was our best audience, due in part to her own West Indian heritage, and was often reduced to near-hysterics as our "back home" dialogue progressed.

We became adept at timing our spot amidst the ongoing bus chatter. Wynton, strategically seated halfway back, would shout out to me as I sat up front, "Boy, where your fatha from?" (Ella's face would immediately become buried in her hands.)

"St Lucia!" I would shout back. "Dung de way by Sandy Point where de big Man o' War used to hol' up." (Ella's head is now bobbing back and forth, her face bathed in tears as her road assistant Georgie digs into her pocket book for more Kleenex.)

---

*Wynton Kelly was trumpeter Miles Davis' pianist from 1959 to 1963.

"You too loi [lie]!" retorts Wynton, with true West Indian vengeance. (Ella now starts to heave backwards and forward in her seat, as Norman makes his way forward to shut us up and save her from seizure.) "I goin' dance on yo' face with dese size elevens!" shouts Wynton; then Norman calls time, cautioning us about making Lady Fitz sick. We give up the dialogue and gradually normalcy returns.

That is the Wynton Kelly whom I grew to love personally. Musically, I feel he had no peers as a comping pianist. As a soloist, Wynton had a fluidity of invention beyond that of most of his fellows. His linear ideas had an unusual lope that gave his phrasing an individual and unusual shape; not so much broken as redirected from time to time, as the inspiration took him—his inventions were unique. Many of his compositions (another area in which he excelled) reflect this original pianism. I still miss Wynton Kelly, the Brimsha Man.

47

IN THE STUDIO: THE PROVING GROUND

No account of my life in jazz would be complete without some further reference to the profusion of studio dates I was fortunate to be part of, even if I cannot now recall every single one. The parade of artists reads like a *Who's Who* of the jazz world: Louis Armstrong, Fred Astaire, Bill Basie, Benny Carter, Roy Eldridge, Ella Fitzgerald, Stan Getz, Dizzy Gillespie, Toni Harper, Coleman Hawkins, Johnny Hodges, Billie Holiday, Freddie Hubbard, Anita O'Day, Charlie Parker, Stuff Smith, Sonny Stitt, Sarah Vaughan, T-Bone Walker, Ben Webster—and on and on. What an education it was for me to accompany these great stars, for they each brought their own brand of musical expertise and wisdom into my life, allowing me to nurture myself on their individual gifts and grow artistically as a result. And almost without exception they were a gas to play with.

T-Bone Walker was a man who simply could not envision any musical obstacles—"Let's go on and do it." He had no need to talk over musical approaches or harmonic directions, unshakably confident that it would all sort itself out in the playing.

Johnny Hodges had a similar laconic confidence. He'd stand around nonchalantly as we tried to settle on routines, keys, order of solos, and so on, blithely determined to perform exactly as he had already decided. If he and the rhythm section should part harmonic company for a moment or two, this was no big deal, for during the playback he'd just laugh, commenting, "Sounded a little modern there to me." Even though we others might be bothered by such varied direction, he'd quietly insist, "I like that, I like that," thus ending all further discussion.

Billie Holiday was totally in charge of her record dates from the word go. She'd enter the studio, have a sip of whatever, joke with the members of the group that she knew well, and go straight into the first tune. On our first session, I must admit to being full of trepidation: I'd heard she could be a hellion to work with. To my surprised delight, however, she turned out to be the complete opposite. She was full of praise for my playing even before we began, and indeed seemed almost in awe of me; nevertheless, she knew precisely what backgrounds she wanted, even trotting out some suggested riffs on her own, scatted in her uniquely succinct way. She had Herbie on tenterhooks for awhile: he too had heard how tough she could be, especially on guitarists! But she was more than affable to him, complimenting him on his quick perception and the quality of his solos. Brown was cool from the start: he gave her one of his "Ice-Cream Charlie" grins, got a "Ray Brown, you sure are pretty" in return, and from then on everything was serene between them. The date was a great, high-humoured success; Norman was so pleased with it that he took everyone out to dinner that night.

The session with Dorothy Dandridge was, to put it mildly, rather less successful. At the time she was enjoying considerable movie-stardom, but she seemed extremely uneasy in the recording studio, and after a short while the reason became all too clear. She had no feeling for jazz, no awareness of its phrasing or idiom, and, in short, seemed something of an anachronism to us, used as we were to such jazz naturals as Billie and Ella. Perhaps it was we who failed her; certainly, we found it very hard to adjust to her approach. And our increasingly strenuous efforts were not aided by her artless exuberance. At one point she squeaked admiringly, "Oh, Oscar, I absolutely love your playing: it's so Icky-Picky-Poo," a remark that immediately demolished Brown, rendering him a useless giggling hulk. I sensed somehow that the session wasn't going to progress much further after that; luckily, Norman took the same view and diplomatically brought it to a close.

Recording with Ella was very special, not least because she was totally different from how one might expect a great vocalist to behave. Fitz usually entered the studio with uncertainty, even apprehension, looking to her accompanists for support and reassurance. Her vocal stylings were invariably flawless, yet she would often question whether she got this right harmonically or that right lyrically; such modesty was charming but strange, given her absolute musical authority. Indeed, she conducted each date with her voice.

An attribute of Fitz's that I came particularly to admire was a ploy she used on "challenges" with instrumentalists. For a while she'd respond to the eight-bar exchanges with phrases of her own; then, suddenly, she'd repeat a phrase just played by the other soloist, which almost always threw him for a moment. And next time she'd repeat the treatment in a host of tonal ranges. Few linear players could cope with this, and if sensible they would bow out of the challenge. As Pres once observed, trying to cut Ella when she was "kicking ass" was a fool's game.

Ella was a jazz musician first and a vocalist second. She had natural musical savvy, and could use her voice in an almost endless variety of ways, from lyric purity to horn-like abandon. We shall never see her like again.

Amongst my sharpest and most enduring memories of studio work is the recording of *The Astaire Story*. It started with a call from Norman: "I've had an idea"—a pet phrase that predicated virtually limitless possibilities, from where to have lunch that day to moving the Golden Gate Bridge, girder by girder, from San Francisco to Sebastopol. On this occasion he wanted to commemorate Fred Astaire's matchless contribution to American popular song.

"Not too many people realize how many of our great standards were either introduced by Fred or centrally featured in his movies," Norman said, "and it would certainly be interesting to hear him recreate them in a jazz setting."

I agreed it would certainly be different, even inspired, and Norman asked me to come to LA to meet Fred and talk a few things through before the full group assembled.

As soon as I arrived I was struck by the meticulous preparation and research Norman had done. He'd chosen the musicians for versatility, studio know-how, and breadth of idiomatic grasp. Thus Alvin Stoller, a widely experienced studio drummer and a fine jazzman, joined Ray, Barney Kessel, and me in the rhythm section, while the horns were Flip Phillips and Charlie Shavers—both essentially Swing players who had fully absorbed the innovations of bop and who could adapt their sound to a wide variety of contexts. Norman had also studied carefully all the songs likely to be used—including obscure or forgotten verses—and had canvassed Fred's opinion of them in considerable detail. The groundwork had been well and truly laid, and as I waited for Fred I started toying with a few phrases I thought unusual or difficult (*Top Hat*, for example) to quieten my own unease.

As I sat there engrossed, I became aware of a presence nearby, and looked up into the smiling face of Astaire himself. He wore a tweed sports jacket, a soft pair of brown slacks engagingly held up by a man's tie, and a hat set at an almost rakish angle. He was at once immensely likeable and awe-inspiring: sensing my diffidence, he said kindly, "Sounds awfully good to me, Oscar." Norman broke the ice further by kidding, "Fred was saying he wants to spell you by playing on some of the tunes, OP," at which Fred roared with laughter:

"I'll have my hands full getting through all these songs singing, let alone trying to play along with Oscar!"

This initial rehearsal and talk-through went very well. Although Fred voiced some doubts about his competence as a vocalist, he was very clear on the feel and treatment he wanted on most of the songs; on others he was less sure and would wonder aloud, "I've never understood why he wrote that kind of lyric for this particular tune" or "I've never felt comfortable with this passage," telling you precisely why. Norman was invaluable in these latter instances: he'd outline the kind of background Fred would receive while offering productive suggestions as to how he might best treat the lyric with the overall group-meld in mind. Above all, Norman was sensitive to the fact that Fred was out of his true element: here was arguably one of the greatest dancers of the century, faced with an ambitious and sophisticated project in which his greatest talent could not be used. Both Norman and I were determined to help him in every way possible and make the date a notable success.

It would be idle to pretend that the sessions passed without a hitch. For all his rhythmic feel, Fred was not naturally attuned to jazz phrasing, and it was at times perilously easy to throw him via the wrong intro or a misplaced fill. We learned to gauge our ad lib lines around and behind him very carefully, giving him enough time to hear his place of re-entry coming up; we also stuck firmly to the normal harmonic clusters, as any kind of "modern" dissonance could phase him or make him worried about his own intonation.

I found it fascinating to discover how different were Fred's senses of time as vocalist and as dancer. Dancing, his time was so strict that he could make an accompaniment sound early or late; his vocal time, however, was very loose, uninhibited, and unmeasured. I found the best way to accompany him was to give him a long harmonic chord-cushion and let him take his natural liberties with metronomic time. It was also riveting to watch him on some of the slow ballads. His normal posture was to hold one hand cupped over his ear as he sang, but on some tunes he would lower the hand and instinctively fall into a semi-swirl, so familiar from his gliding ballroom performances. And we were all touched by his nervous, boyish anxiety: he'd rush to the piano after almost every take, asking "How was that?" or "Did I stay in tune?" He invariably left the final judgement to Norman, and he was equally humble in asking for practice or allowing us to rewrite the arrangements.

One or two surprises remained. We found out that he loved playing drums (Norman later told us that Fred had a full drum set in his living-room) and we cajoled him into sitting in during a rehearsal. It was a riot! To hear his time in conjunction with Ray's vast sound was quite an event, and the look of rapt intent on his face was a joy to behold. And then Norman had another "idea": to include some dance sequences on the album. This was easier said than done. Think of Astaire and you at once visualize long flowing leaps, wonderfully inventive gliding sequences, and an almost unreal rapport with the leading lady; then you remember that doing all that he spent a good proportion of the time in the air—and air doesn't record too easily! But Fred also had tremendous facility as a tap dancer, and although these tracks were not easy to do (not least because nobody had tried such a thing before) they eventually came off, and I treasure them as genuine musical moments rather than any kind of intriguing oddity.

At the end of the final session, Fred presented each member of the group with a beautiful gold identification bracelet which he'd autographed. I have worn mine ever since; years later, when I met Fred at a party Frank Sinatra was giving for me, he told me he'd seen me on television a few nights before and had been thrilled to see I was wearing his bracelet. He was an honour to know and a joy to work with, and every time I turn my wrist and see the words "With thanks; Fred A" I always feel it is I who should be the one saying thank you.

THE VERVE CHARLIE PARKER JAM SESSION

N orman Granz always enjoyed pitting musicians of different styles and traditions against each other, confident that the musical outcome would invariably be as successful as illuminating. That was personified by all his JATP line-ups, and his insatiable hunger for sparking off musical challenges extended to many studio sessions as well. Some people have seen this as mechanical, or even an affection, but I know that he was motivated solely by the desire to bring about an improvisational musical summit. That certainly applied when he chose five saxophonists for what has become known as the Charlie Parker Jam Session.

At the time (1952) Charlie "Bird" Parker was riding high, enjoying a jazz fame second to none; Norman partnered him with Benny Carter, Ben Webster, Johnny Hodges, and Flip Phillips, and added trumpeter Charlie Shavers for good measure. Benny was seen as the epitome of musicality. His wonderful alto sound and virtuosity were now legendary, as were his gifts as a composer and arranger. Ben Webster had become the definitive breathy, big-sounding tenor saxophonist, having made his name with Ellington's peerless early-1940s orchestra. Alto saxophonist Johnny Hodges was revered for his incomparably smooth tone and unique legato delivery; he was also distinguished by his cool, unperturbed attitude to the world. Flip Phillips, having established his reputation with Woody Herman's First Herd, was at this time chiefly renowned for his JATP recording of Juan Tizol's *Perdido*. And Charlie Shavers was even more happy-go-lucky than usual—happy to be the trumpet player on the date, and lucky that he did not have to tangle with any of the saxophonists! The rhythm section comprised Ray Brown, Barney Kessel, drummer J.C. Heard, and me.

Norman and the horns quickly settled which tunes were to be used and the date proceeded smoothly enough, but I became increasingly aware that a couple of the soloists were reluctant to follow Bird after his solo. This reticence was not shared by Carter and Hodges; indeed, Johnny volunteered to follow Bird at any time and on any tune. That was his nature. He knew no fear, and for all his respect for Charlie, he also knew that he would lose nothing in the comparison. Interestingly, I also believe that Charlie himself was oblivious to the others' reticence. He just seemed to be having a ball, listening intently to each of his fellow saxophonists, his head tilted to one side with a look of appreciation on his face. The rhythm section likewise enjoyed things to the full; it was a challenge to tailor our playing for each man, and it was fascinating to be able to evaluate each soloist's endeavours as they played.

When the recording was finished, everyone seemed elated at the outcome. I don't think anyone got musically bruised, for each soloist spoke in his voice and set out his all to maximum effect.

49

THE ROLE OF THE ACCOMPANIST

W hen I originally joined JATP I was featured as one of the soloists in the concerts. I would come out and do a set with Ray Brown. The gig of playing for the horns was originally handled by a favourite of mine in the piano field, Hank Jones. I happily recall standing in the wings many nights, listening to the way that Hank handled the piano in a supportive capacity. His primary calling was as Ella's accompanist; however, he happily supplied the horns on the first part of the show with some of the most intelligent and sensitive backing that I have ever heard—his solos were also a complete joy to listen to. He had such sensitivity and crystalline touch in everything he did, and his lines were exquisite. I learned a hell of a lot from Hank, not least because those sessions began my insight into some of jazz's greatest soloists from a very unusual angle—the inside. Playing for JATP from year to year allowed me to develop an ability to switch backgrounds, instantaneously if need be, from player to player—an essential facility in view of the tour's constantly changing parade of soloists and their varying styles.

Lester Young was perhaps the most relaxed type of player aboard, yet he wanted to lead the rhythm section through the changes as he perceived them. He would stand there and repeat a phrase until he got the sequence of harmonic changes that he wanted from the rhythm section. He also seemed to love sitting on top of the section, much like a kid poaching a ride on the back of a truck with his bike. As the rhythm section pulsed, he would run his lines across it in that relaxed, almost nonchalant style of his. Pres also had a particular idiosyncrasy: he would saunter over to his spot in front of us and then he would half-turn and listen to us for almost eight bars at times, often even passing a comment such as, "Ugh! You bitches sure are skating tonight!" Ray would usually throw a taunt back at him, such as "And what are you going to do about it, Pres?" He usually answered by smoking his way through four or five choruses. In his prime days on the tours he seldom played more than that amount. It wasn't until his waning years that he started playing much longer, as if to reassure himself that he was still capable. Many players seemed to go that way.

Coleman Hawkins on the other hand would step up and challenge the section head on. He would go immediately to the mike and launch into his solo almost oblivious of our presence. We would sometimes throw some different harmonic cadences at him just to hear his reaction. And we would too! He would usually roar through them as if he had written them himself. Occasionally, as is only natural, we would hang him, and he would grunt between lines. However, at the end of his solo, he would start laughing, and come past the piano. "Say, Oscar," he would say in that booming tone of his, seemingly completely unaware that one of his front-line buddies was now at the mike doing his solo thing. "What in the hell were those changes that you people laid on me?" More laughter. Finally, I would say, "I'll run them down for you after the set, Hawk." He would chuckle some more and finally return to his place in the front line.

Another thing that one had to be ready for at all times with Hawk was that he had a way of suddenly changing his ballads into different keys from the ones usually used for those tunes. After having played *September Song* in the key of C for two weeks, he would breeze by me on his way to the microphone and say as he kept walking, "Put *September Song* in F sharp for me," as if it meant absolutely nothing. Those of you that play know that playing anything in the key of F sharp is not exactly easy, and will get your attention. Coleman loved to do this, and revelled inwardly if he sensed any strife at all. Needless to say, we attempted at all times to negate his chances of giggling at any discomfort on our part. His little joke served to make us all better equipped players.

Some players demanded total autonomy over the section virtually always, wanting this chord here and this kind of time here, along with a change of key right at this particular juncture. We catered to this as any good rhythm section should, and sublimated our own feelings in order to satisfy the player. This did not mean that we couldn't or didn't make suggestions to the players in an attempt to improve their performances. I must say that in practically all cases, the players were receptive to the majority of our suggestions.

Any top-calibre accompanist must be able to spot discomfort at once and correct the deficiency, and this is especially true when backing such an extra-sensitive musician as Benny Carter. Being a great arranger and composer in his own right, with an innate feel for correct and apposite harmony, Benny can pose a problem to any renegade rhythm section. You don't scoot around tunes with Benny up front. He knows not only the proper harmonic content but also something that escapes many players: the correct and original melodic line. Should you by chance err in any of these aspects while playing for King, you will immediately receive a quiet "Would you be so kind to run that tune down with me again, please?" from him. When you arrive at the portion of the tune that you shucked your way through melodically or harmonically, you will then get a polite "Oh, is that the way you're going to play that there?"

This courteous act of putting himself in the wrong forces you into the role of teacher—which is almost certainly the last thing you want at such a moment! Your only recourse is to ask him immediately what the correct line or sequence is, which invariably evokes the response "Oh, I've always known it to go this way." If you have your full senses about you, along with the proper respect for Benny's bottomless musical knowledge, you will accept this proffered information and enter it in your library of musical things learned on tour. It is best advisable to leave it at that. I have played with Benny Carter over many years on different occasions, and have no recourse but to say that he is living proof that you not only mature but also improve and grow as you add years to your life. In 1985 I was fortunate enough to have Benny join me during a concert in Italy. I still don't believe what I heard. I left that venue raving about Benny Carter's playing that night, and still have it vividly etched in my memory.

Charlie Parker was capable of playing with any kind of rhythm section, good or bad, though obviously he preferred the better ones. Bird's playing was such that no matter what you played for him, he would inevitably take your musical building blocks and nonchalantly build his house on them. You couldn't faze him harmonically by throwing things like augmented 11th chords at him, because he would immediately take hold of them and lead you somewhere else with the phrases that he used to make his own very special musical shapes. Bird didn't swing on a section in the same way that I think of Lester Young or Eddie Lockjaw Davis doing. Bird's phrases swung *within themselves*; this meant that should you stumble in supplying him the time, you'd be the one in trouble and he would sound better than anyone else could in comparable circumstances.

Even Bird was human, however, and could be stymied at times. I recall one night when Ray Brown and I went uptown to hear some other players, one of whom happened to be a tenor man by the name of "Big Nick" Nicholson, who might be termed a musical instigator. You had to be very careful messing with such men, because they would often choose tunes that were difficult or unusual. That night Bird walked in a few moments after we did, and Big Nick immediately called all three of us up to the stand. Bird happened to have his horn with him, which he uncased while walking up and saying good evening to everybody.

Big Nick called *The Song Is You* and I launched the group into it at breakneck speed. My mind at once scanned past the first part of the tune, looking for whatever it was that Nick intended to hang us all up on, and it didn't take long to surface. He had called it in the key of C major, which puts the long, tedious bridge into E major, a difficult key anyway and especially so for certain instruments.

Nick played the first chorus, which flew by like a freight train passing a hobo, and then handed it over to a bewildered Charlie Parker. He was not alone in his disquiet: there was enough of a scuffle going on in the rhythm section as we tried to straighten out the changes. We managed to do this, but Bird was left out there naked, stumbling his way through the bridge as Nick eyed him with a sly look of feigned astonishment on his face. Bird briefly excused himself and walked away from the mike towards a corner of the room as the group continued playing. We could faintly hear him as he put the bell of his horn into the corner, and in a very determined way played through the song, stating phrases very close to the tune's true melodic line.

Then he returned to the mike—and to describe what he did musically is near to impossible. It was as if someone had pulled the plug underneath a 2000-gallon tank of music. The phrases and reiteration of phrases streamed from Bird's horn with unerring accuracy and determination, and after playing about five memorable choruses, he pointed to Nick and said through the applause, "Go ahead, Nick," and walked to the bar. Bird had left only one thing to play, which Nick wisely did. One chorus of melody and a bow. He—and everyone else in the room—knew beyond doubt that Charlie Parker had solved one of the hardest puzzles in Big Nick's library, and done so with utter mastery.

Playing for Dizzy Gillespie was always a challenge because he was not only a composer but also dabbled (he'd have loved me for that one!) with the piano; consequently, he was very aware of voicings and harmonic clusters. His harmonic perception was unique because he did not hear the final point of resolution in a sequence at the same place that other composers do. He tended to stretch the harmonic tension that he'd created with unusual voicings, and then wait until practically the last moment to resolve it. Furthermore, the resolution itself often did not end where you would expect it to, but landed on a different key centre. Dizzy loved brute force behind him when he was ready for it; however, he did not like to be forced down into it, preferring instead to have a few choruses of lighter rhythmic involvement, which allowed him to create his flights of linear fancy (many times with a mute) and then open up the floodgates of rhythmic impetus on the listener. For anyone watching him during these creative flights, the most visible giveaway of the point at which he was going for it was when he rocked back on his right foot.

Roy Eldridge, on the other hand, took a little more time to warm up into the musical fury that he could create. He loved starting with what he called strollers (just him and the bass player), and then enjoyed having the rest of the rhythm section added one instrument at a time. As the rhythm section thickened up with the addition of each instrument, his playing became ever more incisive, cutting through the pulsation with that rapier quality that he alone possessed. Roy looked primarily for straight-up four–four time, and it had better *be* four–four and not three and seven-eighths or four and one-sixteenth. He wants it dead on!

Sonny Stitt was always a player that you had to be very careful with because he was so prolific in his linear invention that you tended to get caught up in what he was doing and become one of the listeners, instead of one of the participants. I remember one night in England when Sonny's creativity on his horn reached such astonishing heights that when he finally boarded the bus, and he was usually one of the last members to do so, to a person every member of JATP rose and gave him a standing ovation. I can't think of anyone that ever deserved it more than Sonny did that night.

Buddy DeFranco was another member of JATP who thrived on the steam treatment. The more you singed him with tight cutting time, the more he seemed to enjoy it, and the more he would get down into the solo end of his playing. The clarinet is a very difficult instrument on which to achieve that kind of excitement; it is more easily generated on a trumpet, for instance. Playing for Buddy I found that punctuating his phrases with sharp rhythmic figures directly within his range of playing tended to add to the excitement and movement, and aided him in his competition with the other soloists.

To play for Ben Webster was a unique and joyful experience. Belonging to that school of the big tenor sound, he would walk to the mike and, if we were playing a ballad at the time, his sound was so huge that it really necessitated a very sparse harmonic approach behind him. On the other hand, when he played on the up tempos, I once again would resort to the sharp staccato-like fills at various times so that the piano would not mush into his mellow tenor sound, remaining a distinct voice in the background. Ben Webster was also quite a pianist and would forever be challenging the various horn players about playing in some of the very rough keys. He seemed to get a kick out of this, although occasionally he'd call for a tune in one of these rough keys and get himself smothered with its difficulty in turn! He was a very fine stride piano player, and I can still see that huge frame swinging from left to right as he fairgrounded and exaggerated the difficulty of the stride he was playing.

J.J. Johnson and Bill Harris both seemed to have the same needs from a rhythm section. Bill wanted simplicity behind him and an uncluttered rhythmic concept in order to allow him to do his graceful slides and delays. He hated any kind of a rhythm section prone to speeding, for this impeded his line of thought whenever he wanted to effect these musical nuances and tricks unique to him. J.J. Johnson was a very direct and almost staccato player, whose notes—in contrast to Bill Harris'—were played dead on the head, leaving no room for any kind of glissing. He wanted his time the same way. Dead on. At no time would he tolerate any kind of vacillation rhythmically speaking from the section, and should he have detected any deviation, even while someone else was playing, the head came around and the right hand started popping in an effort to redirect the time to where he thought it should be.

I found playing for Johnny Hodges a unique experience, because his mastery was so deceptive. Sitting listening to Johnny deludes you into thinking that he is lying back on the time, playing behind the beat; as soon as you play with him that musical mirage evaporates. For although he employs highly elongated slides from note to note, his time is both undeniably direct and impeccable, strict to the exact sense of the meter. On the cooking things there is no question about where one is; he takes you there, and deposits you with a firm, unquestionably direct delivery of his solo lines. His sound is so big that as an accompanist you dare not tamper with it by using too much pedal or sustained harmonies behind him, unless the melodic line warrants it. His attitude while at the mike from a close-up position was one of almost distraction and boredom, but underneath, Johnny's playing was always emotionally intense and melodically moving, as all careful listeners will testify.

To have played for these and other behemoths of the music world certainly served to educate me in areas in which that type of education simply just isn't available. More importantly, the repetitious schedule of nightly involvement with listening to the inventiveness and the skillful use of musical dexterity and integrity served to deepen my true realization of the immensity of the music we know as jazz. To go out there every night and lay oneself open to possible frustration and, needless to say, personal and mental upheaval, should one have failed in your own mind, is in my mind an act of musical courage. Even beyond that, it is a belief in one's depth as a player of consequence.

PART TWO

MORE KEYS: THE 1960S ONWARD

50

THE PERCUSSIVE GROUP: RAY
BROWN AND ED THIGPEN

Herb Ellis' departure from the Trio for the West Coast created a terrible void. That group with Herb and Ray had become such a well-oiled intuitive outfit, and Herb's guitar such a matchless and central component in all our arrangements, that I found it hard to imagine starting over with a completely new group, let alone a group containing not guitar but drums.

I spoke disappointedly to various close friends, wondering aloud what my next move could be. The person to come up with the most lucid evaluation of the situation was—wouldn't you know it?—Norman Granz. Norman was always at his best whenever an apparently insurmountable problem arose. He exuded total control, and his voice would take on a quasi-casual, but highly determined, candour; furthermore, he took clever care to ensure he was not interrupted. After asking about my future plans, he at once demolished my worries about finding another guitarist by issuing a completely new challenge. He informed me that a lot of people—players and listeners alike—were curious to see if I could retain my command of the piano and the group if Ray's immense sound were to be complemented by a drummer. This challenge was couched with great tact, for he never suggested a lack of faith in me. On the contrary, he believed I would greatly benefit from the change: he thought it of the utmost importance never to "coast" or rest on one's laurels, and he felt that I had possibly reached a stage where I was doing just that—settling for a comfortable environment rather than making maximum and proper use of my creative potential.

I came to realize later that such things are indeed central to the growth of any artist; at the time, however, I was infuriated by the idea that I had become distracted and cosseted, and I took exception to any doubts that I could meet this new challenge. And, of course, this reaction was exactly what Norman had played for: subconsciously I was already starting to formulate a trio concept with drums, instinctively outlining formats that could be used with such a combination that were not possible with a piano/bass/guitar set-up.

Shortly thereafter I made the decision: a drummer it would be. Initially I used Gene Gammage, an engaging man who afterwards continued to follow the Trio's fortunes right up to his untimely death in 1989. He worked well with Ray and me on the 1958 *My Fair Lady* album, but his tenure, though stylish and tasteful, was always going to be a transitional one, and early in 1959 I called in Ed Thigpen.

Ed was a soft-spoken young man whom I had first met when he was in uniform, on duty in Japan. On his return to civilian life he had told Ray in no uncertain terms that he wanted the third spot in the Trio. I had admired his work with Billy Taylor, and knew him to be a master with brushes, so I was happy to offer him the spot—the more so when he showed up for his first rehearsal full of wide-eyed awe and admiration for Ray and myself, more like an adoring fan than our new drummer!

From the outset Ray outlined what he knew I expected from them as my rhythmical driving force. This had nothing to do with the various lines Ray and I would play together, which left spaces for Ed to punctuate and embellish, but hinged on what we call "burning time," when the soloist (in this case, of course, me) launches into his improvisation following the initial theme statement and arranged trio interplay. (The equivalent term in classical music would be the development section.) In addition to our trio rehearsals, therefore, Ray would call his own rehearsals in his or Ed's room and they would simply practise "time." They created a flexible and multi-faceted rhythmical language that they could apply to any musical statement I might make and enhance any direction I might choose. In short, they practised "all the possibles."

Their command of different levels of pulsation was really something. For instance, on what we call the "two" choruses, where Ray would in essence be playing a two–four rhythm, Ed would employ brushes, showing his genius with every silken sweep; this would often graduate to a medium-drive four–four beat from Ray, with Ed's brushes now more forceful. Then came the gear-change into "high," when Ed switched seamlessly to sticks and ride cymbal, and we were off into the "steaming zone," which brought out in me the deepest levels of my groove playing, driven by this incomparable engine behind me.

Even on the bandstand at night Ray remained relentless in this pursuit of a musical meld. "Come on, Thags," he would exhort, "Let's tighten him up!" (Translation: "Come on Ed, let's really put it together so that he hears only one kind of time behind him.") If the rhythm section's time is not totally cohesive in this way, the soloist can easily become disrupted: if you're subconsciously aware of two different grooves, your lines of invention will start to falter. That is one ailment I am happy to say my group didn't suffer from. The worst that would happen was that occasionally the "snap" would go from their timekeeping; however, they always knew when it had happened and would readjust at once.

Turning to another aspect of Ed's playing, he had great taste and imagination in his fills and backup lines behind me. He saw most musical figures as shapes and would try to create shapes that complemented those he heard from Ray and me. I must single out his work in this regard on the 1964 album with Clark Terry, *Oscar Peterson Trio Plus One*, particularly his breaks on *Mack The Knife*, which are as fine as anything I've heard.

This Trio grew and grew the more we got to know each other musically. Thanks to the rhythmic power and density I referred to earlier, we had no problem playing the larger festivals and auditoria. Various other musicians used to marvel at the fact that we could go out on a festival and almost immediately attain a solid groove throughout the whole performance. This came about because we left nothing to chance: we practised for specific venues and rehearsed dynamics as well as lines. After our sets at Chicago's London House, for example, we'd sip coffee until the staff left, and then rehearse from 4.30 to 7.00 (a.m.!). That might sound gruelling; however, for us it had been integral to putting together what we felt was the best trio in jazz, and was now an accepted, even pleasurable honing process.

Editor's Note: The Trio with Ed Thigpen and Ray Brown operated for some six and a half years, from early 1959 to the summer of 1965. Ed Thigpen left then, to settle in Toronto, and was replaced by drummer Louis Hayes; a few months later, Peterson's 15-year partnership with Ray Brown ended when the bassist declared himself worn out by the Trio's demanding touring schedules. Ray settled in Los Angeles, and was replaced by Sam Jones.

Many devotees of Peterson's music think that the work he recorded with Brown and Thigpen is amongst his very finest. Certainly, Night Train *(see the next chapter),* West Side Story, Porgy And Bess, *and* Affinity *represent the best of his studio work thus far; in addition, the 1994 issue of a six-CD set of 1960s live recordings made in concert in Paris (on the French Europe 1 label) demonstrate to near-perfection this Trio's huge repertoire, commanding élan, and sonorous range.*

51

THE *NIGHT TRAIN* ALBUM

N orman Granz had an unquenchable thirst for the blues. His appreciation of the form is rooted in the era of the original blues players, such as Leadbelly and Joe Turner, and I cannot remember a single occasion in all my many recording sessions in his studios when he did not suggest a blues selection.

The *Night Train* album, made in December 1962, featured quite an assortment of tunes, but they all took on a blues flavour in performance. *Night Train* itself had long been one of Norman's favourite tunes, and he specifically asked for it to be included on the album and be treated as a full-blooded blues. The session went very well: everybody felt good and there were no problems with the different takes. Some way through the date, Norman came out of the control booth and said, "Why don't you do a really slow blues tune? Whatever you choose, but make it slow." I couldn't think of an example straight off, so I decided to compose one on the spot. I played the first chorus on my own, and the Trio fell in behind me on the subsequent choruses. Since the tune had an almost church-like feel to it, and as by this time the Civil Rights movement had come into being, I decided to call it *The Hymn To Freedom*—a musical salute to the brave and persevering leaders of that movement, especially the Rev. Martin Luther King.

Night Train turned out to be one of our best-selling albums ever, and it is still in the catalogue to this day. I find that particularly gratifying, for I think its music profoundly reflects some of the emotions and issues that were current in America at the time.

52

MEMBERSHIP FLOW IN THE TRIO (2): 1960S AND 1970S

During 1965 it seems as if I imported what originally was the Cannonball Adderley Quintet rhythm section, for my drummer at that time was Louis Hayes and my bassist was Sam Jones. I was very fortunate in having at my immediate disposal a ready-made rhythm section. We were operational almost at once, for Louis and

Sam did not have to go through the trauma of accustoming themselves to each other's playing; they already had a set of signals to deal with how they played for me as a rhythm section, and—no less important— they had a personal rapport that was carried over from Cannon's group to mine.

I liked this rhythm section because of the tightness and familiarity with each other. They made me play differently without injuring my perception or infringing on my linear ideas; in particular, they influenced how I articulated my ideas against their time. Louis' fills were more post-bop in style than Ed's had been, and they were also thrown in at different intervals from what I had been accustomed to. By the same token, I am certain that Louis had to make some re-organization in his playing in order to effect a total meld with all of us in the group. Sam Jones, on the other hand, was not that far from what Ray Brown had been doing for me, having himself come out of the Jimmy Blanton School, and also being a practitioner of the famous "long note." His time was a little more laid back than I had been playing with, but the impetus of his notes was such that there was no time-hassle, for Sam could instill in you the belief that the only rhythmical way to go was his way. With these two men behind me it was almost inconceivable to envisage any kind of rhythmic disarray or uncertainty.

Sam's time was unusual. Once they hear you count off the tune, most bass players will begin playing—only to fluctuate in their time during the first chorus or so. But Sam had the ability concretely to register your count within himself, and from bar one run at a frighteningly steady pace throughout the tune. I recall on many occasions looking down in awe at that right heel of his as it always seemed to come down directly on the count. Not before it, not after it. Precisely on the count.

Also from the word go I could not help but realize, just simply from his fixed facial expression, that he was locked into the time slot that I had called, and he gave all the impression that nothing would sway him from this. The irony of this unusual ability of Sam's was that if by chance I did call the tempo a mite slow or fast, it was virtually impossible to unlock the rhythm door with Sam and readjust the time! This in turn made me much more aware of my starting count, bearing in mind the fact that there was no second chance at renegotiating it.

In many ways Sam's personal makeup was much the same as his time: staunch and immovable on whatever subject. He made his mind up and it was near to impossible to get him to change his opinion. The only saving grace in this personal trait was that Sam was a good man and a decent person. He also had a beautiful quality that I would like to see reflected in many of the young bassists of today.

He loved the low register of his instrument and would use it with consummate skill; occasionally, and only occasionally, working up the finger part to the higher register. This outlook in itself gave a much bigger root position to our trio, so that when we really wanted to stomp the foundation he was always there as the foundation.

It broke my heart when Louis Hayes and I had to part company; however, one happy fact is that to this day we are as close as we ever have been, and perhaps, just perhaps, one day we may even get back to being musical partners.

On one of my early appearances at Ronnie Scott's club in London, I got to meet Martin Drew, who at that time was working with Ronnie's quartet. Martin is a very happy-go-lucky, joke-quoting person who has a special dedication to music. He lives and breathes it night and day. This was my perception from the very first time I met him. Being curious about what it would be like to play with him, I slipped into the piano seat on one of their last sets and played the last tune with them. Right away Martin seemed to acquire a different kind of interest in his rhythmic playing as we fed one another as rhythm sections do. When I came off, Ronnie had a very funny line to lay on me. As he passed my dressing-room he looked in and said "Thank you, Oscar, we'll let you know." Apart from Ronnie's gag line, Martin came in full of smiles and excitement and informed me how much he enjoyed playing with me.

At some point down the road, after having had Bobby Durham in the group, I called on Martin to join a trio that would consist of myself and Niels-Henning Ørsted Pedersen. I feel that this Trio distinguished itself primarily for its musicality, for here we were three specifically defined players who were now going to execute as one. Martin's crisp delivery of the lines required of him lent a new sparkle to the group, punctuated by Niels' astonishingly inventive bass solos and support lines. It was great fun writing for this group, for it had almost a European flavour to it, seasoned with my North American musical approach. I feel that Martin Drew is without a doubt the consummate big band and studio musician. Some of the parts required of him in small-group work seem to inhibit his natural flair, but he is never anything but conscientious in such a context. If you want to hear Martin at his best, it's on the *Royal Wedding Suite* album, not only with the small group but also in the way that he enhanced and controlled the larger London Orchestra.

I first heard Bobby Durham with Duke Ellington and was immensely impressed with his ease and flair with the big band, especially when considering the intricacy of the library. He is certainly first a rhythmic player, with tremendous drive and equal dexterity across his drums. There are few drummers around today with his kind of total confidence in their ability to execute musically no matter what they are asked to do. When Bobby came into the group, it was as if he had been in it for years; he was able to anticipate things that we had to practically write out for other players. I remember him taunting Ray and myself, when we were in different groups on JATP, about being part of the "over the hill mob," and we kept inviting him down into the Trio, which he managed to sidestep from night to night.

Speaking candidly, I feel that Bobby Durham did not realize his musical capabilities to the full, for at times he would almost shrug off something that he perhaps thought did not mean anything. I have no ill words for Bobby even though we parted company, other than to say that perhaps if he were to re-evaluate some of his capabilities, coupled with the returns that he could enjoy were he to call upon them, his perception of his own worth perhaps would intensify and aid his output.

Canadian David Young does not at present realize, I think, how much potential he has. He is a tremendous bassist and an unusually musical soloist whose playing is richly dimensioned. In addition, he is a master of the long long note—a quality that one rarely meets nowadays.

David tends to have a lope to his playing which you can groove with, as long as you don't lean too hard on its time cycle for this can cause you to retard your own conception of the time being played. I have always enjoyed playing with David Young for he is very venturesome in the solo work and enjoys the challenge of running lines with me or against me. He has one quality that I selfishly revel in. During the times that he was not in my trio or quartet, he remained interested enough to learn many of our various arrangements, and have them in hand should he ever be called upon. His execution is filled with the true joy of playing and it reveals itself in the exuberance and intent that flows through his trio part.

I love David Young for he has afforded me many happy nights of trio playing.

53

THE LONG AND THE SHORT OF IT

I used to call Sam Jones and Bobby Durham Mutt and Jeff, and had you seen them walking down the street together, you'd have understood why. Sam Jones' six-foot slim frame alongside Bobby's chunky Lilliputian figure made a highly comic contrast, even if they themselves weren't aware of it.

I had also nicknamed Bobby "Thug," simply because he came from the toughest neighbourhoods in Philadelphia, added to the fact that he had done some boxing in his earlier days, and was quite a tough cookie.

In my personal dealings with Bobby I always tried to reach the softer side of his nature which I knew to be there, even though he hated to show it. At first he responded to these attempts of mine by adopting a harsh and cynical exterior; but once he realized that I knew it was all a charade, he lightened up, and a strong bond developed between us. In later years, whenever we met I would insist that he kiss me on the cheek, regardless of who was present. This embarrassed him no end; however, realizing that the alternative might mean my kissing him, he always complied. It was good to bring out the gentler nature of this man, for he normally hides it behind tough ring-talk and a macho swagger.

Sam Jones, on the other hand, retained a quiet, almost totally silent presence for the most part, and spoke in a very deep, hesitant voice, choosing his words carefully. He was the epitome of gentleness and whenever he would break up laughing, would cover his mouth and, in effect, guffaw in an almost silent manner.

Bobby and Sam were the best of friends as well as being members of my trio; nevertheless, they had their occasional disagreements and once, on a train ride through Switzerland, fell out in no uncertain fashion, exchanging harsh and ever-uglier words; Bobby even threatened Sam physically. Finally I became disgusted by it all, ordered them out onto the platform and, in pure rage, threatened to smother the two of them physically if they didn't stop it. This did manage to silence them and we continued our train ride in a kind of glum tentative tranquillity.

Several years later, during one of our tours with Ella and her group, we were all standing backstage yakking about this and that, when I reminded Bobby about that train incident. Niels Pedersen had replaced Sam in the group by this time and on hearing this story, asked Bobby how in the world he had expected to win against Sam, given their tremendous difference in height. Bobby's reply exemplified the ghetto resolve of his generation: "You don't understand the scene at all," said Bobby, somewhat annoyed but not in the least fazed. "I know how tall Sam is, but what you don't understand, man, is the way I was thinking.

You see, I intended to work on all this stuff that's here in front of me."
He indicated that Sam's middle would be just short of his eye level, and
punctuated his remarks with his swinging fists. "Once you work on all
this stuff here hard enough, all that other stuff up above that I couldn't
reach before has got to finally come down here where I can deal with it,
Jim!" Upon hearing this we all cracked up in gales of unrestrained
laughter at his graphic logic. Yet I couldn't help thinking that this very
logic, such relentlessly tough thinking, is what enables people like
Bobby Durham to overcome the heavy odds of their ghetto origins and
become the kind of talent that he is.

54

THE MPS YEARS

Sometime after Norman sold his record company Verve to
MGM, he came to me while setting up a European tour for the
Trio and spoke of an inquiry he had had from a gentleman in Villingen,
Germany, asking if I would consider playing a private party at his home
there. He was prepared to pay my concert fee, and would also provide
transportation for the group. When Norman first checked the
schedule, it appeared that the only time for such an appearance would
be after a concert that we were giving in Zurich. We wondered if the
group would be too tired, but decided that we could do it, since we
would not thereby be taking on another complete concert. "Leave it
with me," counselled Norman in his affirmative way, and as usual I did
just that.

Shortly afterwards, I learned that my forthcoming host had asked if
he could record the performance for his own enjoyment, having
undertaken to sign a guarantee that he would never issue the recorded

material or allow anyone access to it. I agreed to this arrangement, and in the fall of 1963 we were driven, as scheduled, to Villingen for my first meeting with Hans Georg Brunner-Schwer.

The first thing I noticed when the cars pulled in was that the grounds belonged to a manufacturing company whose name I had often seen on audio equipment throughout Europe: SABA. We drove past the surveillance guard, took a turn to the left, and pulled up at the front door of a beautiful-looking dwelling. A man with reddish brown hair, cut in a very modest crewcut, a round face, and a boyish grin came towards me as I alighted. "Oskar!" he exclaimed, with noticeable excitement and exuberance, "Welcome to my home. I am Hans Georg and I am so happy to have you here." He introduced me to his shy, pretty wife Marlise and to his two sons, one nearing his teens and one looking to be around seven or eight years of age. My wife Sandy was with us and she was taken off by Marlise to freshen up after the journey.

I was ushered into quite a large anteroom where several guests were standing talking, and then into a large sitting-room of immense proportions, where I would say approximately 20 to 30 people were dispersed around the room talking and drinking. There was a huge concert grand piano situated in front of the wall-to-wall picture window that looked out onto a beautiful back lawn and on further to an immense treed backdrop. There was a controlled opulence here—many beautiful things and yet nothing sickeningly ornate about the surroundings. Everything was precisely arranged, but was also eminently comfortable. I met many of Hans Georg's friends as he and I went to the bar to have some refreshment. He complained that he could not speak English that well, but promised that if I would consent to return regularly, he would make an effort to improve his command of the language.

As I glanced around the room I inevitably subjected the piano to close scrutiny and could not help noticing the four to six Telefunken mikes that were set up in an almost equidistant fashion just slightly above the hammers of the instrument; there were also other mikes strategically placed away from the piano in a configuration that I had not seen used before. The group consisted of Ray Brown and Ed Thigpen, and after some refreshments and chatter, we sat down to our instruments. Everything felt very easy and relaxed. The room was totally hushed, even through the most pulsating parts of the music, and I couldn't help noticing the looks of disbelief and awe on the faces of the audience as they listened to our arrangements and solos. A couple of men drew in their breath during some of Ray's bass solos. They were seated just to one side of him, and as Ray would do occasionally, he ended a passage by dropping down to the low open A string on his bass, which had an all-encompassing finality to it. The sensitivity of Ed Thigpen's brushwork brought on nods of wonderment as he swept through our charts.

Hans Georg had disappeared from the room and wasn't seen again until after the performance was over. He came downstairs, his jacket removed, shirt sleeves rolled up to his elbows, tie removed, and collar open and threw his hands up in the air with a look of ecstasy on his face. "Wonderful! Wonderful!" he exclaimed. "I am so happy." He thanked me and the group for honouring him with our visit, and took us into the dining-room for some food. We were joined by a man by the name of Willi Frukt, who went on to become his chief A&R man later on when Hans Georg formed MPS Records, and his translator/lawyer, Bernard Falk and his wife, who resided in San Francisco. It was a very enjoyable evening which concluded with us returning to Zurich in the wee hours of the morning in order to rest up for the tour that continued next day.

This concert procedure was to be repeated again and again in the following years, although at the time I didn't realize it would evolve into the association that it did. Norman called me the following day to check on how the party had gone and was more than pleased to hear of its success; the next thing I knew is that he received a call from Hans Georg saying that he would dearly love to do a repeat performance the next time the Trio was in Europe. And another development followed. Shortly after these first concerts, Norman told me that Hans Georg had formed a record company and was most interested in putting out some of the recordings that he had made at these parties. I agreed, on condition that I be allowed to select the material and be present at the mixdown. Hans Georg immediately complied and dates were set whereby I would go to Villingen and spend some time listening to the playbacks and choosing the best takes for the forthcoming LPs.

It was during these solo visits of mine that Hans Georg and I became much closer friends. We found out that we were both Leos, that we both loved hearty laughter along with good food and, of course, good music. Hans Georg was a man who was never satisfied with anything that he considered second best, no matter what he was dealing with. As an example, after my first visit, he asked what would be my favourite piano if I had total freedom of choice. At that time I had recently ended my association with one piano company and had begun developing a love for the sound of the beautiful Hamburg Steinway pianos. On my very next visit to his home, he told me he had a surprise for me, and as I rounded the doorway into the music-room, there sitting in its midst was a brand-spanking-new Hamburg Steinway, waiting for someone to play it. I sat down to the piano in eager anticipation and it did not disappoint me. Hans Georg walked around the room, both hands jammed into his pants pockets (his usual listening posture), shaking his head from side to side as this marvellous instrument pealed off its immaculate sounds. "It's you, it's you, Oskar!" he said in excitement. "We must record with this. I have some new techniques we must use for recording the piano."

He had a technician named Mr Donner, who was his right-hand man in the control-room, located on the second floor of his home. Hans Georg's equipment was peerless. There was one very noticeable factor that characterized all the music in his home. He played it all at a very high volume: it was as if music had become a kind of narcotic for him. He would clench his fists and make his whole body vibrate at various junctures during our selections, and there was one thing that he waited for with particular hunger: block chords. Whenever I broke into the block chord technique (introduced to the jazz world by Milt

Buckner), he would rock intensely from side to side, his eyes closed in ecstasy as the rolling phrases cascaded across the room. "Fantastic, fantastic!" he would shout in English, and then say something to Willi Frukt in German in a very excited way. This man was a music addict to the point where he could sing some of my solos; later, I found out that he played some piano and was trying to play some of the block chord choruses that I had used on the recordings.

I spent several happy vacations in Villingen with Hans Georg, for he shared my deep involvement in jazz, and we had many hours discussing various players and recordings that had impressed us. By this time, he had formed MPS Records and was associated with many other jazz musicians; as a result, his already much-improved English was further enriched by a good deal of jazz argot. I recall asking him once about a particular automobile that had just come out. "Ah, beautiful," he said, "Beautiful, Oskar. But a lot of bread!" I broke up with laughter at this utterance. It struck me as peculiar, hearing him lapse from the Germanic pronunciation of my name into the street slang of America to describe money.

As our association deepened he asked me about some of the people that I thought he should be recording. I suggested several players, including my little West Indian counterpart, Monty Alexander; however, one suggestion came about in a remarkable way. In 1968, I received a fantastic Christmas card. It was a tape wrapped up as a Christmas present from Gene and Helen Puerling, whom I had seen the summer past at Audrey and Stuart Genovese's home.* I rushed to my recorder and put the tape on, only to be overwhelmed by the most beautiful rendition of "Silent Night" I have ever heard in my life. I don't believe that anyone writes as well as Gene Puerling does for the Singers Unlimited. I also do not believe that any group can sing the almost impossible harmonic changes with the delicacy and intuitive sensitivity that this singing group does: they are incomparable.

---

*See "Backup Friends," in Chapter 65.

I was so taken by this beautiful Christmas card that on my next visit to Germany I took the tape with me to Hans Georg's house. As it played he sat there transfixed; his wife Marlise came to tears, and when it was over he excitedly said, "Oskar, you must get them for me. I must record them." I am proud that I was involved in initiating Gene and the Singers' association with MPS, especially since their many albums have been so beautiful. The Singers' many fans also owe a great debt to Lady Audrey in Chicago (my landlady) who coerced Gene Puerling to continue writing and singing with the group when he was at a low ebb, forlornly wondering if there was room in the music world for the Singers Unlimited.

During my tenure with MPS the group changed personnel several times. Ray Brown's spot was taken by Sam Jones, and Ed Thigpen's by Louis Hayes and eventually Bobby Durham. Czech bassist George Mraz appeared on several albums, along with drummer Ray Price, who had a short stint in the group. Herbie Ellis and Milt Jackson were brought in for two special albums, while another used charts by that very talented composer, arranger, and conductor Claus Ogerman. The final group on MPS was Niels-Henning and Louis Hayes. We even managed to put together a charming meeting of the Trio and the Singers Unlimited. Quite apart from the music itself, people revelled in the sheer magnificence of the piano sound that Hans Georg attained on these albums. I must say that he was a man dedicated to reproducing on record what he had heard in his music-room.

As I returned to Villingen for some of the later recordings I sensed a change in our relationship, or more precisely a tension on his part. He had always exhibited a fierce pride in our association, but now I got the feeling that he was convinced that my association with Norman Granz as friend, manager, and advisor was driving a wedge in my friendship with him. At first he spoke of Norman in fearful tones; later, it became more of a diatribe of criticism of him—and of course this led to arguments, since I was not about to listen to my best friend being pilloried in such a fashion.

When our association ended contractually in 1972, we bumped

into each other a couple of times in the Eden au Lac hotel in Zurich. On the last such meeting I vividly remember having dinner there at a table adjacent to his. At the conclusion of the meal, I stopped at his table and said good-night in a cordial fashion, retiring to my room with Sandy. She and I sat and talked for about half an hour and then Sandy walked out on the balcony of our room, which overlooked the sidewalk in front of the hotel. Suddenly I heard her calling my name in a whispered and excited fashion at the bathroom door. I came out as quickly as I could and asked what the problem was. "Come and see this," she said, "Come and see this. You won't believe it." She led me out onto the small balcony and pointed to the street below.

There, to my consternation and surprise, was Hans Georg with his head in one hand leaning across the roof of his Mercedes, while smacking the car roof with the other hand in desperation as Marlise tried to console him. I could not hear what he was saying, but from the exaggerated emotional raps of his hand and the tears streaming down his face, I instinctively knew that it had something to do with our now-dissolved friendship. During this period, Norman had started litigation with MPS over the interpretation of royalty payments on my contracts, so my remarks to him in the restaurant had been as short as possible, given the circumstances. This all culminated years later in larger litigation, which was finally resolved in the courts.

I don't know how to summarize my friendship with Hans Georg. It started off like most friendly business relationships but grew into a much more personal involvement, in which we shared our deepest thoughts on a wide variety of matters. Yet there was often something slightly off-key about it all—perhaps best typified by a rather strange weekend I spent at his invitation in his cottage at the lake of Como in northern Italy.

It was taken up by him showing me through his beautiful country home; having photographs taken of us with the local people in their district costumes; listening to what he called the perfect sound—which entailed going out to a garage-like structure with him explaining on the way out there that we would be listening in mono, and then being ushered into this building that housed a speaker that went from ceiling to floor and right wall to left wall: the size of this unbelievable piece of equipment was, at a guess, 15-feet square. He then told me that he liked fishing, as I did; however, our "fishing trip" that weekend was confined to Mr Donner bringing his boat from the boathouse down to the lake by electric railway, a break-neck ride around the lake, a return to shore, and then a pause as we watched Mr Donner return the boat up the railway into the boathouse once more!

During my wanderings with him around the property, I kept seeing some huge objects which I resisted asking about but was, nevertheless, very puzzled by. I found myself trying to connect them with the extraordinary present that his lawyer, Herr Falk, had given him two years earlier: a full-scale wartime searchlight. Very odd, you might think; but my hunch turned out to be strangely appropriate. For those huge objects turned out to be a collection of air-raid sirens strewn all around the grounds!

55

THOSE UNRELENTING BASSISTS

Over the years I have been blessed in being able to draw on a host of supremely talented bassists. Each one deserves a separate portrait.

My very first working bass player was Bert Brown from Montreal. He recorded my first RCA–Victor sides with me. Bert was primarily a studio bassist while also playing at night in Maynard Ferguson's orchestra. A player with a big sound, he gave me the confidence I needed to fulfil those first recordings.

The bass spot in my first *bona fide* Canadian trio belonged to Austin Roberts from Toronto. "Ossie" greatly loved and admired Jimmy Blanton and Oscar Pettiford (both of Ellington's era) and had a musical determination that was near-unreal. He would refuse to give up on a bass part no matter how difficult it was. Along with a great walking style, he developed what was for us at that time a genuine mastery of his instrument. Ossie was an introvert but enormously resolute, and my memories of our early musical struggles together are very fond ones.

Another bassist who passed through our group in the early Montreal years was a happy-go-lucky player named Bob Rudd. Bob had a most distinctive and recognizable approach to bass playing. His walk was almost a lazy one, but the time was there. He used a lot of cross-positioning fingering (a technique not employed too often in jazz in those days) and did a lot of slurring between the notes he chose, which in turn increased the feeling of a really relaxed line. His attitude matched his style: he was a very carefree person about commitment, and in the end sadly that meant that we were forced to part company.

The first bassist of my American groups was Major Holley—"Mule," as he was known in the music circles. I remember him as a very blustery man, who underneath had a deep and kind feeling for people. This didn't stop him from ranting and raving if he thought that he could win the point in dispute. I got to recognize the fact that most of this was a cover-up for situations of which he was unsure, and so learned to ride out these storms and put across my point. My mother loved Major or "Mr Mule" as he became known to her. Somehow, I feel that she may have at some time or the other heard him referring to his "Mama," and that it struck some kind of a chord in her for him. She proceeded to become his "Housemom," and would try to cater for his various whims and fancies.

Mule had a huge sound on his instrument, and an excellent sense of time. His sonorous attack allowed me to hang various phrases and lines together, tethered only by his huge resonances as he walked his lines behind me. His solo lines were intriguing—reminiscent of Oscar Pettiford and Jimmy Blanton in articulation and attack, but differing greatly from those players in sound and choice of notes. I recorded my early Mercury sides with him, and also more than a few cuts for Clef (later Verve).

Mule's recent demise saddened me very much. I had a great respect and love for him: he brought a happy and comfortable approach to his role in the Trio, and our times together were characterized by laughter and good humour. He was almost six feet tall, with huge hands and a deadly stare, which was considerably aided by the immense pair of horn-rimmed glasses that adorned his face. And he invariably wore simply a T-shirt, jeans, and loafers—a feature that underscores this next story, which captures the "True Mule" at his most inimitable.

At one time he and I played a resort in Quebec known as Lac des Piles. This name emanates from the piles of cut timber that they used to float down the lake to the sawmill. I was also given to understand that the lake was exceedingly deep, and in some places the depth was unknown. I cautioned Mule about this and received a "pooh-pooh" response from him. A few days after starting the gig, we were sitting around the luncheon room with the manager of the resort, and Mule made some inquiry about a couple of canoes that were lying about. The manager again tried to caution him about the dangers of storms and capsizing and so forth. Mule immediately launched into a prolonged dialogue on his days in the US Navy and the like, which seemed to last forever. Finally he stopped, and the manager walked away shrugging his shoulders and muttering to himself.

Mule asked me if I wanted to come along on the canoe ride and I quickly declined. I am to this day a non-swimmer and also, at that particular time of my life, I weighed approximately 290 pounds. Having been raised in Quebec and having several friends with cottages in the lake areas around the Laurentian mountains, I was well-acquainted with the do's and don'ts of canoeing, such as "Do make sure you stay away from canoes if you are a non-swimmer" and "Don't be stupid enough to be lured into a canoe with someone as stubborn as Mule." I had to listen to another lecture on non-confidence in him as a former US sailor and as a person, and after this was over, I said that I was going to have a nap and left him to his own devices, retiring to my room on the third floor.

I slept for about an hour-and-a-half, arose, and went downstairs to the lounge. As I walked down, I happened to glance up at one of the lines used for drying guest laundry, and ended up holding on to the railing so as not to fall down the staircase from laughing. There, neatly held on by clothes-pins, were the following items of apparel: a pair of jeans, a T-shirt, a pair of underwear briefs, a pair of socks, a pair of loafers, and, I kid you not, a pair of horn-rimmed glasses! There seated at the foot of the stairs was Mule wrapped in a blanket, muttering under his breath, "God-damn canoe! God-damn canoe!" Thus ended the affair of the great canoe ride at Lac des Piles.

The record for the longest stint in the Trio by anyone is still held by Ray Brown. Fifteen years of continual musical dedication and devotion on his part allowed me to have what I think was the finest trio in Jazz. I can say this unequivocally because I kept a very close eye on the various groups around us. We had but one credo in those formative years: outplay the competition! It was almost like the old gunfighter syndrome: whenever we met up with any of our competitors we would systematically set out to intimidate and destroy them musically. Ray believed wholeheartedly in this principle and would expect me fully to execute it, launched by the driving force that he and the third member (whoever he was) supplied for me.

Ray Brown is probably one of the greatest talents ever on his particular instrument. He has a natural, intuitive feel for anything he approaches musically, and his sound is so huge and personal that listeners recognize it almost automatically. It has a very warm and lasting tonal quality to it, which has a most profound effect on whomever he plays with.

One of the things that sets Ray apart from other bassists is that he not only commands so many different idioms and styles of attack: he is also able to change his sound according to what and how he is playing. For instance, when he is playing behind you on a ballad, his attack seems to allow the bass note to swell and engulf your phrase within its tonal colour. On the other hand, when he is "walking" behind you on a medium tempo, his notes become more directional in their attack, while the sound drops just enough of its length to give each note a little more "snap" and intent. When he moves to up-tempo level, his attack becomes even more fierce, and yet the tonal quality is not compromised.

But the most awesome side of Ray's talent is his timing. It is something that I never took for granted when we played together: I was delighted to benefit from it, but I had to learn not to lean too heavily on it, because this would make it impossible for me to play with other bassists. One interesting thing is that Ray did sometimes speed up or slow down as he played; we are all human. However, no one ever swung so hard while speeding or slowing!

When we were first together as a duo, I started to give Ray what could almost be perceived as guitar lines. He finally said to me one day, "In case you haven't noticed, there are no God-dammed frets on this axe." (Translation: "This is a bass, not a guitar.") I must confess that because of Ray's prowess on his instrument and his tremendous musicality, I tended to "stretch" him musically sometimes in the manner in which I expected certain things from him. Even though this sometimes caused temporary conflict, the growth that we both enjoyed from these excursions into the "almost impossible" was immeasurable. It is in these periods of strain and perseverance that true artistry evolves, and the fruits of all of our endeavours ripen into musical genius. This is what I saw and heard in Ray Brown.

RAY BROWN

He plays with the ease of a tiger on stalk
His time resolute, devoid of any balk
His fingers seek out notes with grace and surety,
His sound absolute, with strength and purity.

This is Ray Brown with the handsome face,
Handling his bass with infinite grace.
His power and dexterity leave little to be desired,
And whose immense musical talent by now has inspired
Countless thousands of bassists the whole world round,
To work untold hours trying to emulate his sound.

Well, what of this man whose boyish looks
Belie his huge talent not found in books?
I have known his for years now, many though they may be,
And in no way is he any mystery to me.
For Ray is a man who was destined to be
Exactly what he personifies quite truthfully.
A man who is happy to stand up with pride,
And amaze the whole world, his instrument at his side.
This is his calling and he knows it full well,
And he will doggedly pursue it come heaven or hell.

He has tirelessly addressed his musical quest
For perfection by giving his absolute best
By probing and searching the harmonic abyss,
Not just from Gillespie, but as far back as Lizst.
His hunger for chord trails as yet unexplored,
Has kept many soloists from ever being bored
By the musical paths he gave them to travel,
Amid musical ploys they had to unravel.

He solos with ease and with endless incentive
His lines ever rhythmic yet harmonically inventive
His solos are punctuated with huge blobs of sound,
That echo and reverberate and forever rebound
With a furious attack that crackles like fire
Giving way to those long notes that seem to inspire
The soloist to reach out and stretch way beyond their ability
As they ride the crest of Ray's musical agility.

As he played for me to improvise
It was then that I came to realize
What an immense gift the powers had given,
Yet with all of this Ray has continually striven
To improve it, to mould it, yes, to make it grow
For as we played together, I came to know
How to best use this man with impeccable time,
Whose harmonic sense bordered on the sublime.

As a man, I have held him in great esteem
For he helped me fulfill my own musical dream.
A dream of having a group that not only could soar
Like a graceful eagle, but could also roar
Like a huge jungle beast that knew no bounds
As we roamed musically free on Ray Brown's big sounds.

Sam Jones was a most direct, uncomplicated man. He was also a man of few words. Whenever he said anything, it would only be said after due consideration. He hated brassy and loud situations, and what he chose to call "hokey" music. His taste ran the same in people. He could cope with uncomplicated people and basically believable music. Almost anything else was outside his realm of comprehension.

Sam played exactly the way that he believed. Simply and straight to the point. His sense of time was also utterly rock-solid; however, he seldom ventured into harmonic areas in which he felt unsure. (This was possibly an additional reason for his steadfast time.) He wanted to be sure whenever his hand came down on that note.

I have very strong and loving memories of Sam Jones. One of these is on the occasion of my first solo performance in America: it was at Carnegie Hall in New York, at the then Newport Festival. I was scheduled to follow Mahavarishna and then the Cannonball Adderly Quintet. I was standing in the wings listening, when I sensed a person next to me. I looked around and it was Sam. "Just came to keep you company, Brother P," he said. We stood around backstage talking of various things, and I shall never forget what happened next. Sam leaned over and said, "Look here, P, if you should change your mind about following all of those horns and things, I've got my bass in my car across the street in the garage. Just say the word and I'll go get it and lend you a hand with all of that stuff out there." I was really touched by this quiet and unobtrusive show of support. I thanked him and went on, and ironically had a hell of a reception as a solo player. When I came off stage, Sam was in the wings and as he embraced me he said, "Shoot! I should have known that you wouldn't need any help or else you wouldn't have shown!" I shall always remember that kind deed from the kind, silent man, Sam Jones.

George Mraz is a deceptive bass player. His quiet nature and unassuming manner contrast sharply with his penetrating sound and acute, almost aggressive sense of timing. During his time in my group, he complained most of the time about how hard the parts were: it didn't stop him making them each and every night!

I am, I confess, not a great fan of the bowed bass solo; but George has a sound quality when soloing in this mode that sets him apart. There is a compelling continuity to his arco lines and sound that few other bassists possess, and his balance and innate sensitivity make him one of the finest jazz bassists around today.

In a roundabout way, it was through George that I got to meet Niels-Henning Ørsted Pedersen. We had started a tour of Europe, and George had to leave suddenly for distressingly political reasons. For looking at the schedule one day and seeing Zagreb listed, George (who is Czech) said in his usual quiet way, "Oscar, you know that I can't go back there, don't you?" I replied that I would bring it to Norman Granz's attention and not to worry. Norman said that it would be no problem to get a substitute for him and besides, we had over three weeks to solve it.

But it did turn out to be a problem: most of the bass players that were contacted did not seem to want to take a shot at it. Suddenly, three weeks had shrunk to one, and I started to panic. Norman tried to put my fears at ease by saying that he had one more prospect in mind, and if he consented to do the gig, our troubles were over. When I asked him whom he had in mind, he called Niels' name. I had heard Niels one night for a very brief moment in the Club Momartre in Copenhagen. Ray had been preparing to leave the group and had suggested that I listen to Niels' playing if I had the chance. Ray thought that, as he put it, "He's the only one that I know that might keep up with you."

Happily, Niels was free to do the gig in Zagreb, with no political complications, and so we met for the first time in the hotel salon on the afternoon of the concert to discuss the evening's programme. Naturally, we couldn't do any of my arrangements: there was no time for him to learn them. We merely talked over repertoire, treatment, and tempos while I sat looking at this gentle-mannered young Dane, wondering if he would be able to cut it that night. I soon got my answer.

We opened with some medium tempo standard, and I played a couple of solo ad lib choruses on it in order to establish feeling and harmonic directions. Niels stood studiously by, his head tilted to one side as if he was trying to read my hands. Suddenly, he lit into the tune without any hesitation at all and from there on, it was clear sailing for the rest of the night. I totally enjoyed myself throughout, throwing my all into this new feel behind me. He had a clear ringing sound on his axe, quite different from any of his predecessors in the group. There was a free unbridled movement to his musical cadences; he quickly responded when I left open swatches for him to answer me—his solos were joyful sorties into separate yet attached worlds, and I revelled in his natural feel for time. He settled down into every tempo immediately, and seemed to devote every working note to ensuring that each tune really cooked.

Niels Pedersen is the type of player whose talents on his instrument are such that he is almost unaware of what he does. His virtuosity on the bass surpasses anyone else that I have known. His melodic sense is impeccable, his choice of harmonic sequences is a pure delight to play with, and his time is flawless. I have written things for him to play melodically that I could not have written for many other bassists. I have been able to write only a partial sequence for him knowing full well that his great perceptive sense and knowledge of me would come into play and allow him to finish it for me. He is now arguably the most inventive bassist in jazz; time will show what further greatness awaits him.

John Heard worked with me on numerous occasions during the 1970s, recording several albums with both the Trio and the larger groups with which I was involved. He is a heavy-duty bassist, whose profound musical quality and prodigious chromatic sensitivity were outstanding. Perhaps he lacked the all-out technique of Niels Pedersen or Scott LaFaro (see page 247), but music was so deeply rooted in his soul that everything he played had a truthfulness and simple depth that would make any bassist proud.

His departure from the music field, sad though it may be, is probably the best decision he could have made, as he was a man fighting a battle within himself. For John happens also to be a very talented visual artist, whose pencil drawings have earned him world-wide kudos. He was, I believe, caught between two art forms, and I am glad for him that the struggle is over.

There has always been a noticeable gentleness about David Young. Behind that boyish grin lies a concerned and loving human being—an aspect of his nature never more evident than during my recuperation from my stroke. David of course called to inquire about my progress; he then dumbfounded me by asking casually if I felt like getting together to play a little.

Up to this point in my illness I had been side-stepping the question of whether or not I would be able to play the piano again, even though in other respects my recovery was progressing well enough. I was probably scared of confronting this remaining unknown: I had carefully avoided even going down to my music-room, where my Bosendorfer resides. So after stammering my agreement to David's immensely kind offer, and setting a date the next week for him to come by with his bass, I wondered what I'd let myself in for. Fearing the worst, I decided not to touch my instrument until the rehearsal with David.

When the evening arrived, I was a bundle of nerves. I had not sat to the piano since an attempt months earlier that ended in tears with my therapist trying to console me; I had collapsed over the keyboard after essaying the simple theme of *Love Ballade* and failing miserably. Those images came back to haunt me as David undid his bass cover and tuned up. David must have sensed my inner panic: all he said was, "Now, take it easy on me!" This comment served to help awaken the devil in me: I kicked off into one of my compositions that has a very hard piano and bass unison line. We stumbled through it somehow and both broke into laughter; all at once, I realized that I had played the lines with both hands! We played several more tunes as the mood took us; David continued to encourage me with instinctive understanding—musical and human—and we both came away exhilarated by the success of the evening.

I owe David a huge debt for this unselfish and deeply sensitive overture. Thanks to him, a massive obstacle that I had been dreading facing was now behind me, for although my playing had by no means been perfect, I was confident that it was well on the way back.

As I said at the outset of this chapter, I have been extremely fortunate in the stream of gifted bassists who've come my way these 50 years. Without much doubt, the two greatest were Ray and Niels; but before I attempt a comparative summary of their separate geniuses, I would like to mention some other bass players that I've encountered, either in passing or only on record.

Red Callender is a gentleman who never actually worked in any of my groups; however, having always admired his playing, I was invariably eager whenever in LA to have the chance to jam with him. With his consistent striding mastery, Red had the kind of time most bassists would give their eye-teeth for. His playing reflected his personality—completely natural—and while, sadly, his death a while ago cost us an important asset, as long as jazz has any meaning he will be remembered.

Red Mitchell is another bassist I have only jammed with. He always intrigued me with his fluidly inventive solo work, and his intuitive understanding of running lines would have been sensational in any group. His time ain't exactly bad, either! Had he not been in Europe at the time Ray decided to leave the Trio and settle in Los Angeles, Red most certainly would have got the call.

I never got the opportunity of hearing Scott LaFaro in person, but I certainly enthused about him when I heard the album *The Arrival Of Victor Feldman* (on the Contemporary label). His big sound, coupled with a huge walking thrust, impressed me no end, and I made a big mental note of him. As a soloist Scotty brought a new concept to bass playing: it's very unusual to find someone with that kind of solo ability who is also master of the "big walk"; the only others I can think of are Ray and Niels. Scotty had it all, and the tragedy of his early loss to the jazz world in my mind remains unparalleled.

Charles Mingus and I never got along, either musically or personally. He was always publicly threatening to punch me out (as, I'm told, he had done to various other players), but never lived up to his threats. Even so, I was often anxious about this happening—especially after I found out, following a broadcast in Toronto in which he spoke derogatorily of me, that he was appearing in New York at a club at the same time that I was working in that city; the only difference was that we had different nights off. I decided to bring things to a head and give him the opportunity of venting any pent-up anger he felt towards me.

He happened to be playing with one of my favourite pianists, Phineas Newborn; Ray and I walked in, sat to one side, and listened to a set. Phineas then came over to our table, said hello, and sat down to talk. It quickly became clear that he was for some reason extremely nervous, for he was almost stuttering while we chatted, and seemed to be looking past me at something in the distance. I turned my head just in time to see Mingus standing behind me; without saying hello, I told him that I'd heard he was looking for me. He laughed and said something like, "Me? I'm always looking for good piano players," and that was the end of that.

I've never been a fan of Charles Mingus' bass playing, apart from the recordings he made with Red Norvo's group. And as already said, we never got along: I thought I knew what his feelings were about me, and I sensed he knew my feelings about him. Strangely enough, one night at a festival in the late 1970s, Mingus sat all through one of my performances slightly to the side of the stage, and as I came off he was applauding wildly. He was well into his illness then, for his legs were swollen and you could see the sickness in him. After shaking my hand he looked at me and said, "You know, Oscar, you're about the only pianist that I've never played with." Although I merely shrugged as I departed, I couldn't help saying to myself, "And that ain't never going to change."

CODA: INEVITABLE COMPARISONS

The world of jazz is often the victim of an unfortunate, albeit self-inflicted paradox. Nearly everyone would agree that individuality is a prerequisite in the creative arts, if not indeed a *sine qua non*; yet one of the first things that many jazz listeners and aficionados do is to draw aggressive comparisons between individual musicians. It is as if they are imprisoned by the need to judge one player against another, even though the styles at issue may be vastly different and as diverse in execution.

Such has been the case with Ray Brown and Niels Pedersen. Once Ray had left the group, people watched with interest to see who would get the nod for the spot in the Trio. Sam Jones followed Ray, but because he was a more low-key and straight-ahead player, he did not inspire the interest that Niels did when he joined. Sam had a sparse and direct approach to the instrument; in a sense, the leanness of his playing served as a spotlight to herald Niels' arrival in the Trio. For Niels was a prolific and stunningly gifted soloist: the immediate reaction to his playing was one of near-disbelief. The ease with which he executed linear unison lines with me was a particular cause of astonishment.

From the outset Niels' virtuosity as a soloist was associated with Ray Brown's, almost as if they were seen as rival contenders. In my view, people tended to forget that Ray had executed those same unison lines with the same ease during his tenure with the Trio, and also that the two men brought out different aspects of my own playing. This whole matter of comparison-and-difference is perhaps best illustrated by a record made at Montreux in 1977, where I used both Ray and Niels simultaneously, showcasing the definitive differences between these two titans' playing and their fundamental approach to the bass. For, ultimately, Ray Brown and Niels-Henning Pedersen cannot be compared: their musical and conceptual thinking differs profoundly. Ray's playing derives from a blues-soaked background, whereas Niels had a primarily classical training—although he soon immersed himself in jazz, playing with many great jazzmen early in his life, so immense was his talent. His musical pathways are more harmonically based, laced with a deep feeling for the blues culture that he later became so involved with.

Both are anticipatory time players: the big difference is that Ray's time-base is inherently part of his Negroid background and under-standing, while Niels' is rooted in both the blues format and his European, classical heritage. Ray will play something instinctively; Niels will mentally evaluate it first—which defines a major difference in their concept of time. Niels' tremendous control of the instrument serves to give him a more complex train of thought in solo, while Ray's improvisations hinge on his black heritage and huge percussively resonant sound. He is a true fundamentalist: his inclinations are essentially native, emotionally enriched by the music that he was weaned on. Niels stretches himself because of his great intuitive insight into musical form, and so responds structurally in a more individual way to the jazz phrasing of someone like myself. Ray and Niels will never think alike; nor therefore can they ever be judged by the same musical and conceptual criteria. They are, however, both geniuses endowed with awesome skills, emotional musical reaction, and limitless sensitivity.

To compare a Ferrari and a Mercedes 300SL would ultimately be futile: there is a great difference in both their design-base and their engineering sand handling. Analogously, there is, in the end, little point in trying to compare the playing of Niels-Henning Ørsted Pedersen and Raymond Matthew Brown: I leave you to enjoy them both!

56

PERSUASIVE PERCUSSION

H aving played with a large number of different rhythm sections, on record dates and especially with JATP, I find it fascinating to reflect on various percussionists' different attributes and musical approaches. They all had the same motivation and intent—to meld everything rhythmically, and also to create a properly pulsating environment to which the soloist could respond—but they varied considerably in how they went about achieving this goal. To some it was of the utmost importance to be the main cog in the rhythm section wheel; to others, it was more than enough to supply articulate time interspersed by sporadic "hits," punctuations, and bridges. Yet others envisioned themselves as an integral part of the soloist's lines, and felt religiously obliged to dart in and out of his phrases with drum comments of their own.

Louie Bellson is one of the most imposing drummers I have ever worked with. The key thing about his section playing is that he controls the situation primarily by sound. His choice of a cymbal for parts of different tunes seems to bring a new inspirational "feel" and approach to each tune. His touch is of such a sensitive character that he excels in his dynamic control of a rhythmic situation. This is one of the main reasons that he is such a joy in a big band. He has an intuitive sense of densities and colour, which, added to his awesome facility and strength, make him a commanding force in any jazz group large or small. I believe that it was these qualities that Duke Ellington so loved when Louie was in his orchestra, for if we stop and think about it, who used more colour in their music than Duke? I love to use Louie for the same reasons, and I also feel so relaxed and unworried with him running things back there.

Max Roach is another case altogether. His musical psyche is so masterly that he can seem something of a magician—implying, by figured intent, that he has played something which in reality he hasn't. He sets up this musical illusion by a series of percussive phrases that have a specific continuity to them; then he starts the phrase in question, but does not actually complete it. Were you to question various listeners, they would almost certainly say that they heard the phrase played. Max accomplishes this feat by being the complete master of musical and rhythmical shapes, something that is lacking in many of the so-called "Fusion" players. To me, it is an essential musical component: Tatum had this same ability.

Max also has a flair for "floating" —playing patterns between the soloist's phrases without interfering or disrupting them. This kind of "sensitive intrusion" is a very special gift: only a handful of percussionists can separate themselves bodily from the time in order to add another separate linear, yet rhythmic string of improvisational phrases without altogether shredding the musical fibre of the performance. Max Roach is one of these. Philly Joe Jones was another. Grady Tate is yet another.

I had heard the name Jeff Hamilton any number of times on various trips to LA, and I finally got to hear him play once he became a member of the LA 4 group, and later Ray Brown's trio. Jeff is an elite time-keeper. His playing keeps you within the tempo originally called with absolute certainty, without ever being dully metronomic; in addition, he sincerely revels in the lines that the various soloists in the group play, and does everything he can to enhance those lines and thoughts. Because of this, his contribution to any group is multi-layered; then there are his beautifully interpretive solos. He is one of the very few percussionists around who can actually portray the melodic line of a song while playing a drum solo around it, an aspect of his playing that I revel in. Jeff knows the individual sound of each of his drums, and even though they may not be tuned to the exact notes of the melody, he is able to imply that melody percussively—a remarkable feat. His solos have wonderful shapes to them; but it is his time-keeping that ultimately distinguishes him as amongst the very best. It is a great pleasure to be able to lean back on his time and lay out my solos without fear of fluctuation and uncertainty. I love Jeff Hamilton.

Connie Kay was arguably the #1 sanctified time player. His percussive style was inimitable in its "true grit," purity, and simplicity. There was a formidable calm to his work, a blemishless serenity which may reflect his West Indian heritage; certainly, the musical and almost spiritual satisfaction that such playing offers echoes the effect on me of Lester Young's expressive lines, and it is no accident that Pres chose to work with Connie whenever he could. He particularly enjoyed what he termed Connie's "Tinkty-Boom" beat on the ride cymbal, a famous time-keeping device of which Kenny Clarke was also a master. It is a shame that so many percussionists today seem to overlook this most essential characteristic of jazz playing. In my mind, he who is without it is flawed. Connie Kay was in no way flawed. On the contrary, he was indeed blessed.

Art Blakey's first name should have been "Mash." He was a loaded cylinder of raw power, ready to be unleashed at any given time. He thought power; he loved power. I even think that any moves that he chose to make were predicated on a power base. He played strictly from a total "feel" initiative. When we first met in Birdland in the early

1950s, he said to me, "They say you're the man with those powerful hands; come on and play with us." The tune that he chose was quite fast, and after the two soloists were through, it came around to me. Up to this time, the rhythm section had been steaming behind the two horns, and I assumed that it would pull back somewhat in intensity for the piano. No way! Art just leaned back a bit in order to hear the piano a little better, and continued on his way, egging me on to play more and more choruses until the intensity reached an almost unbelievable point. When we finished, he just smiled at me and, waving his finger, said "Uh huh! You tried to pull some shit on the old man!" He had to be kidding! He had called the tune, he had counted it off, and he had insisted that I keep on playing. Yet here he was, implying that I was trying to get him! No one ever got the old man. He was a power unto himself!

To talk of drummers without speaking of Daddy Jo Jones would be sacrilege. In today's world of almost brushless players, he stands there as a beacon of light from another time past. His hands were magic, his conception of swing ineffable. He had a swan-like grace as he sat behind his drums, and would in turn give them an almost majestic look. He would immediately capture your attention with that flashing broad smile, and would transfix you with the magic sweep of his hands as he switched from sticks to brushes then back to sticks, seemingly never letting go of either. He heard everything as time. A descending gliss from the saxophones, to his thinking, needed a subtle cymbal trill. A shock chord from the brass would bring on a choked cymbal, while a pushed note from a soloist would necessitate two quick closings of his hi-hat. He had it all. Finesse, time, perception, hands, you name it. Perhaps the only thing he lacked was a widespread understanding and appreciation of his awesome genius.

57

JOE PASS: GUITAR ETERNAL

Joe Pass is a great piano player! Such is the depth and tonality of his guitar playing that I often imagine him sitting at my own instrument, for he has truly managed to go "where no man has gone before" on the guitar. It is not merely his command of the instrument that entrances me: it is his complete ease, and exact knowledge of where he is going harmonically and creatively. His musicality is awesome, and he has the rare ability to gain an inside understanding of tunes, thus enabling him to give his listeners that true and unbroken flow of interpretation.

"We have a new Gerald Wilson album in along with some other goodies," said my record dealer that day back in 1962. Little did I know that I was about to be introduced to a unique guitar talent. The playing of the new LP came to an abrupt end the moment that I heard a selection titled "Teri." I replayed it over and over again, slowly ingesting its long fluid lines. I then went out and collected all of the recordings I could featuring Joe; in truth, there weren't too many at that time, but I became a Pass devotee from that moment on.

It was not until ten years later, in 1972, while I was out in LA for some record dates for Norman that I finally got to meet Joe Pass in person. A friend of mine, Eric Smith, had taken me out to dinner, and afterwards asked me if I felt like hearing some music. Off we went to a spot called Dante's in the Valley. It so happened that Joe was the featured artist that weekend, accompanied by Jim Hughart on bass. I sat enraptured by the same thoughtful fluidity that I had heard on the recordings, but it was much more intense hearing it in person. This smallish man with the devilish smile held the room full of people in his spell; after each performance he would embark on a slow, almost ponderous monologue about the tune he had just played.

Then he announced that I was in the room, and invited me up to play. He had already played a tune called *Just Friends* and he had roasted it so badly that I decided that I wanted a piece of it, so we repeated it. I laid out a four-bar intro and we were off. I knew from the moment that we hit into it that Joe and I could be ideal music partners. He took off immediately on a statement of the melody, and I proceeded to feed him harmonically with some short chopped chord sequences. As we rounded the corner of the end of the first chorus and he glanced around at me, I nodded for him to take the first taste, and he effortlessly wove in and out of my sequences with that marvellous way he has of turning phrases around and confronting you with another harmonic side that you didn't expect. He sat with his eyes closed tightly as he worked his way through his last chorus, and released it to me. I decided to continue within the musical vein that he had set out and laid out some elongated phrases to match his earlier ones.

After a few choruses of piano, I left the second eight-bar sequence for him to play. He leapt in like a missile catapulted out of its silo, answering my line with a like phrase. I increased the impetus by using the same pattern, but changed the rhythmic cadence of it. He smiled, and retorted musically by playing the same phrase in a completely different tonal base.

This is the essence of challenge playing. We were now really getting down into it: I decided to answer his tonal deviation by going his way so I laid out a corresponding atonal phrase for my reply. There was a glint in his eyes as he followed my line in his mind, and I sat there wondering if he would take the bait. The audience by this time had become aware of the musical struggle taking place on the stand, and was responding with audible gasps and groans as Joe and I took out after one another. Joe leaned backwards in his chair (a habit of his when he is really getting ready to go for it) and went off on an intricate and deep harmonic sequence with a difficulty factor of perhaps 98. A trick that I had learned from Nat Cole in playing challenges was to let it build in pressure by moving through various harmonic and tonal sequences, then, at the right moment, release it by reverting to a totally rhythmic pattern. I laid out a deep walking rhythm figure, and Joe's face broke out in laughter, accompanied by applause from the audience.

I realized that I had found a true musical relative—someone whose playing had not only intrigued me, but also inspired me so intensely that I seemed to have reached a creative level that might have gone undiscovered without him. Joe Pass helped make me a better player.

Over the years we have worked in various contexts—trio, quartet, and larger combos. Perhaps the greatest moments, though, have occurred in our duo concerts, in which we do a thing called "Dialogue," a musical discussion between the two of us. On these concerts, Joe and I never call the tunes until we hit the stage; we hope thereby to retain the freshness of improvisational creativity—although on one occasion we became almost *too* spontaneous.

It was a Royal Festival Hall concert; we had finished, and the audience insisted on more. We took several bows to no avail, so Norman suggested that we play just one more selection in order to appease the audience. I swear that I spoke to Joe Pass in the wings before returning to the stage. We had agreed to play *Tenderly* as an encore, and that I would play the first chorus. In those days, Joe would sit on a chair at my back. I strode out and played my chorus of *Tenderly*, and moved into a segue in order for Joe to pick it up. I completed it, and ... total silence. As anyone can imagine, dead time on stage is excruciating for a performer: I finally had to break convention and look behind me. To my horror, the chair was empty! I immediately struck out on the total tune; suddenly, the audience started applauding as Joe nonchalantly walked on stage and strapped on his guitar. As he started his chorus, he whispered in my ear, "I had to go to the bathroom."

58

PORGY AND BESS WITH
JOE PASS

A s will be evident by now, I have always numbered myself amongst Joe Pass' greatest admirers, and I count it a further blessing that he and I collaborated for more than seven years in a host of diverse musical enterprises.

The *Porgy And Bess* album we made in 1976 is probably the most unusual one I have ever undertaken. Any project with Joe opened up exciting possibilities, but this one was unique in that I elected to play the clavichord throughout. That decision had its roots in my *Piano Parties* series for British television; one of my guests had been the former British Prime Minister Sir Edward Heath, and he graciously agreed to play the clavichord on the programme. Listening to him conjure such a personal sound on the instrument triggered the idea that I could meld it with Joe's guitar in a stimulating way. I discussed the idea with Norman, who not only gave the go-ahead for the album but soon afterwards gifted me with a beautiful clavichord made in England, which I shall always treasure.

I had to spend some time familiarizing myself with the instrument, which requires a very different technique from the piano, but I gradually built up a rapport with it, encouraging me to think further about how to marry its plangent effects to Joe Pass' sound and ideas. Even so, I was quite apprehensive when the recording day dawned, simply because I'd never done anything quite like this before. But once I'd heard the rundown of the first tune, I knew it would work—and so did Joe and Norman. The album became a kind of landmark for us; I hope also it gave a new dimension to George Gershwin's wonderful opera.

59

HANGOUT IN JAPAN

The Quartet had just finished a concert in Matsue, and our sponsor, Mr Hata, had graciously invited us to join him for an after-concert meal. He is a lean, tall, stately looking man who almost sways with a measured rhythm as he walks. He exudes class, dressing in immaculately tailored striped suits, and always groomed to the nth degree. He is soft-spoken, but inspires respectful caution and courteous awareness in all his subordinates, and indeed in almost all the performing artists he sponsors. All, that is, but Joe Pass.

For some reason Joe had decided to make Mr Hata the object of his affections and humour on this tour. He dubbed him "Hata-san" and addressed him not unlike some very hip musician, even though Mr Hata does not speak English very well despite his endeavours at odd times to do so without an interpreter. Unperturbed, Joe at once taught him the "give me five" greeting, and proceeded good-naturedly to kid Hata-san at every available opportunity. The marvellous thing about all this was that Mr Hata seemed to enjoy it thoroughly and from the outset made Joe his night-time buddy, religiously searching him out each evening so they could launch into their kidding routines.

The rest of the group enjoyed their repartee but for the most part stayed out of it. On this particular evening, Joe's reaction to Mr Hata's dinner invitation was to jump all over him verbally, warning him not to take us out for "some jive Japanese food." Joe went on to lecture Mr Hata (who was feigning a deep interest) that, being a true connoisseur of Japanese cuisine, he did not want to be bored by the usual fare. Having established from his interpreter exactly what Joe was raving about, Mr Hata smiled and attempted to reassure him that the meal would definitely not be boring. This didn't silence Joe, however: he continued to badger Mr Hata even as we walked towards the stage for the second half of the concert, insisting that he wanted something different and exciting. Little did he know how much Mr Hata would take him at his word!

Once we'd finished the concert and the autograph signing, we all bundled into the cars and headed off in anticipation of this vaunted meal. We ended up in a small seafood house that any gastronomically aspiring tourist would have had trouble finding, let alone wandering into by chance. It was on a tiny street where the postman probably knew every house, establishment, and occupant by name. The staff, who I'm certain knew nothing about us, were courteous and enthralled by this unusual group of clients.

Mr Hata positioned himself next to Joe, who continued his talk about what a seasoned veteran he was on the varied foods of Japan. Next to Joe sat Martin Drew, my British percussionist at the time, while next to Martin sat John Heard (my bassist), then Ron Goedvolk (my road manager) and myself.* The opening part of the meal consisted of the normal miniature Japanese salad and assorted taste tempters made up of various kinds of miniature sea life. This was followed in turn by some utterly fantastic Sashimi, made of fresh salmon beautifully marbled. The next course was some marvellously cooked Crab and Salmon Teriyaki, amongst other exotic goodies too hard to describe here. As we enjoyed each course, Mr Hata, being the gracious host that he was, would insist that we be informed about exactly what the various dishes were and their origins. Throughout all this, Joe continued his

---

*It is particularly significant that Martin sat next to Joe. He had a very restricted diet the whole time he was on the road with me: whenever we ate out together, the scenario never varied. He would stare relentlessly at the menu for moments on end, and then "Do you have any smoked salmon?" would be his first query, regardless whether we were in the depths of the African veldt or the Galapagos Islands. Depending on the response, he would then ask for some corned beef, and if he came up empty, his next choice would be steak, and failing that, roast chicken. Upon having made that selection, he would then ask for some bitter lemon or anything that resembled it. His final request would be an earnest plea to one of the staff members as they passed by: "Bread!" he would beg. "Bread and lots of Buttah!!"

banter about "When are we going to get into the real Japanese cuisine, the real soulful dishes?" Mr Hata merely laughed and attempted to soothe Joe by assuring him that there was more to come. Meanwhile, Joe's comrade-in-arms, Martin, had settled for some sort of chicken that the chef graciously and hurriedly cooked up for him. This, along with some bread and orange juice, served to satisfy Martin's needs.

Everything seemed to be proceeding well when suddenly, we were all served almost simultaneously with a deep crock-like disc that seemed to be harbouring some form of forbidding sea life within its confines. The amiable conversation ceased, and everyone became engrossed in finding out exactly what was hiding in its darkened enclosure. I have seldom found myself leery of food served to me by anyone, so quite understandably, when even I momentarily seemed stymied by this ominous dish, Joe jumped on me. "All right, OP!" he shouted from his end of the food bar. "What the hell are you going to do with this? You're the great connoisseur of Japanese food: let me see you eat that!" I had very serious doubts about this unknown body before me, but I knew that I was on the hook with Joe and thought I had better find out exactly what the hell it was!

"It" appeared to be in some sort of shell, not unlike a snail only ten times as large. It was solid and well-immersed in some form of darkened juice or sauce. I attempted to pry it out of its protective shell with a two-pronged fork supplied to us, but this was not going to be easy. "Jesus!" screamed Joe, "I think they served us one of those land turtles! Are you kidding, Hata-san?" he inquired, "I can't eat this! It's alive!" The best that Martin Drew could come up with was, "Jesus, Joe! I think you ate that last week!" My road manager found himself speechless, and contented himself with staring down at it and shaking his head as if to admonish it for its ugliness. I at last decided to make the first move, so with a concerted effort, I energetically pried my Alien from its shell. This mass of dark, unknown, and almost shapeless "thing" hung from my chopsticks as if daring me to put it in my mouth. I inwardly had fears of immediate termination, but somehow I managed to pop it into my mouth. Because of its formidable size, it was almost impossible to chew. I slowly forced a look of surprise and then allowed a look of enjoyment to creep over my face, and began nodding my assent as to its good taste.

"Don't go for it," admonished Joe, "He'd die just to get us to eat this crap! Don't go for it!" I meanwhile managed somehow to chew it into enough of a submissive state to swallow it, and that *really* conjured up visions of Matsue General's intensive care unit. Joe came over to me and said in a confidential tone, "Level with me: it's lousy, isn't it?" I reassured him that it wasn't as bad as he thought and told him that I rather enjoyed the taste. "I can't eat that crap," he insisted. "I gotta family at home."

Mr Hata, meanwhile, was suffering from complete seizure and constrictions from laughing. He had lost all his composure and was reduced to hiding his face in his handkerchief to dry his tears from his unrestrained laughter. Ron Goedvolk was still staring and shaking his head in disbelief. Martin Drew sat there with his face screwed up, and intermittently gave the "creature" the occasional glance of astonishment.

For Joe Pass the moment of truth had arrived. He finally had to bow to pressure from Mr Hata, who chided him about his remarks on the subject of "true" Japanese food. At long last, he reluctantly picked up the thing on his fork, and heaving a protestational sigh, shoved it into his mouth. His face immediately became contorted like a man who had just swallowed the proverbial dose of hemlock. His hands went to his throat and he heaved out of his seat and began weaving about the premises, not unlike a bull in its last throes. He finally swallowed it and after heaving a few times, screamed "Shit! I just ate my shoe!" This set us all off onto uncontrollable gales of laughter. Meanwhile, during the fray, Ron Goedvolk had decided to emulate Joe and had quickly tossed his into his mouth. When the laughter finally subsided, there was Ron still sitting at the bar, relentlessly chewing away at his new found adversary: the giant Japanese Snail!

60

DUKE ELLINGTON:
MONARCH SUPREME

E dward Kennedy Ellington was a man of immense elegance, but to summarize him as such would be a grotesque devaluation of what he was and what he achieved. Yes, his gait and carriage typified self-confidence and control, yet he took that elegance to an entirely different level. It permeated every situation in which he found himself, regardless of context or geography, so that whatever space he occupied at a particular moment became part of his kingdom. Moreover, he exuded an effervescence that warmed everyone in his presence. His speech was as neat, measured, and distinctive in its cadences as were his compositions, and he had the knack of making you part of his intimate entourage just by addressing you.

I first got to meet Duke after I had performed at the Montreal Forum (home of the history-making Montreal Canadiens ice-hockey team). He embraced and lauded me in his customarily regal manner, but I didn't see him again for quite a while, apart from catching a couple of Canadian gigs that he played. I was too reticent to approach him then: I was in awe of him as a musical icon, and I feared he wouldn't even remember me. However, when I made my Carnegie Hall debut some years later under Norman's auspices, I found out that Duke was appearing at the Bop City club that same evening, and rushed over there as soon as that JATP concert was over. Apparently someone told him I was in the audience, whereupon he stopped his set, announced my presence, welcomed me to New York, and then insisted that I come up and play a tune with his orchestra! I was a pack of nerves, and on reaching the stage asked him which tune he was going to call. He gave me that impish, sly gaze, and replied that he was confident I could handle anything he chose. Luckily for me, he decided on *"A" Train*, and kicked off the band on a tune I knew well. As would be confirmed on so many future occasions, Duke Ellington was a magnanimous man.

He was also a man of contradictions. Often he seemed unable to do or say things in a simple, ordinary way; yet for all its sophistication his work was distinguished for its harmonic precision and melodic simplicity. And although his memory was astounding—including the facility for turning past impressions into musical evocations both durable and unique—he sometimes lost track of what he had done. I particularly recall an incident at the end of a JATP tour we were on together. We were sitting backstage waiting for them to finish loading the bus when he asked me to play something for him on the piano that had not yet been wheeled away. I chose one of my favourite Ellington pieces, *Lady Of The Lavender Mist*, and as I played Duke came over, his head cocked on one side; with an almost mystified look on his face he asked me what I was playing. Astonished, I replied, "Duke, that's one of your tunes!" He remained puzzled, saying he still didn't know what it was called. I thought he might be putting me on, so repeated, almost caustically, "It's one of yours: *Lady Of The Lavender Mist!*"

At that point, he sat beside me on the bench and asked me to play it again, and listened with intense concentration. When I'd finished, I kidded him once again about not remembering one of his songs, and a beautiful one too. He countered by saying that he was only concerned with what he was going to compose in the future, rather than dwell on what he had written in the past.

That was a key indication of what made Ellington's mind work and why he achieved so much. His music centred on anticipation and new experience: never content with what he had accomplished yesterday, his paramount concern was always about what he would achieve tomorrow.

61

THE TRUMPET KINGS

Over the years I've had the great pleasure of accompanying a host of jazz soloists; nevertheless, the series that came to be known as *Oscar Peterson Meets The Trumpet Kings* was a very special event for me. This was the latest of Norman's "musical visions," and it was daringly innovative. Usually, sessions of this type would, to all intents and purposes, be jam sessions, with the rhythm section feeding the trumpet soloists and providing helpful ideas and suggestions along the way. But Norman wanted something fresher and more adventurous—something that might plumb the true soul of all the players concerned. Accordingly, he envisaged this series of recordings as one-on-one sessions, and made it known to all the participants that he would not accept any musical fairgrounding: he wanted only the truth.

The field was as heavy as it was broad: Norman had chosen Dizzy Gillespie, Roy Eldridge, Clark Terry, Harry Edison, and Jon Faddis. Since I was going to be the sole supplier of the harmonic and rhythmic background, I started thinking hard about how I was going to go about things. For doing a couple of tunes during a date with that kind of musical sparseness is one thing; to devote an entire album to it is quite another. And I was going to do five! In the end I abandoned any attempt at forward planning, deciding that the best way to operate was to go into the studio with no preconceived ideas and to take each session as it came, as freely and spontaneously as possible.

Dizzy was the first person up; we both happened to be in London during November 1974, and the session took place there and then. I saw Dizzy prior to the date, and he immediately launched into playful threats about what he was going to do to me. When I arrived at the studio that afternoon, Dizzy was already there, supine on the floor and feigning sleep. When I called his name he got up, pretending to be bleary-eyed and not knowing where he was; when I asked what he was doing lying on the floor, he said he'd slept there overnight in order to be in proper shape to waste me musically. Amidst all the laughter and kibbitzing around, I sensed a degree of tension between us, and deduced that Diz was in fact quite apprehensive about how I was going to go about things. I think he was expecting a gladiatorial set-to, each going after the other improvisationally; this notion was fuelled by Carmen McRae who happened to drop by to "watch the blood-letting."

In truth, my plans were very much otherwise: I was looking to give him all the loving musical support I could in order to relieve the tension and make the session a genuinely communal affair. And as soon as Norman called us to order and taping began, I felt Dizzy relax. There was no aggression, no rivalry: I felt only a great warmth and admiration for what Dizzy was doing that day, and would not have dreamed of cutting a path through any of his beautiful lines. The session came to a conclusion, and Dizzy and I embraced each other with deep mutual satisfaction. I think Norman had expected much more in the way of sparks and confrontation from us and he said so; however, we must have been on the right track, for the album won a Grammy and was also nominated Record of the Year in the *Down Beat* Critics' Poll.

Like Dizzy, Roy Eldridge seemed at first to imagine that the purpose of these sessions was primarily confrontational. Speedy came over before the first tune and said something like, "Let's not be hitting the racetrack until I get my chops together."

I assured him that it was not part of my intent to get after him, that I saw it as essentially his date, with me on hand to supply whatever he needed musically. In general, record dates work best if you discuss the repertoire with the other artists and allow them their say on the matter; this leads to a melding of ideas which invariably produces a much more satisfying performance. I adopted this approach with Roy, suggesting tunes in a tentative way rather than as a statement of fact, running over some of them with him just to get their general feel. This seemed to please him; more importantly, it involved him fully, and he began to come up with ideas about how we should approach various tunes. This in turn pleased me no end: we had reached a common ground and were comfortable—and no one swings harder than Speedy when he's comfortable.

Roy's roots were, of course, in the early Swing era, and I tried to fashion my accompaniment accordingly. He relished my old-style piano background, which comprises a bass note in the left hand alternating with a chord in the right hand. Not many players nowadays can handle that kind of background, but to Speedy it was a piece of cake. He waltzed through the tunes with ease, serenely inspired by being able to play exactly the way he felt like playing that day, and the session was a highly fruitful one.

Clark Terry fears no one musically. He is an absolute master of his instrument and has a control matched by very few. Once again, I sensed a certain "cutting contest" apprehension initially, but surmounted this by putting the session in Clark's lap and my playing at his disposal. I'd done this with Roy, but here I was additionally motivated by knowing that you don't play games on a date with Bogen, as we affectionately call Clark. I learned this a long time ago from listening to a set of challenges between him and Gerry Mulligan. Clark was with Gerry's big band at the time, and the leader made the mistake of pressing Clark improvisationally, only to be cut with imperious disdain.

Such homework is essential in the kind of situation I found myself in with the trumpet kings. I knew that it would be madness to challenge Clark to a linear confrontation unless I had everything together, for I knew that he certainly would. However, not a hint of such head-to-head battling occurred. Clark fell into his natural creative groove, and was not only vigorously creative as a soloist but also sassed back at me on his horn as we exchanged lines, and the album was as pleasing and successful in its way as the one with Speedy.

Harry Edison came in and laid it out cold turkey: "Don't try laying any of your intricate shit on me, OP, 'cos it ain't gonna work." With that, Sweets sat down and made the most relaxed of the five albums. Harry used you as part of his instrument, laying down the type of phrases which told you to supply the underpad for his rug with no ifs, ands, or buts. He was entirely his own man musically, and once he was finished with an idea, he simply stopped, leaving you to supply whatever finishing touches were needed to round off the statement. His conception of time was subtly laid-back, and you had to bear this fully in mind as you walked along with him; he dictated the improvisational pace, and it was fatal to pre-think him.

All that may sound like enslavement, but it isn't: he was merely supplying a format that enabled you to become his musical ally and fellow-explorer. Once you recognized that and went along with it, a beautiful musical experience resulted; that was certainly the case with this Harry "Sweets" Edison album, so far as I was concerned.

Jon Faddis arrived early at the studio, and I have to say that his selection for this series was also somewhat premature. On this particular album I felt I was in a total quandary, because the distinction between musical procedure and musical truth arose again and again. I was obliged to rein myself in not only during our dialogues and gambits, but even on the background movements that I supplied behind his solos. I don't believe he was quite ready for the album at that time; however, now that he has found himself and secured his musical footing, I would very much like to try it again.

All in all I feel very proud of this series of albums. Norman's vision worked, and some magnificent music ensued. Most important of all, each trumpet king reigned with dignity and integrity: there were no lies.

62

CLARK TERRY: UNSUNG HERO

In my view, people have not recognized the true genius of Clark Terry. For some strange reason, he has not received the mass recognition that he so richly deserves. Clark has a combination of gifts that most players would give their eye-teeth for. He not only has an enviably high level of performance but also a staggering consistency. His sound on the horn is matchless, and his command of the instrument is numbing. Add, to all this, melodically fruitful ideas, and garnish with unique breathing and range, and you have a fair recipe for instant genius.

I have always been intrigued with Clark: he has a special appeal for rhythm-section players. As accompanists we all listen hard when playing for any soloist; however, the greatest compliment that I can bestow on a player is when I find myself absorbed in his playing as a *listener* rather than as an accompanist. The two contexts are entirely separate. When playing as an accompanist, one has to act musically as a mélange of personalities—as the soloist's censor, critic, musical midwife, even therapist. To fulfill these duties requires a concentrated listening or monitoring process which can only be achieved with years of training. In addition, one has to remain as close as possible in order to select the necessary background phrases and fills to feed the soloist. *This* listening technique is very different from "ordinary" listening. Clark's immense improvisational scope tends to overtake players and, somehow, force them to be total listeners. I had to teach myself to overcome this tendency and learn to cope with Clark as I did with other soloists.

I first got to know Clark back in the late 1950s, when he was in Bill Basie's new Kansas City Five with Buddy DeFranco. I stood transfixed as Bogen (our nickname for him) motored through the various tunes

Basie called from the repertoire. There seemed to be no end to his storehouse of ideas as he soloed, and his rich sound permeated the Brass Rail room as if it were part of the structure.

I grew to love and respect Clark as a man. I found him mildly introverted and someone who recoiled from personal upheaval and turmoil whenever he encountered them. This is not to say that Clark was not a realist, but any kind of controversy seemed to upset him inwardly to a considerable extent. We toured regularly, and recorded on numerous occasions. Whenever we came in contact with one another, it always seemed to be an important moment for both of us. We have both had marital upsets in our lives, and there is an unstated *sympatico* between us on that account as well as through musical admiration.

At one time in the mid-1970s, while preparing for a small tour of Europe, I mentioned to Norman that I hadn't seen Clark for what seemed like a long spell, or Zoot Sims either. Norman casually said, "Well, if you really want to see them and also play with them, why not take them with you to Europe?" After asking him to help me arrange this, I hung up the phone and eagerly awaited his return call telling me that it could be done. Fortunately, both Clark and Scooter (as I affectionately called Zoot) were both able and happy to make the tour with us.

The tour lasted only for a few weeks but I must say that I cannot remember having enjoyed a tour, both musically and personally, as much as this one, and I still regret that not one of the concerts was recorded. It was a perfect mix. The Trio at that time comprised Niels-Henning on bass and Martin Drew on drums; Clark and Zoot were perfectly suited to each other, having played together in other groups such as Gerry Mulligan's. Every night represented walking into heaven, musically speaking: I have always loved Zoot Sims' playing, and Clark is the epitome of trumpet artistry.

There were also many moments of laughter and camaraderie. Zoot bowled us over one night in a restaurant when he related the story about his standing in front of Storyville in Boston one night waiting for a cab to take him somewhere. It was raining and cabs were at a premium. Suddenly out of nowhere this empty cab swooped up to the curb in front of him and stopped. He couldn't believe his luck. As he was about to grab the empty cab before someone else did, he insists that the door opened and George Wein (the noted jazz impresario) got out. With that story, the after-concert dinner came to an immediate hysterical end with us all holding our sides in uncontrollable laughter, while Zoot sat there with that well-known inscrutable look on his face, as if to say, "What are you laughing at? It's true."

Much of this musical and personal happiness was due to Clark Terry. He has a way when he steps to the mike of carrying you with him to wherever he wants to go. We found that he was best showcased by giving him the first three or four choruses, using what we call "strollers," when the rhythm section lays out, allowing just the bass player to "walk" behind the soloist. To my mind this approach brings out the best melodic properties of Clark Terry's playing: because of his beautiful sound and marvellously interpretative and lyrical mind, he can carry the listener to exhilarating heights during this prelude to full group interplay. I have not only felt it myself but have watched the intensity grow in the other members of the rhythm section, the anticipation swelling as Clark heaped chorus upon chorus until, finally, we would burst into action, providing an even deeper rhythmic feel and richer harmonic path.

Clark Terry has everything—amazing technique, astonishing breath control, prodigious imagination, and one of the most versatile (and lovely) sounds jazz has ever known. He takes no prisoners on a bandstand, and is held in awe by his peers. Hopefully, sooner or later, the music world as a whole will learn to appreciate him properly.

63

RONNIE SCOTT: "THE REV"

During my tours of Europe I sat in at Ronnie Scott's on many occasions, and also played a number of seasons there. This gave the group the chance to enjoy London for more than the couple of days our concert appearances afforded; in addition, I enjoyed the club, and I really enjoyed Ronnie. His laconic, almost warped sense of humour greatly appealed to me, and I would sit and listen to his comic routines over and over, even though I'd heard most of the gags before. He bore an uncanny resemblance to a minister from my childhood days whom I loved: the Reverend Charlie Combe. I told Ronnie of this, and almost at once nicknamed him "The Rev."

One night on one of my early visits, Ronnie's group was appearing opposite mine, and were coming to the end of their last set, which would, of course, be followed by ours. He was using a piano-less band at the time, and as I passed the bandstand on the way to my dressing-room, I thought it might be fun to join them on a fast bebop tune that they were burning up very impressively. Ronnie, in mid-solo, swivelled round when he heard the piano comping behind him, then roared into a few more choruses. The tune finished and I went backstage to prepare for my set; there was a knock on my door and Rev stuck his head in. With that famous straight face he said, "Thanks a lot, Oscar; we'll let you know," and vanished. He'd got me, and I swore I'd be avenged; it took a long time, but it was worth the wait!

Over a year later, during another season at the club, I arrived early to find the place buzzing with excitement. When I asked what the upheaval was about, I was told that the Secret Service had been in, for Princess Margaret was due to come in for one of my shows. Things proceeded normally for a while; Ronnie went on for his group's first set, and then towards the end of it the Princess arrived with her entourage of guests, increasing the already formidable crush—as on every night during that engagement, the club was wall-to-wall-people-packed. My first set, introduced as usual by Rev, went very well: we were received so exuberantly that we went slightly over our allotted time. As usual I came off wringing wet, and retired to my dressing-room to freshen up.

A little while later there was a knock at the door and Rev entered in an unusually tentative manner. "Oscar ..." he began hesitantly. "Er ... Princess Margaret is in the room, as you must know, and she has requested that you join her at her table. On the other hand, she has indicated that if you prefer it, she will come back and speak to you here."

Gleefully I realized my moment had come. If there's nothing else left in the world to bank on, one thing remains certain: the English love their royalty and are loyal to and proud of them—"Rev" Ronnie Scott included. I turned to him with the grimmest facial expression I could muster and shouted, "What!! What did you say?" He stumbled backwards for a moment in surprise and began to repeat his remark.

"I was saying that Princess Margaret is in the house and ..."

"Let me tell you something, Ronnie," I cut him off, spitting out the words through gritted teeth, "in case you don't know it, I happen to be Canadian, not British. I don't want to hear anything about your Princess Margaret Rose or anyone else in your Royal family, and furthermore, not only am I not going out there to speak to them, I don't on any account want her or any members of her party back here in my dressing-room!"

It was as if I had shot him. He put his hand to his head as if wounded, staggered back a few steps, and opened the door, muttering in incredulous panic, "Oh my God, what do I do now?" I fell on the sofa, convulsed with laughter—and with triumph at having brought off my return-ploy. When I got myself together, I opened the door, still grim-faced; there was Ronnie, his normally rosy complexion now ashen as he discussed this ghastly crisis with a couple of members of his group. As I walked towards him he semi-recoiled, as if expecting another verbal battering. I pointed my finger at him and said, "Now we're even for your 'We'll let you know, Oscar' gag, Rev!"

He wiped his brow and started to laugh. The stress drained from him as he took me by the arm, saying only, "Come on, let's go say hello to the Princess."

64

MR. PRETTY: ALAN CLAIRE

One of the guests on my BBC-TV series was a leprechaun-like man with a shy demeanour and impish grin and laugh: Alan Claire. I've always loved Alan and held him in great esteem as a pianist: he ought to be a conservatory-professor to whom all aspiring pianists should go in order to learn the correct reading of a ballad. That is an art in itself, and Alan's perception of harmonic resolution and his delicate understanding of hue and texture make him a master.

His knowledge of the great composers is enviable: he is detailedly aware of compositions most players have never heard, let alone the public. As a result, he sees and hears things in a song's structure that pass unnoticed by virtually everyone. "Look at the way Strayhorn changed this cadence the second time around, Oscar," he would say as we talked about repertoire and tunes that intrigued us. "Marvellous, marvellous; and listen to this sequence here—the way he pretends to use that same harmonic direction but suddenly goes another way altogether. Incredible!" Billy Strayhorn is the kind of quietly sensitive genius who particularly appeals to players like Alan: indeed, he relishes Strayhorn's every chord and sequence much as a gourmand revels in the rich essence of a pâté choude. Alan is not a "steamer" like Horace Silver, Wynton Kelly, or Hampton Hawes. He is an "insider," a player that looks to plumb the very vitals of a song and whose deepest pleasure is to savour the lushness of beautiful harmonies and subtle lines.

I spent a memorable night in 1982 with Alan and the late Pat Smythe. After a fair time comparing musical notes and experiences, Alan played me two recently re-discovered Cole Porter tunes, *I Could Kick Myself* and *When A Woman's In Love*, fashioning each one with his inimitable craftsmanship. Pat played beautifully too; I had been an admirer of his ever since my days at Ronnie Scott's, when Pat was often in the group that played opposite us. Once he knocked diffidently on my dressing-room door to compliment me on the set I'd just finished, and that same sensitivity characterized his playing. He too was an introspective, thoughtful "ballad searcher," intent on bringing out all the nuances of a given piece.

Like Pat, Alan too is gone now, and I feel not just great sadness at the demise of two close personal friends: I know how much we need pianists like them—not just in jazz, but in music as a whole. Their intelligent, inquiring approach gives access to the subtle crevices and almost invisible paths that are a feature of the finest composers' terrain, and their lyrically interpretative voices give a dimension to pianism that we can ill-afford to lose.

65

FOUR VIGNETTES

JAMES MASON

I don't know why, but I am always amazed when distinguished members of other professions turn out to be fans of jazz. In awe of what they do, I never imagine that they could be admirers of our own work. Silly, really, but the feeling has never really left me.

The night I looked down into the audience and saw James Mason tapping his foot religiously to Roy Eldridge's solo took me aback: I hadn't expected to play to Field Marshall Erwin Rommel! He came backstage afterwards, and I told him how pleased but surprised I was to see him there; he gave that little half-smile of his and replied, "I enjoyed it so much that you"ll probably see a lot of me from now on."

I thought no more about it for a while, for the Trio was preparing to play a season at Campbell's in London, Ontario. This was a restaurant owned chiefly by the Campbell brothers—Ted, the businessman, and Chris, the frustrated musician who lived to play piano and revelled in what I was doing. They had taken the adventurous step of instigating a live music policy in the dining-room, a brave move, for London at the time was a wealthy, pretty, but quiet-to-the-point-of-sleepiness town. Its conservatism had tended to mean that anyone seeking cultural stimulation simply went to Toronto—though that city's archaic drinking laws and the transient nature of its attractions (individual stars and artistic companies then rarely played a season in Canada but merely passed through) hardly made it a major attraction.

Anyway, our sojourn was a great success, and amongst other things helped cement my friendship with Ruth Robinson and her London family. They were regular patrons during our stay, and adopted Ray and me as if we were two long-lost members of their clan. One evening, Ruth's husband, George, came over to me during the intermission and announced excitedly that James Mason had called, wanting to catch our last set. After he'd done so, we sat and talked until about 3.30 a.m. It became evident that James had a deep-rooted and highly know-ledgeable love of jazz; in addition, he was fascinating about its parallels to acting. He spoke of the importance of improvisation to both art forms, and even wondered if there could ever be a totally improvised stage production with different actors, musicians, and thematic strands every night, each group operating on an absolutely impromptu basis.

I will never forget my times with Jimmy. On his return to Los Angeles, when he found out that I would be there for some record dates, he threw a wonderful party in my honour. He was a marvellous friend whom I never got to see often enough and whose memory I treasure.

JONATHAN WINTERS

The London House, Chicago: the Trio is having a good night. Enter Jonathan Winters, the famed comic. The management give him the seat immediately to the right of the keyboard, which means he sits there three or four feet from my face. He's quiet enough for most of the set, and applauds enthusiastically along with everyone else.

Suddenly, during what we are figuring will be the penultimate tune, he begins muttering under his breath so that only the Trio can hear. We start picking up things like "Play it, you horny devils!" and "God love ya, God love ya!" These are followed by the famous African animal sounds that only he can make. I look around at Ray: he's slowly collapsing over his bass, and Ed Thigpen is laughing uncontrollably, tears in his eyes. I know when I'm beaten: this is no contest, and we quit the stage, leaving everyone else in the room to wonder just what calamity it was that befell us.

CLINT EASTWOOD

It took only one glance, as I gazed around the jazz club in San Francisco where I was performing, to recognize that lean countenance with the piercing eyes that I had seen many times before on movie screens. Clint Eastwood! Sitting here in a jazz club? No guns, no horse, no cowboy outfit; just a look of intense interest from those same eyes, his head slightly cocked to one side as he listened to Niels-Henning's bass solo.

I have always been an admirer of Clint Eastwood, and this turned out to be the first of many occasions when we met at a jazz event. I found him to be a man of quiet depths and great musical appreciation, and my admiration became even greater when I learned of his determination to make a full-length feature film out of Charlie Parker's story. *Bird* was a tremendous undertaking—and a very brave one, for he risked offending many of the jazz people whom I know he loves and admires.

My most recent recollection of him is a perfect cameo. I had just finished a concert at the Hollywood Bowl, and there was that same lean face towering above the heads of fans who had come to express their appreciation.

"Clint!" I called over them.

"How are you doing, Maestro?" he queried with that familiar half-smile.

We talked for a while about the concert, the pressure of playing it, and part of the repertoire, and as suddenly as he had shown up, he vanished.

BACKUP FRIENDS

The people around us in the early stages were able to watch the development of the Trio into a truly formidable group; but they also shared in that development and, indeed, helped to effect it. For creating music is not just an aesthetic and technical pursuit: there is a profound human side to it too, and many loved and valued friends took over where the performing end stopped—people like Morey and Daisy Kessler, Eric and Lucille Smith, Frank and Ruby Bell. They may all be unknown names to readers of this book, but they were intensely important to the three of us. We were nourished by their generosity and caring concern which went beyond music: they worried about us as men thrust into a swirling world of incessant airports, hotels, train stations, restaurants, and the like.

They went out of their way to make us feel special and needed as friends. Morey and Daisy would open their home to us whenever we were in town, throwing parties galore to which our musical colleagues were always invited, and sharing countless Sunday afternoons with us, just sitting around yakking and listening to music. Eric and Lucille did the same kind of thing on many occasions, while Eric and Morey would at times show up in the most unlikely places imaginable. I remember checking into a hotel in Rome and glancing at the lobby area, only to be saluted by Eric raising his glass at the bar. On another trip we landed in Israel, and both Eric and Morey were atop the spectators' balcony, waving flags at us! And Frank and Ruby Bell gave us the kind of moral support, trust, and belief in us that meant a very great deal (and still does).

Throughout my years at the London House in Chicago, I became good friends with a lady who, from time to time, would enchant us as the alternating performer in the room. Her name: Audrey Morris. Vocalist nonpareil in my book. Without a doubt, Audrey had the deepest repertoire of great songs of any vocalist of her kind.

We became friends at once. Audrey's husband, Stuart Genovese, a local saxophonist and flutist, also became a close friend. During our time off I would nightly sit in the room to listen to her interpretation of some of the great songs of our time, many of them not always familiar to her listening public. Unfortunately, the London House was not at this time known for the quiet attention one would think its public would give to the performing artist. The Trio often had to curtail its set until it became quiet; however, Audrey had no such problems, invariably gaining the room's full and rapt attention. She has a way of reading a lyric that rivets her listeners. I learned new respect for various ballads that she sang because of her lyrical interpretations.

My friendship with Audrey and Stuart deepened, the eventual result being that I ended up as a houseguest at their home whenever I returned to Chicago to perform. My previous nickname for her, "Odd Job," gave way therefore to "My Landlady." We spent countless hours, on my nights off, staying up until daybreak listening to various records that we loved. Stuart was a music teacher at the time at a school in Chicago, and managed to survive through these late-hour music sessions as best he could, being due in school in the mornings. Not only did Audrey become "my landlady": they became my family in Chicago.

There were others, too, who reached out to us and made road-life warmer and easier. Sammy Berger, the sad-faced owner of the Town Tavern in Toronto, who allowed himself to be made the butt of many of our gags; Ed Sarkesian and his lovely wife, Laurie, who owned the Rouge Lounge in Dearborn, Michigan, who appointed themselves our guardians whenever we played Detroit; and Clarence Baker of Baker's Keyboard Lounge, who—unlike so many night-club owners—would dedicatedly listen to our every note from his usual spot at the end of the bar.

I often look at young groups today and wonder whether they get the same kind of support and, if so, where they find it. If they are as lucky as we were, then they're unusually blessed.

66

PAUL DE MARKY'S
CHOPIN-LIKE EGGS

I have always wondered how pianists endeavour to play Chopin's Minute Waltz within the confines of its title. When I started to learn it, I attempted always to keep its performance time to the 60 seconds the title demands. It wasn't until I came under the tutelage of Mr de Marky that it took on a special meaning for me.

I had just managed to escape injury from a lesson with him and we were sitting conversing when he suddenly arose from his chair (gods are the only people that arise from anywhere or anything), sat at the piano, and started playing the *Minute Waltz*. As he played, he started to slowly rock back and forth as he sometimes did, telling me that nearly all his students had struggled to keep within one minute, and that some even resorted to practising with a stop-watch.

"I used to make use of this tune daily for the preparation of my breakfast," he said. As I looked at him quizzically, he explained, "I found that if I put my eggs on to boil and played the Waltz twice at exactly the proper rate, my eggs came out perfectly done. I have never had a problem playing the *Minute Waltz* simply because I love eggs much too much!"

Some people have the uncanny ability to find a solution for almost any problem. Paul de Marky certainly had it.

67

BENNY GREEN: CRITIC SUPREME

Throughout my musical career I have been reviewed by pundits all over the world, and my work has prompted many articles and critiques. I have to say that for the most part I have ignored much of what has about written about me, primarily because the authors knew little about the culture they were claiming to evaluate. At times, too, I thought their involvement with jazz to be not only ignorant but also less than honest. There are exceptions, though, and Benny Green was an outstanding one.

Before I even met him, I was an ardent admirer of his work, whether it be concert reviews or analysis of recordings. His sheer knowledge of music was authoritative enough, but his staunch and committed love of jazz impressed me even more; in addition, I marvelled at his command of the English language and his ability to harness that to his intense appreciation of jazz and its players. He was unfailingly honest: if he didn't enjoy something, he said so. That didn't prevent him from forming friendships with most jazz musicians, for they too acknowledged his wit, knowledge, and dedication. He once told me that these warm relationships were sometimes problematic when he had to review a performance that did not register with him. In addition, he was always sadly sympathetic to players who had fallen prey to narcotics. It pained him deeply to witness their struggles, empathizing with their attempts to get their true talent to transcend their addiction.

Never unnecessarily caustic, he was nevertheless definitively reliable in his musical evaluation. I count myself fortunate to have been his friend, and also to have won such praise from him for my records and concerts. The jazz world has lost a great and gifted voice that communicated to everyone with a feeling for the music.

68

"OSCAR'S PIANO PARTIES"

In 1976 a special "first" took place in my career: I was contracted by the BBC in London to host my own television series. True, I had already done a series for BCTV Vancouver, featuring guests such as Carmen McRae, Dizzy Gillespie, and many other JATP alumni, but this BBC show was to be very different, casting me in the role of chat-show host. Norman was very stimulated by this imaginative advance from just another modern music show with intermittent patter, and at one of the pre-show meetings he went on to suggest: "We should invite some guests who are not involved in the music business as such but who are nevertheless interesting and musical people, and see how OP handles it. After all, if we're to show there is another dimension to him, let's at least give him some challenges."

Benny Green had been brought in as a consultant for the series, at Norman's suggestion, for his skills as an author and his ability to provide background on our guests through his profound knowledge of the music world would prove invaluable. He agreed with Norman's conception of the shows, adding that the programs should provide a happy mélange of dialogue with the guests and whatever musical performances were needed and appropriate. He was sure that our jazz guests would be more likely to open up to me than to anyone not in the profession, and he also assured me that in the case of other visitors, with whose life and work I was less familiar, he would be on hand with all the necessary backup and information.

I later learned that the idea of the program was conceived as a result of some remarks I made in a 1974 *Omnibus* show with André Previn. I had referred then to the now-defunct "Piano Parties," in which any number of pianists would get together in a pre-determined place and have it out musically. This phrase had stuck in my new producer's mind, and he hit upon the idea of a show primarily featuring pianists as my guests, or people associated with the instrument.

I was of course nervous at the start of the very first show; but on the whole my main emotion was curiosity rather than anxiety—the desire to find out, before and on air, as much as I could about the various guests. The show ran for three series, and the guest list became ever-more diversified, partly because we started to run out of pianists, and partly because we made a determined attempt to mine as broad a musical seam as we could. Many interviews remain clearly etched on my mind, for all kinds of reasons; but if I had to nominate my absolute favourite, it would be the one with Bill Basie.

I remember as if it were this afternoon his arriving in the studio. He was already growing fragile, and we had a wheelchair waiting for him at the artists' entrance. It was an honour to wheel him into the studio, especially as there was nothing frail about his spirit or his humour: he was in very capricious mood and after me from the word go—they should have had the cameras rolling!

He was anxious about the stiffness creeping through his hands. "I hope I don't embarrass you today," he confided, "but the old fingers haven't been operating too well recently. I just don't seem to be able to feel the board the way I like, and sometimes my hands feel cold, so cold." I took his hands in mine and massaged them, saying that I was sure he'd be in his usual fine fettle. Suddenly his mood changed: he pulled his hands away, looked at me with that famous stare, and said, "Knowing you and your gorilla self, that ain't gonna stop you from washing me away! So why are you sitting here trying to con me into believing you're going to take pity on me?" He gave one of his famous sardonic laughs and went on, "I know that ain't going to stop you from doing what you got to do as soon as you get to that monster over there." More laughter. "That's the way you got to be, see, that's the way you just got to be."

All this was very funny, but it wasn't true: I felt nothing but love and comradeship for this idol and mentor of mine. Because of my own arthritis I could identify closely with this pain and frustration: that creeping growth of stiffness is the ailment pianists fear most of all. As we rehearsed, however, I sensed a certain relaxation flowing into Bill's playing. He seemed to enjoy the Bosendorfer that we had brought in for him, and in between tunes chatted to me about the instrument and the nature of true piano talent. "People don't realize what it takes to be able to play one of these babies here," he remarked. "Each one has its own personality and speaks to you with its own voice." He ran his fingers lovingly across the keys as he sat contemplating this behemoth sprawled before him. "It's really something when you can have a great conversation with a sweetie like this lady," he mused. "That's why I love you and Art. Neither one of you was afraid of playing these instruments. It takes the likes of you two to show people what these pianos really sound like."

We had some very tender moments together that afternoon before the taping took place. I shall always remember how he sat there at the piano—this beautiful man, slightly hunched, at last beginning to show the wear and tear of nearly 50 years on the road (or perhaps I had refused to recognize the signs until now).

"You know, P," he said softly, "it just hurts so much sometimes not to be able to play things I used to do practically in my sleep before. Because the hands won't do it anymore. Sometimes I wake up at night and this hand here hurts so bad you wouldn't believe it." He gingerly held his right hand between the palm and thumb of his left hand and massaged it tentatively, as if afraid of hurting it in the process. I sympathized deeply, and wondered how many of his admirers knew what this man was putting himself through every night when he climbed onto the bandstand and fronted the orchestra. Yet I knew that, even though he could no longer possibly play the things he wanted to play the way he wanted to play them, just his presence would make the evening a success; for with all due respect to the band as it now attempts to carry on without him, under Frank Foster's leadership, there is no Basie band without Bill Basie.

BASIE

"Hmmmmm" is not a word that signifies consent
Nor is it necessarily an indication of dissent
But when used by a person as part of their norm
It then takes on quite a varied form.

It can say that a person is vaguely in touch
But, then again, that isn't saying very much
For it can say that they knew all of this up front
Or, it simply could have been a satisfied grunt.

Bill Basie was a master of this type of fare
For with craft and cunning he'd set out his snare
Which entailed looking sleepy, most unaware
Of the quite varied scenes taking place in his lair.

He'd sit and he'd nod, all the while playing possum
While waiting for the intrigue to thicken and blossom
Into a full-grown scene, which would come to a halt
As one eye opened slowly, not unlike a bank vault.

"Say listen here!" would for the most part be the phrase
That he would use quite effectively to cut through the haze
Of argument and upheaval that pervaded the room,
And yet it still didn't seem to matter exactly whom
It was directed at, for each separate person on his own
Would fall to silence, or at least lower his tone
As each one waited almost apprehensively
While inwardly wondering, "Is he looking at me?"

It was then that Bill would lay out his trap
Sitting back while waiting for someone to snap
At the bait, which would usually not take too long
And would generally end in causing the throng
Of onlookers to jump on this hapless prey
As Bill would rise slowly, shake his head and walk away.

When we played as a team, his attitude didn't differ
If anything at all, his resolve became stiffer.
His approach was direct, his intent resolute,
And he'd size up each tune in a manner most astute.

He'd start in a way one could deem apologetic
Yet back in his mind, the ending was prophetic.
For he knew how to play me as he twisted and turned,
And he'd throw off my cadences like a lover long spurned.

The pattern continued this way for some time
Until just by chance, I happened to climb
On top of a phrase he had left undone
So I finished it off with a true Basie run.

He looked up startled, and was visibly shaken
As though he could not believe I had taken
A page from the book of the master and so
Had dealt him a cruel and unexpected blow.

I seized on the moment and spewed out a line
That dipsied and doodled and was difficult to define
He hesitated a moment, then replied in kind
With the simplest of ideas that came to his mind.
I countered once more with a true Basie invention
Hoping for an end to this musical contention
But, squaring his shoulders as if calling on pride,
He uttered a growl and lit into some stride.

This was Bill Basie at his pianistic best
And as those of us fortunate to be present can attest
This man who saw humour in his own special way
Had a feel for the piano that even to this day
Remains unchallenged and, I happily say,
It will forever and ever remain that way.

Edward Heath seemed quite on edge when he came into the studio to guest on one of the shows. I had the feeling that he didn't quite know what was expected of him, but his apprehension seemed to evaporate as I asked him about his interests in music and how he was able to meld them into the busy schedule of his political life. He talked of the impending vote concerning Britain's joining the European Common Market, and how he used music as a soothing balm for his anguish on the night of the Parliamentary division. He had played some pieces on his clavichord, he said, and proceeded to play a selection on that instrument in the studio; the highly introspective and delicately personal sound he elicited held everyone in rapt attention. I was so moved by its sound that in the following week I visited an instrument maker in London and had them make one for me. Norman got wind of this and persuaded the manufacturer to let him buy it for me as a gift. I repaid him in some small way, I hope, with the Pablo album discussed in "Porgy And Bess" (see Chapter 58).

The show I am perhaps most proud of is the one where Ella was my guest. I've seen Fitz interviewed on many occasions, and hardly ever has the interviewer been able to penetrate that invisible barrier that surrounds her. I didn't want to add myself to that list, and decided on a cagily off-hand strategy. As soon as she arrived, I assumed a carefree "We'll get it done somehow" attitude, and did not press for the strict rehearsals that normally attend any show involving musical numbers. As a result, Ella perhaps felt relaxed and able to let her guard down; in any event the show was a huge success. I don't think I've seen Ella emote more than she did on that taping. We talked of her earlier years in the most natural fashion possible; she even volunteered information about herself I hadn't delved for. In addition, she was in such fantastic vocal form that I felt moved to interrupt her and pay her a verbal and musical tribute on the spot. This buoyed her spirits further and she responded with even greater effervescence. Norman and Benny Green were ecstatic when the show was over, as was I: we all felt we had inspired and witnessed an exquisite cameo—a perfect microcosm of Ella's greatness as an artist and a person.

One person who turned out to be a revelation was Twiggy. I had no particular pre-show thoughts: to be frank, I had no idea how I was going to communicate with her in any meaningful way, our worlds being so far apart. But she was a complete joy: her grace and warmth charmed us all, and again I felt compelled to pay her compliments on the show.

Twiggy brought a new dimension to the series; others brought that special something too. The late Anthony Burgess' marvellous eccentricity and formidable intellect, not to mention his beautiful composition then being featured at the Mermaid Theatre; John Williams' honesty as he confessed to Joe Pass that he felt almost helpless playing jazz; the unexpected honour of being told by Richard Rodney Bennett of his labours at the piano to learn my version of *All The Things You Are*. And behind it all, the comfort afforded by Benny and Norman, and the freedom of being able to present my group in whatever setting I chose throughout the series.

These series formed an unforgettable part of my musical life, and they occasioned only one regret. The Canadian networks purchased all kinds of shows from various countries around the world, but not once was any of these BBC programs picked to be shown on Canadian television. That made me wonder; and it still hurts.

69

THE HANDS HASSLE

F rom the moment that I commenced learning the piano, I became aware of the hassle incurred by all pianistic beginners in their attempt to figure out which finger should be where at what time. This dilemma continued to bug me until I was approximately nine or ten years of age and rapidly approaching total frustration with the instrument. From time to time I would sit to the piano and attempt to play various figures and lines, only to end up either running out of fingers or being so totally mixed up digitally that I had no idea as to what to play next. This wasn't a problem with any of the classical pieces that I was playing at that time, because the correct fingering was usually indicated within the manuscript. The problem seemed to arise when I tried to improvise something that popped into my mind, and find the way to deliver my musical idea via the keyboard. I finally decided to analyse what it was that was causing this block.

The first discovery I made had virtually no connection to digital placement, but concerned the almost fathomless relationship between the initial thought process or conception of a line and its finalization on the keyboard itself. The first realization I had was almost a subconscious reaction, while turning out to be musically realistic when finally thought out all the way. I found that the improvisational mechanism of the mind had to be set in motion far enough in front of the physical delivery (via the fingers in this case) to allow the player to quickly formulate the digital pattern needed in order to make a musical passage take place. This element varies from player to player dependent on their musical virtuosity and facility on the instrument.

Identifying the problem was one thing; solving it was another. Taking a good look at my hands on the keyboard, I began studying what seemed to be normal movement in the delivery of a phrase. I became aware that many players seemed to initiate a lot of their descending lines and runs off of the thumb, index, and second fingers. I imitated some of these things that I had heard up to that time and came to the conclusion that this form of technique in the right hand was incorrect and detrimental to my own selfish linear needs. I reasoned that it was a much more natural and controllable method to descend on the keyboard off the back of the right hand, for various reasons. First and foremost, I felt that the third and fourth fingers were the weakest digits and that by utilizing this method, I would immediately begin strengthening these fingers. Second, the natural impetus or flow of movement in the right hand in the descending direction using this technique creates a much more normal ergonomic movement from a physical viewpoint. One thing became very noticeable to me from the outset: I tended to have much better control of individual articulation within my descending runs using this type of fingering. Last and far from least, it became amazingly easy to reverse direction and start back up the keyboard without the slightest hesitation: because I had started on the back end of the hand, it was a totally normal motion to start upwards on the keyboard utilizing the thumb and index finger in their most natural motion. Once again, I found that articulation became much easier and decisive using this method.

I now tackled the problem of matching the left hand to the motion of the right hand in doubling the right-hand lines. Once more as I studied the natural motions of my left hand on the piano, I found that my tendencies differed from the system being taught to most pianists.

If we place both hands on the piano reasonably close together, we immediately become aware that the thumbs of both hands sit within reasonable proximity to one another. I repudiated that system and started making myself believe that the fourth or little finger on my left hand was the thumb of my left hand, and should instinctively behave in the same manner as the thumb of my right hand in the playing of these phrases. I tried to explain this on several occasions to various players in my earlier years with little success; for some reason, people cannot visualize that although their hands look digitally different left to right, at various times it becomes mandatory for us to see them as two right hands. I proceeded to break myself of this one-handed disability by singing phrases out loud, then playing them with the right hand, then with the same line repeated by the left hand (badly at first), and then finally by both hands.

I made a couple of further discoveries. The first was that in descending the keyboard with the right hand (starting with the third and fourth fingers), the same thinking applied when ascending the keyboard with the left hand. The second was that articulation is of the utmost importance in the playing of double lines. I have only heard one pianist (Phineas Newborn) who had the double octaves mastered to the point where all his lines were totally convincing in their articulation. Another discovery in linear playing and invention pertains to the harmonic clusters (from the left hand) that most pianists seem to play from. In my opinion the harmonic clusters laid down in the left hand prior to the delivery of any linear patterns in the right hand are of the utmost importance from a voicing standpoint. It is these clusters that primarily govern the linear patterns and direction that the right hand will take, so that in essence we are virtually playing from left to right when using this method.

For years people have remarked about the ease with which I seem to play the piano and the abundance of technique that they seem to think I have. In addressing this aspect of my playing, I must say that it is my firm belief that the best pianists in jazz conquered most of the pitfalls inherent in playing the instrument very early in their studies in order to be able to go on with their inventions, and thus express themselves without stuttering and stammering all over the keyboard while leaving the majority of the intended invention to the imagination of the listener. Just as I believe that speech should come from the mouth of the orator and influence the mind of the listener, I also believe that in the case of a performing pianist, the musical invention should come from the emotional and intellectual conception of the mind and heart and should be coupled with the best possible digital capability in order to enunciate their ideas for the listener. I have heard pianists who are basically sparse players by intention (Bill Basie and Jimmy Jones, for example), but I have also heard pianists who are barren players due to their ineptitude on the instrument. I decided a long time ago not to be a member of the latter club.

70

PREPARATION FOR SOLO
PIANO PERFORMANCE

During the years of my various trios and quartets, I was so engrossed in the group format that I never gave any detailed thought to solo piano. It was a medium that I happened to enjoy, and occasionally I would drop in the odd solo tune to serve as a contrast to the rhythmic pulsation of the Trio. Such selections were usually fairly short; they required some preparation, but certainly not the tremendous amount of work that is required to perform a complete evening of solo piano.

I went merrily along my way until Norman asked me why I didn't go out on stage and perform the first part of the set by myself. "Get away from the rigidity and uniformity of the Trio and give yourself some breathing room. You never know just what you might come up with." Anyone who knows Norman Granz will be aware that he is forever seeking challenges for the musicians around him. On record dates he would come into the studio after we had finished a take that we were satisfied with and would say something like, "Well, that's fine if you don't want to come up with something new or fresh and you're content to keep on operating in the same old comfortable way. If you're interested in trying something a little different, what about ___," and he would name some tune that the group had almost certainly never played. This kind of reasoning lay behind his remarks about solo piano, and he continued to harangue me about it.

In contrast to Norman's friendly carping, it came as a surprise one night on a tour with Duke Ellington when Duke sidled up to me in the wings and started complimenting me on the virtuosity of my trio. He paused for a moment, then said, "You know, Maestro, that your piano virtuosity is comparable to fine caviar. However, have you ever stopped to think that some people like to get down to the essence of the caviar and consequently enjoy it without the eggs and the onions." With that he patted me on the shoulder and walked away. His remark shook me so much that I didn't even stop to wonder if there had been any collusion between Duke and Norman; later on, knowing my friend Smedley as I do, it struck me as obvious that they had talked about this while I was on stage.

Norman continued goading me until we were on tour in Europe and also due to perform several concerts in the Beirut area. "If you're worried about tearing it in front of your peers at home, why not try it out while we're in Lebanon? In fact, I think that's the way I'll set it up," said Norman with his usual decisive assurance, and was off as if he were going to make the public announcement at that very moment. I decided that it was something I should at least try; if it failed or did not come off the way I intended, I could always return to the trio format and be quite happy. I shared the bill that night with Lady Ella and I have to confess to extreme trepidation before performing. When finished, I felt that I had broken the ice from a performing standpoint, but in no way was I pleased with the musical tonality of it. My playing was constricted, apprehensive, and sluggish, and for a very simple reason: I had not prepared properly for it. To add to my dissatisfaction, I felt untold shame whenever people congratulated me that night because to my mind I had failed miserably. I resolved to return to the same boyhood attitudes that I had when initially studying the piano, and thus rid myself of the inadequacies that my solo playing was suffering from.

The first adjustment I had to make is, I think, a most interesting one. For years I had operated as a highly successful jazz pianist, but *in a group*; I was sure of myself, but much of this assurance derived from my confident reliance on the other members. I realized that I could no longer be so comfortably reliant, and needed to resume the kind of inquisitiveness usually found only in students and listeners.

Having been a teacher myself for some time, working with professional players, I was aware that often their biggest obstacle to progress was an inability to look at their weaknesses objectively, but that their momentum rose tremendously once they overcame that problem, allowing them to make remarkable strides in their musical self-improvement. Now *I* needed to do the same thing; and once I did so, I found I could delve into my solo work's shortcomings and work on them productively.

The first major target I addressed was the ability to accompany myself comfortably, with no impression of tension or unevenness. I remembered one night playing a concert in Carmel using just Ray Brown, without a drummer or guitarist. During the performance (which was shortly after the Beirut concert), I launched into some solo things. After I finished the concert, Ray queried me about what direction I was going in musically and if I intended to continue doing solo concerts. I said yes; he thought for a few moments then said, "You know, it takes awhile before someone can really attain that feeling of ease in the left hand because it has to be so smooth that it's totally believable." It goes without saying that I respect Ray's opinion in most things, and I got the message, resolving to make sure that he would soon be entirely comfortable with that aspect of my playing.

The first thing that I had to attack was the intended bass movement supplied by the left hand. Not only were the initial bass notes important, but even more important was the harmonic cluster that is the upper half of the bass pattern. This may sound very easy to bring about but, believe me, it is not! It meant untold hours—and I mean hours—of repeating these patterns in various sequences until they became second nature to me. Slowly but surely I began to see and hear the development taking place. Once this growth was initiated, I then set to playing lines and runs against these patterns and listened dedicatedly to make certain that there was truth and conviction in all of my right-hand meandering. At any point that I sensed tension or dishevelment in my right-hand lines, I would stop immediately and, instead of looking at what I'd played with my right hand, would investigate what bass note I had played as a root, and what harmonic cluster I had used to answer it. (It's worth repeating that, contrary to many players' belief, the fundamental harmonic direction and melodic ideas emanate from the expressions of the left hand. In other words, the question is asked by the left hand and the answer is delivered—at length if need be—by the right hand.)

The next step of the procedure is to figure out how to terminate right-hand ideas in the neatest fashion possible: I couldn't afford them to sound choked off or wandering into a never-never land that had no relation to what the left hand was doing. To effect this, I played through different selections, being careful at all times to be aware of where the right hand wanted to terminate its line, and whereabouts the left hand would be both rhythmically and harmonically. I would then stop and replay the improvised line as best I could and attempt to integrate or tuck the very end of the line into the phraseology and rhythmic intent of the left hand, sometimes allowing the left hand actually to finish the line for me.

This is something that has to be done individually by each player in order to retain his or her own temperament and creative impetus, rather than sounding like a rehash of previous players. I found also that the double lines referred to in the previous chapter became most useful in solo playing when used as dividers or connectors between harmonic segments of a tune.

The next area of solo pianism that I worked on was one that I feel many young jazz pianists neglect terribly: the "inner voicings" and their movement. By this I mean that each pianist should have such a thorough harmonic understanding of what *all* the harmonic voices within chord structures are doing, at all times, that they are able to realize that many marvellous things can be accomplished within a "harmonic sequence" that is being held, rather than repositioning the whole harmonic structure. The fact that we retain the outer voices while moving the textures within the structure creates a rich and interesting harmonic mosaic that can lead to more interesting lines being played off them by the right hand. This takes a great deal of investigatory practice, and also enormous patience. At the outset, it is perhaps best for the player to return to the four-part chord and work from there, until the harmonic growth that this method will develop ultimately materializes.

Lastly, I did a total re-evaluation of my pedalling techniques that I had learned in classical music, combined with those I was using for jazz playing, in order to extend the harmonic sounds that I would now need for solo playing. Incidentally, this is something that I think all pianists should do from time to time, since there is a temptation to take this particular technique for granted.

After spending a long time on all these aspects, I began employing them in performance, and found to my pleasure that solo piano had become just as natural as playing trios. Looking back, however, I can say that my greatest moment of satisfaction occurred some two years later, during an engagement at the Blue Note in New York with Ray, Joe Pass, and Martin Drew. We had been steaming through a set when I suddenly decided it was ballad time and instinctively moved into a chorus of *Old Folks* out of tempo. In then establishing the in-tempo section, I went into the classic stride left-hand patterns that not only complement the right-hand inventions but are indeed their essential foundation. I was taking the tune at a medium, loping pace when all at once Ray Brown burst out: "Yeah, shit! Ain't but a few guys know how to do that. It takes a long time to get that natural lope. Go on, don't stop now!"

With all due and grateful respect to the ovations I've received for my solo concerts, this was uniquely gratifying. Like a number of bassists, Ray is a capable pianist, and a total devotee of that kind of solo piano; moreover, I sensed that he had not intended to speak those thoughts out loud but was so overwhelmed that he had voiced them unconsciously—an involuntary tribute that made my pride and delight all the more intense.

Playing solo piano, like any other form of development, takes patient research; sensitive awareness of harmonic structures and movement; the ability to integrate both hands in a believable and innovative manner; a means of tying all this together with immaculate time and intelligent pedalling; and finally, total control of articulation and touch. Then, and only then, can one truthfully say, "I played solo piano."

71

PIANOS: MY LIFELONG FRIENDS

I t was immense to me, and seemed to be forever smiling to itself, as if it knew that I would be forever addicted to it. It was certainly not the most elegant instrument that I would ever play; nevertheless, it was the family's prime musical mainstay and all of us kids were required to get involved with it sooner or later. I marvelled at it from the outset; in particular, I wondered why it could sound so good when some people sat to it, and so horrible when others did.

One of the earliest things I noticed about most of the players that came through our house was the way they belaboured the sustain pedal. They seemed to imagine that its use would automatically straighten out their directionless meanderings and bad chords. Naturally, this didn't happen, but they sailed on undeterred—perhaps hoping to effect Roy Eldridge's motto: "Straight ahead, and strive for tone"! Another inane habit concerned the determined use of (fairly terrible) runs whenever the player became harmonically unsure or out of his depth: he'd reach for these runs as a kind of comforter, no matter what the harmonic or melodic needs of the piece were at the time. And these performances weren't just disagreeable to listen to: I used to think they were hurting my piano. (I feel the same way today when I run into a bad lounge player.)

The family's first piano was an upright with an almost forbiddingly dark hue. It served all the Peterson clan from Fred to May, the baby of the family, and stayed with us until I was about 15. At that juncture I won the *Ken Sobel Amateur Show*, which entailed a cash prize. It was decided to spend most of it on a new piano. We couldn't afford a brand-new one, only a second-hand job; but comparing it to the state our grand old lady was now in, it was new in every way that mattered, and it gave us joyous service for many years.

Early on I imagined that all the pianos I would play would be uprights. Not so! One day I was sent to the auditorium of my High School on an errand, and there stood a beautiful baby grand piano. I couldn't resist it: the errand vanished from my mind as I sat down to play this exquisite discovery. It was fantastic! The sound from its horizontal strings was a revelation after the vertical, harp-like strings I was used to: it seemed to reach inside me and grab at the pit of my stomach. The bell-like treble end particularly intrigued me, as I tried out numerous harmonic clusters in my left hand against moving phrases in the upper register, and I came away determined that one day one of these musical marvels would be mine. My own grand piano.

I took the first steps towards this goal when I purchased for $50 what was then known as a "square grand"—a flat, rectangular instrument whose keyboard was set off to the left rather than in the centre. It had been the property of the old Coliseum in Montreal, where I had played on occasion, so when I got word that the management was looking to sell it just to be rid of it, I was confident that my bid would be looked on favourably. The deal concluded, the piano was installed in my apartment in Montreal North. I no longer remember the name of the make, but I do recall that it was battered and beaten, that there were strings missing, that the remaining ivories were turning yellow, and that it was loaded with dust. Yet when I sat down to it that first afternoon it tried its very best to sing for me. Some of the bass strings rattled from improper alignment, the pedal carriage was loose, and the casing was scratched and scarred. All this meant nothing to me: it was mine, and since I could sense what a grand lady she must have been once upon a time, I vowed to bring her back to life.

I had just started my first trio and was not too flush with money, so I had to wait about six months before I could afford a technician to come in and appraise the instrument. It turned out a very bad day. My wife and I had spent hours cleaning the piano up, and the technician meticulously looked it over for a good half-hour before turning to me with the words, "Oscar, if this is a whim of yours or the lack of something better to do, that's one thing; but if you're seriously thinking of having me try to put this into a really playable condition, forget it. As your friend I wouldn't allow you to waste your time and money: it's not worth it."

I felt as if I'd been hit in the stomach with a sledgehammer. But after he left I sat and played that piano for about half an hour, and it felt good. He had attempted to tune it as best he could, and indeed had done a fine job considering how long it had sat neglected in that building; but it wasn't anywhere close to the A440 that I was accustomed to hearing. It clanked and twanged; yet sometimes, when I managed to touch the parts where she wasn't ailing, she once again became a grand old lady for a couple of bars.

There is one piano that I could never play: it belonged to my teacher, Paul de Marky. During my lessons I would sit and listen to him play that instrument and draw from it huge sonorous shapes that hung in the air like huge Chinese lanterns hanging in the night. Mr de Marky knew his lady, and would shamelessly make love to her in my presence, while I sat consumed with jealousy. She would never play that way for me, I thought, and that was true: she treated me as a good friend, but never as a lover. She loved Paul de Marky.

I was determined, before I invested in my first proper grand piano, to master the techniques of pedalling. I would watch and listen to Paul de Marky as he used them to enhance the wonders he could entice with his hands. A tinge of sustain here; there a phrase played with the sostenuto pedal subtly introduced. He would produce a myriad of notes in the treble clef over a chord held by that mysterious middle pedal while the left hand answered statements already articulated by the right hand. The only other pianist I know who has a similar mastery of pedalling is a gentleman who honoured me by guesting on one of my London TV shows, and with whom I later shared a privileged half-hour on a show for CBC—the late Jorge Bolet. Some people passed him off as a "Romantic," understanding neither the word nor his playing: his huge hands, emotional depth, and sensitive feet combined in passionate conversation with his instrument. Certainly, I learned more from those two pianists about the vital artistry of pedalling than from anyone else.

As my concert, radio, and television engagements increased, I had the opportunity of playing more and more grand pianos. For a while I experienced considerable difficulty coping with the different "feel" of these curved giants, and I found it valuable to look at the way other pianists I admired went about it. The producer of my first series with CBC, Rusty Davis, was a classically trained virtuoso whom I respected highly, not least for his adoration of Tatum and his ability to execute, note-perfect, various recorded Arthur T solos. He was a great help to me, both in what he showed me and in his warm encouragement: he repeatedly told me how intimidated my playing made him feel, and that it was only a matter of time before I solved the "grand mystery."

Rusty was involved in one of the funnier episodes during that CBC series. I had frittered away too much time at home, and all at once realized I had cut it fine if I was to arrive for the broadcast on time. The taxi driver did all he could to help, and we were making good progress when we suddenly got rear-ended by another cab. Irate and frustrated, my cabby jumped out to have a few words with his colleague; I sat biting my nails and looking at the time. Finally I got out and pleaded with the driver to continue his run. Off we went again, but traffic was heavy and in next to no time it was 8.30 and we were still a good five minutes from the studio. I groaned: I had never missed an engagement, let alone a broadcast. In my anguish I had the driver tune in to the local radio station, only to hear the announcer saying "... and enjoy 15 minutes of scintillating piano music from Montreal's own Oscar Peterson."

I gasped, traumatized. Then the announcer went on to say, in his customarily jaunty manner, that I was going to take the audience through a version of *Exactly Like You* that I had just conjured up. I heard an intro and then the opening chorus: it may not have been exactly the way I would have approached it, but it was very close. By this time we had reached the station and I careened into the lobby, up the elevator, and into the studio—to find an absorbed Rusty Davis, head down, eyes closed, cavorting through *Exactly Like You*. Sensing me, he opened his eyes and motioned with his head for me to get over to the piano. I slipped out of my raincoat and tiptoed to the piano bench, at which point Rusty hit a harmonic cluster with his left hand and launched into one of his ascending Tatum runs that culminates in a dazzling cascade down the keyboard. As he started, he slid off the stool to the right, and by the time he had commenced the descending finale, had moved on to the stool from the left; I finished Rusty's figure and went on to complete what was now *his* version of *Exactly Like You*.

When the show was over, Rusty came over with his almost comic-book walk, cigarette in hand, head cocked back, laughing and said, "I told you we'd make the greatest piano team in the world!" Amidst my relieved laughter I was stunned by this man's versatility, and somehow the episode increased my determination to learn the personality and temperament of each instrument that I came across. Pianos are closely akin to humans: they need a lot of understanding and a clear appreciation of their strengths and weaknesses.

Once I was with JATP my income both increased and stabilized, and I decided to make the big move. I called up Eaton's store in Montreal, informed them I wanted to purchase a grand, and made an appointment for a week later.

When I arrived, the manager said, "Mr Peterson, I told Steinway of your desire to buy a grand piano, and they asked if you would allow Mr Steinway himself to send you the piano he'd like you to have." I stood transfixed for a minute or two; then recovering my composure, I replied that of course I would wait till Mr Steinway had made his choice. About two and a half months later, Eaton's moved this glorious grand piano into my Montreal home. I was almost afraid to touch it—for two reasons: the fear of the unknown, and what I would say and do if I didn't like his choice. I deliberated for a few moments; then sat cautiously down and began to play one of my favourite ballads.

From the first few notes I knew that this Steinway was meant to be mine. The luminosity and richness of its tone was something I had never experienced before, and even in her new state she responded immediately to my light pedal suggestions. It occurred to me—sentimentally, perhaps—that the spirit of that ill old lady from the Coliseum had been reborn in this beautiful new ebonized and gold body. In any event, this new lady—reborn or not—taught me a lot about love; I felt totally confident with her and began to feel that at last I could develop into a player of importance.

In the mid-1960s I met a friend of Ray Brown's from Cincinnati, John Breen. He was a gifted scientist and we quickly became close; whenever the Trio visited Cincinnati, John would have us by his house (his wife Martha was a sensational cook!), and he and we would spend the evening needling each other about our pet fad, hi-fi equipment. I knew he was with the Baldwin company, and he would constantly wonder aloud why I wasn't playing a "good" instrument like a Baldwin. Gradually the mutual kidding grew into something more.

For it so happened that I was now experiencing problems with Steinway: for reasons I never quite got to the bottom of, there were occasions when pianos that should have been provided for concerts failed to materialize. And when Baldwin introduced their new SD-10 concert grand, John insisted that I at least try one. I agreed, though not too enthusiastically: hitherto I had found Baldwin pianos tonally cold.

To my delighted amazement, the SD-10 responded with unusual tonal warmth; the striking action had also been vastly improved. As a result of this revelation, I became a Baldwin artist—an arrangement that lasted for over a decade.

I ran across a lot of European pianos in my JATP years. The two I remember best were a lovely instrument in Denmark made by Hornung and Mueller, and the Viennese-made Bosendorfer. Sadly, the former piano did not prosper in the Canadian atmosphere, refusing to retain its tuning, and despite its lovely feel, I was forced to part with it. But the Bosendorfer was something else—especially the one I encountered in the late 1970s.

This piano was called "The Imperial." At the end of the set I walked off during the applause and went straight over to Norman Granz in the wings, frightening him out of his wits by screaming, "God-dammit, Norman, where did that box come from?! I gotta have one of those!" He looked at me with his normal calm and replied, "If you like it so much, why don't you go back out there and play a couple of encores on it?"

I duly complied: in fact, we played at least four encores, for I couldn't get enough of that piano and, that night at least, could do no wrong on it. My bassist Niels Pedersen's only remark was, "Damn! Why did they have to send you such a good piano? Now we're paying for it, because you're never going to leave!"

He was almost right. Normally, unless it's absolutely necessary (sound-checks in a studio, for example), I seldom go out on stage before a concert. Checking out the piano might lead to preconditioned ideas, and they can in turn interfere with the creative process so essential to a successful jazz concert. Niels and Ray Brown, good pianists in their own rights, would usually try out the instrument while setting up their bass on the stage, and report their findings to me. I'd pooh-pooh these, turning them into jokes in order to keep a clear mind for the approaching tasks. By the same token, I would hardly ever return to play after a concert was over, feeling that I had said all I had to say during the concert. But that night in Vienna was different. I stalled around until the audience had gone, then virtually sprinted back to the piano to bask once more in its incredible tonal quality.

Norman was so overwhelmed by my initial reaction that he had forgotten to tell me that a representative from the Bosendorfer company had been in attendance to find out whether I had enjoyed the instrument they'd provided. They subsequently contacted me, asking me to choose the piano of my liking the next time I was in Vienna—very much an offer I could not refuse!

On my next visit to Vienna I was picked up at the hotel and driven to what had been an old monastery in the heart of the city. Our party was given a tour of the whole manufacturing process, from where the piano is born to where it comes to completion. The craftsmen were totally dedicated to their different tasks, and we were duly impressed by their meticulous workmanship: no cut corners, no feeling of haste or careless substitution; just the quiet and enveloping ambience of people working together to produce the finest product they could.

Finally we were ushered into the piano salon. This was it! Before me stood an array of 15 to 20 grands—and I mean grands! They were akin to a herd of beautiful Arabian horses, waiting to be chosen for their unique individual qualities. I was told to start trying them, one after the other, in order to isolate my final preference. Almost overcome with excitement, I began my analysis. It was truly unbelievable: instrument after instrument offered itself to me in an unselfish, fulfilling way, each one speaking with its own special voice. I glanced at Norman with what must have been a look of bewilderment and awe, for he strolled over and said quietly, "Take your time, OP: you don't even have to make your choice today. If you can't decide, you can easily come back after the tour and choose then. In fact," he continued, "that might be an easier way to do it, without pressing yourself now."

At this point Niels Pedersen, who had been trying out the various instruments, whispered in my ear, "They're all great, but there's a real beauty farther down the line." I asked him not to tip his hand as to which one he meant, and continued my trials.

Suddenly I touched this one instrument, and it spoke to me in a way

I'd never heard before: the sound seemed to run through my fingers, straight up my arms, and into my whole body. "This is mine!" I shouted in excitement. "This is the one!"

The Bosendorfer gentlemen, Dr Radler and Mr Lemell, exchanged glances, which meant nothing to me at the time, and politely suggested I complete my appraisal of the remainder. As a courtesy to them, I did; however, I kept returning to that same instrument, and finally they let me stay there. I tried out various selections on her, and she faithfully reproduced each idea with a matchless, wondrous clarity of tone. Niels and Norman were as entranced by her crystalline spell as I was, and I turned to Dr Radler and Mr Lemell with the plea, "I love this one."

It was then that they explained their earlier, knowing nods. "We are so pleased, Mr Peterson," Mr Lemell said. "You see, you've picked out the one piano that has a special and entirely new technology to it. The clarity and beauty of sound are the results of long and complex research, and you have made us very happy in proving that technology a success." I must confess that at that moment I wasn't too interested in the technical background: all I knew was that I had found the most beautiful instrument I had ever played, and I wanted to make her mine. My heart pounded within me as they agreed on my choice and that, after final checks and tunings, they would ship it to me in Toronto.

Sometime after it had arrived and I had spent some time alone with my lady, I decided to throw a party at my home in her honour. I invited some of my special friends to welcome a new citizen to Canada, and after a few drinks someone asked where this immigrant was and when were they going to get to meet him or her. I ushered them all downstairs into the music-room and stood like a proud father as they all gasped in astonishment at this ten-foot wonder sitting quietly at one end. When everyone was comfortably settled I played a few ballads to show off my lady. A close and dear friend, Morey Kessler, stood in the middle of the room with his back to the piano next to another dear friend, Ruby Bell. When I'd finished playing I walked over to them, aware of the silence that had descended onto the room. Ruby turned to me, her face bathed in tears. "Oscar, my love, she's just gorgeous." Morey turned too, and he also had a tear in his eye as he said, "OP, you've moved me many times in the past, but I think that's the most moving moment musically I've ever known." And everyone else said similar things.

Reluctantly, I had to rid myself of my Steinway: I didn't have room for two pianos at the time. Even there, however, I had good fortune, for a very dear friend, Gary Gross, insisted that I sell the Steinway to him. He would have it no other way, and it was gratifying to know that it was going from my loving hands to his. It was even more gratifying to know that I had found that very special musical lady from whom I would never be divorced.

72

THE ELECTRONIC REVOLUTION

W hen in the 1970s I purchased my first electronic instrument I knew I was entering a new musical world. I felt no trepidation about what I was getting into, only excitement. The make was an ARP 2600; it was monophonic and had no keyboard. (I suppose if you'd told any of my musical colleagues that Oscar had bought an instrument devoid of a keyboard, they'd have laughed you out of the building!) The salesman who assisted me was curious about how I planned to use it; I replied, "I'm going back to the hotel to make some music."

Little did I know what was in store for me! I beetled back to the hotel and had an early dinner in order to devote the rest of the evening to my new toy. I set it up (I assumed correctly) with the patch chords, and turned up the volume. I was met with the weirdest howling sound imaginable. I quickly shut it down and started over. To cut a long and tedious evening short, I got nowhere, and after midnight gave it up as a bad job. Next day I sought urgent help and instruction from a friend, and eventually I teased some sounds from the unit. This eased my frustration; my education in the electronic musical world had truly begun.

Once the word was out that I was even vaguely interested in electronic keyboards, various manufacturers were after me; I was inundated by calls—and by instruments. This was the worst thing that could have happened: I was suddenly immersed in a sea of instruction manuals, few of which were properly written, and I struggled vainly to keep up with all this wondrous new hardware. Moreover, I hadn't yet acquired a firm-enough understanding of the basic principles of synthesis, and I soon found myself confused and lost. I thought there must be something wrong with me, and indeed there was: electronic burn-out. I decided to back off for a while; I left the instruments alone and read no more manuals. This proved a wise move; after a few weeks away from the mad swirl of vcos, vcfs, and vcas, my curiosity about electronics became refreshed, and I resolved to try again. This renewed interest was nourished by two important developments.

The first was an ad that intrigued me no end: "This is the only synthesizer you'll ever need." Given the raft of instruments now available, I was sceptical, but nevertheless placed a call to New England Digital and spoke to Brad Naples, then the sales manager and now the company's President. He was very surprised that I had called, but within a week appeared at my home, along with an engineer and the instrument in question, the Synclavier.

That was the second development: I fell totally in love with this instrument. We spent two and a half marvellous days exploring it: I could hardly believe the all-encompassing facilities it offered. I could record instantly on it, with 16 tracks available; it solved all kinds of metronomic problems that were beyond my or anyone else's capacity; and it had the most wonderfully ethereal sound that I'd ever heard. It was a joy to compose on, printing out the music as I wrote and responding with lightning speed to my detailed editing.

Such a banquet was almost too much, but it convinced me that instruments of this kind would change the complexion of the musical world in a decisive way. Soon afterwards I met Taro Kakehashi of Roland, a giant contributor to the field of electronic music who has subsequently become a dear friend. He taught me a great deal more about synthesizers, and I also admired him for two splendidly complementary qualities: he was a perfectionist who constantly sought to improve and enhance his sophisticated instruments, but he was also enormously generous to younger and poorer musicians who could not yet afford his hi-tech wonders—loaning them out and offering wisely productive advice.

Electronic music is here to stay. I would be appalled if anyone thought it would render the great "acoustic" instruments obsolete: I could never imagine a musical world where there was not a central and honoured place for the piano, the violin, the flute, and so on. But I cannot agree with those musicians who feel that synthesizers have no place in our music world; nor do I feel threatened by them, as some seem to be.

It would be idle for me to pretend that the advent of so much new technology does not have its disturbing side or its dangers. Chief amongst the latter are banal commercialism and greed: too much electronic music is lacklustre Muzak, and too many manufacturers flood the market every few months with allegedly breakthrough innovations that can only serve to bewilder young players and composers (and cost them a great deal of money in the interim). There have also been unfortunate cases of working musicians being replaced by these same synths. These are real problems, and it is to be hoped that both manufacturers and record producers will devote their prime energies to genuine creativity, rather than quick-buck exploitation.

Speaking for myself, these marvels or monsters (depending on your point of view) have proved nothing but beneficial: my composing has increased ten-fold and I learn something new every day; I firmly believe that the opportunities they afford all instrumentalists are excitingly liberating. Young players need not feel confined by conventional sounds—nor do they need to abandon them entirely: the scope for creative merging is enormous, and new and different dimensions to music beckon. Furthermore, through synthesizers we now have available to us the instrumental sounds of other lands; we Westerners no longer have any excuse for parochialism, for global music is now a facility available to all dedicated practitioners. That alone is a major boon, and may well prove to be electronics' greatest contribution to music.

73
PROMOTERS AND THEIR WAYS

It is impossible for artists to distance themselves completely from promoters year in, year out. Most managers worry at least occasionally about an artist's relationship with an impresario, fearing that the latter will somehow manoeuvre the former into some kind of unacceptable agreement; there have of course been cases where artists have been lured away from their original manager by some opportunistic or conniving promoter. On the other hand, I have met many promoters with whom I've become friendly and where all arrangements were hassle-free. I've been lucky to have Norman as my own personal manager and best friend: most of the promoters who have become personal friends I met through him.

Frank Tenot, from Paris, presented Ella Fitzgerald, JATP, and me to the French public countless times. Good-looking, on the small side, and with a rich, deep voice seemingly made for radio broadcasting, Frank became a cherished friend via lunches at such gastronomic havens as Chez Ami Louis and Chez Allard, where he, Norman, and I would discuss everything from current world politics to the conceptual difference between Lester Young's and Coleman Hawkins' solos. Frank, an incomparable gourmand and a great lover of jazz, was also deeply interested in Spanish music. I came to realize that it was primarily its simple plaintivism that so attracted him—a quality that also characterizes two of his jazz favourites, Bill Basie and Erroll Garner, both of them uncluttered, plaintively linear players. Frank is also devoted to Norman, and our friendship has both blossomed and deepened over the years.

Sabine Lovatelli of Brazil heads the Mozarteum Brasileiro concert agency, and has presented us in several concerts in South America. She is unbelievable! When it comes to new promoters, I usually try to stay in the background as much as possible, letting my road manager deal with the immediate details. That might seem unfriendly, but I believe it to be necessary: it stops me from taking anyone for granted, and also, should the person turn out to be someone I dislike, it allows things to be kept on a strictly business basis. Such a policy was impossible from the start with Sabine. She completely disarmed me with her charm and natural warmth; in addition, as a businesswoman she has that rare gift: low-key authority. She is fully aware of what needs to be done for the artist *and* for the public, and she simply does it. I was particularly struck by her handling of press conferences. She would start them with a quietly sincere welcome, and end them just as unobtrusively with an aside to me that would go, "I think we'll finish after the next question so that you have enough time to rest before the performance"—a consideration that, unfortunately, many other presenters forget or ignore. Her manner during the concert is the same quiet, controlled confidence, intermingled with a teenage exuberance for the music. After the concert, her husband, Carlo, appears—a tall, happy-natured man—and the fun begins. They go to great lengths to show their appreciation for the music we provided: nothing is too much trouble. Their friends immediately become our friends, and wonderful friends they are.

One evening, towards the end of our visit, I was amazed when the other trio members and my road manager made a short speech of thanks dedicated to Sabine, and presented her with a huge bouquet of gorgeous roses. I had never seen the group react like that before (certainly not to a promoter), and the incident illustrates how much her warmth and caring touched everyone with whom she dealt.

There's one strange thing about Sabine's relationship with us. She and Norman have had innumerable phone conversations (from London, Paris, Geneva, and so on), during which they have concluded various deals, and there is complete faith and trust between them. Yet they have never met face to face! Sabine speaks of "the mythical Norman," while he reverently calls her "the Contessa."

Frank and Sabine—and Norman, of course—are special in that with them friendship has come to transcend business. With other promoters it isn't always easy to combine (or indeed separate) the two; nevertheless, many remain my friends, and it would be absurd to suggest that I harbour a dislike for the breed in general. However, there is one anomaly that still puzzles me.

Let's suppose I'm due to play a concert somewhere which is advertised as starting at 8.30. Should the promoter decide to delay the concert by 5, 10, 15 minutes or more, it is his or her prerogative to do so. Artists normally accept this and will make up for the late start at the end of the performance, usually with no flak or resentment, and everything is fine. Let's now reverse the situation and assume that I arrive 15, 20, or 30 minutes late. Promoters invariably see that as a serious misdemeanor or, worse yet, a breach of contract, which can often lead to talk of refunding part of the fee and so on. This is a show-business anachronism that I have never understood. In Chapter 85, "Great Hotels of the World," you'll find my account of an incident concerning a French promoter that gives some indication of what performers have to cope with from time to time; yet such hassles are rarely reported in the newspapers—or certainly not as often as the late appearance of an artist is. Surely what's sauce for the goose ought to be sauce for the gander?

74

THE ROYAL WEDDING ALBUM

I n early 1981 I was touring Australia with the Trio. It quickly became clear to me that in every city we visited there was an unquenchable excitement about the impending wedding of Prince Charles and Lady Diana Spencer; everywhere I went it was an almost unrelenting topic of conversation. It had a profound effect on me—so much so that I decided to compose and dedicate an album to the couple and the occasion. I called Norman Granz in California, and agreeing that it would be an interesting departure for me musically, he gave the go-ahead to the project.

From the start I felt that the album must have a regal aura to it, which underscored the opening selection, *Announcement*. In it I tried to capture various aspects of the coming event and also to portray the excitement the Australian people had so evidently felt. Nevertheless, my own favourite selections now are *London Gets Ready*, *Heraldry* (which was a special compositional challenge), and *Lady Di's Waltz*, in which I tried to portray the inner beauty that Diana was later to impart to the whole world. The final tune, *Empty Cathedral*, was written from conjured-up memories of the many times I had ridden by St Paul's Cathedral late at night; its imposing stature always affected me deeply, and I hope I managed to evoke that in my piece.

The album was recorded in London, and many members of the orchestra came to me during and after the sessions to say how much they had enjoyed playing my compositions. But my highest satisfaction came ten years later in 1991, when I had the opportunity of dining on the Royal yacht *Britannia* in Toronto with the Prince and Princess, and to experience her outgoing warmth and beauty in person.

75

THE NEW QUARTET

O ver the years I have been more than fortunate in being able to call on exceptional talent to form my various groups. Each one has had its own personality and musical temperature, and it was a joy to revel in their separate strengths. Now, however, I would like to celebrate my current group, known as the NATO Group.

I had called on the services of British drummer Martin Drew after I suffered a stroke; he had gigged with us on several earlier occasions, and I admired his talents and contributions. When I felt ready to return to the concert stage after a period of rehabilitation, I was confident that the combination of Martin and Niels would provide the cushion I would need for such a comeback. We operated as a trio for a while, but then I happened to hear a guitarist who reminded me—delightedly—of Wes Montgomery. His name is Ulf Wakenius, and he had everything one could want in a small-group player. He joined us and at once became an inspiration both to me and to the others, resulting in nightly solo challenges between Niels, Ulf, and myself. In addition to his extrovert power he has great harmonic sensitivity on ballads, both as a soloist and accompanist; his quality in the latter regard is beautifully illustrated on my compositions *When Summer Comes* and *Evening Song*, to be found on our Munich recording for Telarc.

If I had to choose one word that comes to mind when I think about this group, it would be "exuberance." The Quartet not only offers all the musical challenges I could ever desire, but also embodies the same kind of personal love and respect that characterized my earliest groups. I shall always retain a great love for these guys, for they typify everything I look for in friends, and fulfill all that I have always looked for in musical colleagues. I love my quartet.

76

THE ORDER OF CANADA

B eing chosen in 1972 to receive the Order of Canada was the highest honour in my career. Aware of the vastness of my country and its youth (together with a certain naïveté in some respects), I somehow never thought of myself as a suitable nominee; nevertheless, from the outset the Order has always commanded my unreserved admiration. I particularly warmed to the fact that any Canadian is eligible, not just parliamentarians: there is profound merit in the notion that anyone and everyone can perform out-standing service and deserve recognition for it. When I read the correspondence informing me of my government's decision, I lapsed into a state of semi-shock for a while; then a great warmth crept through me—one that remained even after the eventual ceremonies. I felt as if I had climbed a mountain and was drinking in an awe-inspiring, breathtaking view from the top of the world. This was something beyond the acclaim of an audience: this had an aura of magic, of overwhelming reverence.

As my name was called and I walked up to take my place in front of the then Governor-General, the Right Honourable Roland Michener, I felt an indescribable urge to call my Mom and Dad, who had both passed away some years before. I desperately wanted them to be here with me for this great moment in my life. The feeling grew as one of the Governor-General's aides read out the decree stating the facts of my life and citing my accomplishments, and I stayed in this other world right up to the moment when Roland Michener placed the medal around my neck and said, "I hope you realize how proud you have made us all feel as Canadians." My focus and time suddenly returned and I managed a timid "Thank you, Sir."

It is still my most important memory, surmounting all the other awards and honours I have received, grateful though I am for them all. For nothing can surpass recognition by one's homeland and all the people within its boundaries.

77

THE GLENN GOULD PRIZE

In May 1993 I was accorded the Glenn Gould Prize, the first of several unexpected and unusual awards. To my knowledge this prize was primarily endowed in order to honour members of the classical world, so it was not something I had ever envisioned being eligible for. The prize itself was honour enough, but it seemed even greater when I was informed that the decision of the voting committee—comprising judges from seven different countries—was unanimous in my case. Although various classical players over the years have acclaimed my playing, as a jazz musician I had not expected this kind of formal recognition.

Almost as soon as I was told of the award, I thought of my beloved teacher Paul de Marky, and what a shame it was that he had not lived to see me achieve this unique recognition in his own field of music. Ever since that moment I have privately dedicated the award to him, for his influence on the way I came to approach playing the piano was as decisive as profound.

78

THE PRAEMIUM IMPERIALE

Although I have just cited the Glenn Gould Prize as a totally unexpected honour, I must confess that in March 1999 I was even more stunned by the accolade bestowed on me by the Japan Arts Association, whose Governor is Prince Hitachi (brother of the present Emperor). I was on a writing retreat in Barbados when word arrived from my office asking if I would accept the Praemium Imperiale medal, and thus join the laureates of the order. Sometime later I learned that the benefactors who endowed the Praemium Imperiale wished to create a musical equivalent to the Nobel Prize, which primarily honours achievements in literature and the sciences, and that increased my awed pleasure in being honoured in such a way.

The ceremony, which I was privileged to attend, was held at the Lincoln Center, New York. It was quite an experience to listen to Prince Hitachi, former Prime Minister Nakasone, former German President Richard von Weizsäcker, Sir Edward Heath, David Rockefeller Jr., and various other dignitaries make the formal announcement of this year's laureates. Moments like these are special anyway, and particularly so if you are a jazz musician and composer—a type that hardly dares dream of such awards. And I felt doubly honoured: not only was I the first jazz artist to be welcomed into such prestigious company, but also the first (and so far the only) Canadian to be inducted. I like to think that my parents were present in spirit, for they made possible all the satisfactions I have come to know as a jazz pianist—including the award of the Unesco International Music Prize, which followed some time later.

PART THREE

MATTERS POLITICAL

79

BIGOTRY STARTS EARLY

As the time neared for my first child Lynn to enter kindergarten, excitement rapidly grew each day for her mother, Lil, and myself. We were very curious about exactly how our daughter would react to the totally new environment that she would now be entering. I had made certain that I would be home in order to accompany her to school on her very first day. Her Mom had fussed and fretted almost uncontrollably for days before, wondering which outfit to select for this most auspicious occasion—the entrance of our first offspring into the public school system.

When registration day finally arrived, the family arose extra early in order not to hinder Lynn's departure, and assisted in the preparations. Finally, the time came and Lynn and I proudly departed our house, heading for this new era in all of our lives.

We had been residents of Notre Dame de Grace, a suburb of Montreal, for quite a few years now and were familiar with the area, which was typical of Canada's suburban community. It nestled between other suburbs and the big Ville de Montreal, fighting for its constitutional life in the teeth of threats of punitive taxation. The population comprised primarily English-speaking families with a smaller number of French-speakers. Incomes varied hugely, from sub-breadline casualties to upper-middle-class salaried professionals. It was in this sort of neighbourhood that Lynn's school was situated.

As we arrived at the school, Lynn quite naturally became more and more exuberant and I could almost judge her level of anticipation by the way that she squeezed my hand as she excitedly interrogated me about all that she would be doing here from day to day. I attempted to calm her, and finally we took our places in one of the numerous lines of new enrollees. Immediately in front of us was another father with his daughter, who was also decked out for the occasion. As Lynn and I waited for our turn to come, the daughter in front carried on a sporadic conversation with her Dad; then, in a quiet moment, she turned and for the first time became aware of Lynn. She stared at Lynn relentlessly for what seemed like an hour, and then looked up at me. Lynn immediately smiled at the youngster and, when that failed to bring on a response, simply added a hello. The girl then wiggled her father's hand to get his attention, looked up at him and said, "Daddy, she's a nigger!" in an almost reproachful tone of anger. Her father ignored her. Enraged at not eliciting a response, she then turned on Lynn and proceeded to chant, "You're a nigger! You're a nigger!" over and over again.

My immediate thought was to make a cripple out of her Dad; suddenly, I more or less came to my senses and refocused on Lynn. I knelt down and embraced her as she started to cry. I did whatever I could to comfort her while attempting to reassure her that there was nothing wrong with her. I also tried to convince her that not all of the children in the school were like that and certainly did not dislike her. The brat in front suddenly whirled and spat at Lynn; I was forced to threaten her stupid father with bodily harm if he didn't call off his daughter.

Lynn was certainly crushed for the time, but thankfully, like most children of that early an age, she recovered her composure and managed to get back into the mood of the event. But it was hideously unfair that Lynn's schooldays had to commence with such an ugly event simply because of these parents' stupid bigotry—a disease that would now be carried into another generation by a daughter infected with the bacteria of racial hatred and intolerance.

Many whites have wondered over the years why blacks seem to have a distrust or innate apprehension of them when they first meet. They sense a reluctance to be totally "up front" in a new friendship by openly displaying a readiness to "go all the way." There is a perfectly good reason for this. Much like the unfortunate and almost brutal instance stated above, many have been the times when I have set out to have an evening's enjoyment, only to run into some form of bigotry. Perhaps it merely might have been something a maître d'hôtel said or did; it would nevertheless be enough to cast a pall over what was to have been a happy time. On other occasions, I have received the famous "cold shoulder" treatment, where an ostensibly open discussion panned out in my being repeatedly and noticeably ignored by certain parties within the group. Such occurrences serve to repress any initial openness on the part of many blacks. It is a form of preventative insurance taken out by people who have too often been victimized.

There is also a form of bigotry that I categorize as "comfortable racism." This entails people unknowingly tolerating and perpetuating a form of behaviour that has been accepted within a society, yet is racist and therefore absolutely unacceptable to millions of the world's citizens. Unless one fully confronts it, this form of insult and repression will continue to flourish.

On one of my first trips to England, while enjoying a few days off in London, I got lucky and won some money at a local gaming club. The next day I decided to purchase some sweaters that I had noticed at one of the better-known men's stores on Piccadilly. I went in and almost immediately a young man came forward to wait on me, politely inquiring as to what kind of merchandise I wanted. I told him that I wanted to purchase some sweaters and inquired how many shades the particular style that I fancied was available in. He reeled off about eight different descriptive colours, including one that he termed "nigger brown."

At first, refusing to believe my ears, I asked him to repeat my choices, and he dutifully acquiesced by repeating the same list, more slowly this time, once again ending up with "nigger brown." I was angry at first, but suddenly realized that he was not trying to be smart, and was merely employing a descriptive sales phrase that was acceptable in this country. I immediately asked him to call for the manager, which he did, and continued a normal conversation with me as though nothing at all was wrong. His attitude confirmed to me that he saw nothing wrong with the terminology he had employed. When the manager arrived and asked if he could be of service, I asked him if he was aware of the various shades of sweaters that he had available for sale in the store. Puzzled, he managed a weak "Yes, I am, sir," then went on to ask me what my problem was. I asked his junior to do a repeat performance of his sales pitch on the sweaters. It was only when the manager issued an embarrassed, horrified gasp after hearing the word "nigger" in my presence that the young sales clerk suddenly got the point.

That anecdote illustrates how easy it is for young people to grow up with various forms of racial debasement taking place around them. They learn subliminally all the while to accept this as part of the status quo, and then subconsciously integrate these ideas into their own lives and those of their families, never aware of how much racial upheaval they are spreading. Unfortunately, it is only when blacks rebel violently against this type of plantation-like treatment that some, and only some, of these racially unknowing young people learn a very harsh but valuable lesson.

80

NIGGER!

I should have known after two incidents on a particular tour that things were not going to go well no matter what I tried. First, I had to do a date with Dizzy Gillespie almost immediately upon my return from Europe. I knew that I was tired and working on jet lag, but all I had left was this gig with Dizzy in Washington and a flight to LA the very next morning for an appearance in the Hollywood Bowl. After which I intended to take a two-month vacation and go to my cottage.

It all started at the concert in Washington when the promoter, rather than giving Dizzy his just deserts as a personality, over-reacted to my presence, and made a big deal about me being there while virtually ignoring Dizzy. This naturally put me on tenterhooks for the evening and I became quite upset. Instead of going home in preparation for my early flight the next morning, I went out to hear some music, hoping to relax and free my mind from the earlier embarrassments. Then I returned to my hotel exhausted at 3.00 a.m. and suddenly realized that I had not packed. Adhering to my rule about packing the night before a flight, I set to the task and finally fell into bed around 4.15 a.m. Reluctantly rising at 7.00 a.m., bleary-eyed and disoriented, I somehow managed to make it to the airport, consoling myself the whole way there that I would be able to spend some comfort-time in the airline lounge and get myself together.

The first stroke of bad luck occurred when I dragged myself up two flights of stairs to the lounge, only to find, to my horror, a sign that said, "Lounge does not open until 10 a.m." My flight of course was departing at 9.30 a.m. There I was—tired, disgruntled, and totally out of whack, standing on the staircase debating my next move. I opted to walk back to the terminal area and wearily began the trek. Stopping at the newsagent I purchased the morning paper and asked for some film— only to be told that the only place I could obtain it was in the souvenir shop at the other end of the airport. I made the walk, purchased the film, and returned to the gate area.

As I did so I became aware of a woman begging her husband to take a picture of the family because this was their first trip on the then new 747 jet. Daddy responded with the fact he was out of the type of film that he needed, and that the newsagent did not sell it any more. Guess what? Good Samaritan Oscar jumped in, started to say that film could be purchased at the souvenir shop, and was suddenly fixed by one of the most powerful stares of hatred from the wife that one could imagine. The only thing that could possibly follow this would be a call for the police. Retreating in embarrassment and dismay I decided to sit out the remaining time on a secluded wall seat in the area.

Departure time came; I boarded the flight, gratefully took my seat, and fell asleep at once. I obviously slept quite soundly and long, for I woke to hear the Captain's voice announcing we were approaching the Grand Canyon and that on this day, due to unusually good weather conditions, we would have a great view from the right side of the aircraft—the side I was happened to be seated on. In my semi-stupor I lay there neither asleep nor awake, my eyes still closed. I suddenly became aware of intermittent bright flashes coupled with the sound of what had to be a camera. I opened my eyes to see one of our hostesses at the window seat immediately in front of me busily snapping flash shots of the Canyon. What a waste of battery power! Oscar rides to the rescue! Lifting myself out of my seat I softly tapped the hostess on the shoulder. She looked back, and I informed her that she was wasting battery power due to the fact that the flash meant nothing some 25,000 feet away from her subject. With a look of disdain she informed me that she had always used flash from the air and that her pictures had come out just fine, thank you *very* much! That did it! Never again. I'd sit out the rest of the trip and help no other humans, no matter what their problems. The rest of the flight thankfully went by without any further incident and we finally landed in LA.

Then, of course, there was the inevitable tedious wait for my baggage. As I stood there in the collection area, I saw two ladies being met by two gentlemen, all of them pictures of the perfect stereotype tourist. One of the ladies was quite a bit shorter than the other and her hair was done in tight ringlets that terminated in bangs across her forehead. The two men that met them spent the next few minutes announcing their intended vacation itinerary to them, which apparently would culminate in a visit to Las Vegas. These announcements were punctuated with excited squeals of delight from the two females. I should have recognized the mental level of the group by reflecting properly on the fact that *both* men left to get the car while leaving the women to cope with the baggage: they immediately started to panic, not knowing which of the three huge turnstiles their baggage would appear on. I felt sorry for them, having been marooned myself in various airports in my earlier travels and being well aware of the terror of not knowing what one's next move should be. No way around it, they definitely needed help. I strolled over to where they were standing in their misery and said, "Your bags will be on turnstile number three, ladies."

Suddenly the little one took a long, deliberate look at me from the tip of my toes to the top of my head and shouted, "FUCK OFF, NIGGER!"

81

MY FAVOURITE POLITICIAN

For better or worse, I have never courted people in the political environment. On the other hand, I have always had a great interest in watching the game of chess in which they daily engage while going about their governmental chores. Members of various world governments have attended my concerts from time to time, and have often come backstage to chat with me. Many of them turned out to be frustrated or interested players. Many of these people I have admired politically, while disagreeing with them on more than a few issues.

One such regular listener of mine happens to be my all-time favourite personage in the political world—Canada's former Prime Minister, the late Pierre Elliott Trudeau. I always had an unbridled admiration for this gifted and yet controversial man, whose depth of perception and passionate beliefs about Canada helped cause his decline in popularity. He was certainly charismatic, but, more importantly, he enjoyed a form of worldwide respect and adoration by the masses that come only to a special few—for instance, Duke Ellington, the Queen Mother, Vladimir Horowitz, John F. Kennedy, or Carl Sandburg.

As a Canadian often far removed from my homeland, I can readily attest to the way people moan and groan about the lack of political candidates to choose from; this was at its most striking during the US presidential elections that coincided with Mr Trudeau's tenure as Prime Minister. Invariably, they would sooner or later turn to me and say something like, "You're so lucky to have a true statesman running your country," or "I wish he were running in our race." Mind you, I can imagine what some members of the conservative wing of the Republican Party some years ago might have had to say about our free-swinging Pierre! Somehow, I could never envision him winning the endorsement of people such as Jesse Helms or Pat Buchanan. Yet Mr Trudeau was made of the kind of fibre and resilience that his adversaries recognized and respected, knowing full well that they were confronting a player equipped with all the necessary accoutrements and skills needed to deal with their kind. To draw an analogy, this would not be too far removed from one of the unskilled pretenders to the jazz throne confronting someone such as Art Tatum, Charlie Parker, or the like: another form of self-annihilation.

82

PITFALLS OF THE PROFESSION

I have always detested the look of night clubs in the daytime hours: they all seem so seedy and dirty in the innocent and fresh light of day. At night, the low lights and smoky atmosphere inevitably attracts, amongst others, the shadowy people of the streets; and I suppose it's equally inevitable that some jazz players fell in with such people. For ever since the 1930s this has been the jazz player's standard environment—a far cry from the hygenic confines and "sensible" hours that characterize a conservatoire student or the life of a classical player—and at its worst it positively breeds corruption and addiction.

Most young jazz musicians felt compelled to migrate to the great cities and meccas of jazz in order to prove and improve their musical skills; few were adequately prepared for the hardships and general viciousness they would encounter. There were no sorority houses or dorms here—just sleazy hotels that harboured drug dealers and other underworld predators. Sadly, many of these youngsters could not admit to or cope with such hardships, and fell prey to the dope-world pythons.

With all that in mind, I have to say that I was exceptionally fortunate in the way I was brought up. Without being fully conscious of it, I drew great strength and comfort from the prescribed guidelines Mom and Dad laid down, to which there were never any exceptions. Their rules exemplified West Indian custom and belief: you were never to behave in an unacceptable or discourteous manner, and that was that! I also owe a great debt to the minister of the first church my family attended in Canada—Reverend Combe. He seemed almost like a saint to me, with his shock of silvery hair and the unforgettable tenor voice, tinged with a slight English accent and always faintly hoarse. His influence on me was indelible; the image of him in my mind was always an extra shield whenever I came into contact with drug pedlars and the like. Without those sources of strength and discipline to draw on, things might have been very different for me.

I will never forget, on one of my first working visits to the USA, watching one of my idols—one of the most gifted drummers there has ever been—inject heroin into his system. It took something out of me seeing that; I went home disappointed and angry, unable to understand how this supremely talented man could humiliate himself and his body in such a fashion. I remember feeling that if this was the price of "making it," it was way too high for me.

On the same trip, the night I played Carnegie Hall, I rushed over to Birdland to hear a saxophone genius who was due to appear there that night. As I was being led to my seat, I passed a corner booth and did a second take. There, propped up against the back of the seat, eyes closed in a stupor, was the man I'd come to hear. To add to his indignity, someone had hung a "Do Not Disturb" sign around his neck. I can't properly describe the rage and hurt I felt at that moment.

It was outside that same club that years later I stood with Sonny Clark, begging him to shape up and put his life in order, after he had hit me with the inevitable plea for two dollars. Shortly afterwards on a return visit, I asked after Sonny, only to be told that he had killed himself via a drug overdose. Useless human waste—and far from the only casualty. I grew to know and love Hampton Hawes in LA. He told me I was an inspiration to him and marvelled at what our trio was into musically. I encouraged him and tried to help with advice whenever I could. One day I noticed an extra glint to those bright eyes of his. I tried to rationalize away what I thought I saw, but deep down I knew: addiction had struck. His wife begged me to have faith in his ability to fight and recover, but the drug dragon had sunk its fangs too deeply into my friend for me to be very hopeful. Sadly, I was right: a few years later I lost my blues-playing buddy for ever.

I have seen how players can succumb to this false crutch, especially when their careers seem stagnated or suspended. I have observed the raft of famous but misguided players follow their idols into drug-abuse, and often into death as a result. I have watched talent being traded for little packets of cocaine by ruthless club-owners and mobsters. I have lost friendships simply because I could not accept this surrender of the mind to the mindless. The problem is still around, of course: not enough has been learned from that past carnage. If I had to advise any young musician, I'd say that your instrument should be your needle, and music your addiction. It is mine.

83

CULTURAL POLITICS: THE
BETRAYAL OF JAZZ

For most of my life as a working musician I have been forced to watch gloomily as Western society emasculated or simply ignored the culture and unique phenomenon we call jazz. It is very difficult to understand why it has been so profoundly denied as an artistic force; but I am quite clear about one thing—the treatment of jazz is deeply indicative of society's values, and also its fears and prejudices.

North America has never been able to lay claim to a classical music talent the size of Bach, Mozart, or Beethoven; perhaps this explains both its musical diffidence and its warm devotion to European composers and players, who are in constant demand in our concert halls, sometimes at the behest of heads of nations. But America did invent *an entire musical form*—jazz; and it seems to me that almost from the outset it was suppressed by the racist American white who would have no part of this "jungle music." Such aesthetic sabotage has proved a more complex matter than mere fascist censorship, however: it has also been effected through commercial dilution and exploitation. Even more remarkable—and distressing—has been Western blacks' acquiescence in this process, almost conniving at the appropriation of something inherently their own and its repackaging into bland hybrids masquerading as new music.

From the beginning, there were certain white bandleaders who heard something in the music of the great early blacks and attempted to build a musical empire from it. However, the talent of those innovatory blacks was so immense that it broke through to the American public, with two cheering results: black musicians were increasingly to be found in white orchestras, while the greatest practitioners—figures such as Armstrong, Waller, Ellington, and Basie—were able to make it almost entirely on their own.

As jazz grew in commercial viability and attracted the interest of white show-business tycoons, blacks were able to make their way into areas of the entertainment world previously denied them, thus exposing more and more Americans to black genius and the message of the ghetto. The Swing bands opened up the nation's ballrooms to this burgeoning black talent, rapidly alerting people to the quality of such men as Lester Young, Coleman Hawkins, and Roy Eldridge, and causing them to be regarded as major performers in their own right. Another significant figure was Teddy Wilson, the articulate and distinctive black pianist who fuelled Benny Goodman's outfits large and small. Benny ran the most popular band of the time, and Teddy's central role was an important racial signal. And all the while, radio was growing bigger and bigger throughout North America and reaching across the waters to Europe. To the casual observer, it might have seemed that jazz had simultaneously acquired international recognition and established its status as the indigenous music of America.

Yet such a view would have been much too optimistic. Long before Goodman's triumphs, it had become clear that America as a whole was in no mood to recognize jazz as its own true music (nor has it ever done so). Many Americans could not stomach the idea that blacks could produce anything of aesthetic or cultural worth. Worse, such a response was not confined to obvious bigots and racist cretins. The English historian Arnold Toynbee wrote in the 1930s:

> When we classify mankind by colour, the only one of the primary races ... which has not made a single creative contribution to any of our 21 civilisations is the black race.
>
> (A Study of History)

Toynbee would have called himself a liberal, and he was certainly a cultivated and learned man; to read those words of his is not just an insulting shock but proof, perhaps, of how widespread were the vast majority of people's ignorance and embarrassment when confronted by jazz. Possibly the music's earthy affirmation discomfited the more staid liberals; maybe anything that reminded Americans of slavery and their nation's grim past was just too uncomfortable. Either way, jazz was culturally marginalized from an early stage, and its brief explosion into mass popularity during the Swing era did nothing to alter that.

Such an embarrassed, or openly hostile, response led to further woes. Jazz could not, it seemed, be properly honoured; it could, however, be fully exploited. Booking agencies began to proliferate in the 1930s, peopled by operators who soon laid claim to an ownership of jazz orchestras and artists. They wasted no time in draining off profits that performers never got to see, and were much assisted in this by the practice of "double-contracting": an orchestra leader would be contracted for one fee, while the hirer of the band got another contract and a much higher fee, leaving the agent to pocket the difference—in addition to his 25 per cent or more from unsuspecting musicians. Little did agents care about the insane and debilitating itineraries forced upon the people they were supposed to represent and look after. Little did they worry about the squalor of the hotels or the damp and cold band buses, which I am sure helped bring about the early deaths of so many players, through tuberculosis and the like. And little did they care about the humiliation and terror heaped on performers during their treks through the South. Why should they, since many were themselves bigots of the first order?

Despite all this, jazz refused to lie down. In the late 1930s and early 1940s, as the boom in big bands declined somewhat and the cost of spiriting them around the globe escalated, a new phenomenon emerged—the Jazz Concert. Initiated by John Hammond and Norman Granz, and taken up by other impresarios such as Gene Norman, this development had a profoundly liberating effect on a number of important jazz soloists. Hitherto, people had listened to big band repertoires—performances that only occasionally allowed them to hear snatches of inspiration from their favourite soloists. Even on phonograph records (a big industry by now) the soloists only got to perform after the bands had finished their ensemble cadences and exercises, and were usually limited to eight or sixteen bars. Now, with the rise not only of jazz concerts but also of jazz clubs, the soloists left their frustrations behind them—and those of their admirers—being able to appear in groups of their own, playing material of their choice, for as long as they wanted. This in turn nurtured a lot of other musicians, especially pianists, many of whom went on to considerable prominence, establishing the "piano era" of the late 1940s and early 1950s.

By this time the jazz world had become probably the most integrated community in American society. I have heard claims of earlier integration made by other professions and cultures; however, I am convinced that the jazz world was the leader in this respect. There was a profound egalitarianism wherever one looked: a promoter like Norman Granz was interested only in talent, only in presenting on stage the people he wanted to hear, regardless of their racial origin; in the same way, white musicians such as Gerry Mulligan happily recognized that to be able to play within the black community was the jazz equivalent of getting a Harvard education. Of course, there were bad feelings from time to time; but such blots were invariably a matter of individual clashes rather than a threat to the prevailing atmosphere, and the overall picture in the jazz world was one of thorough—albeit unheralded—integration, long before people started swapping bus seats in the South.

This achievement is all the more impressive, and sadly ironic, if one looks at other aspects of American musical culture at this time. The countless studio bands, financed by the various networks in all the major cities, were characterized by a dearth of black players. The situation in the movie studios was even starker: in their music departments one might possibly find a very lonely Benny Carter, but not much else. And the classical picture was no better: yet another snow-capped winter scene. On the basis of skill and ability, one might expect to find 20 black players in a symphony orchestra, and at least a smattering of African-American conductors. Not a bit of it: from Dean

Dixon onwards, black symphonic musicians of unquestioned talent have found American classical society apparently unable to cope with the concept of a mixed orchestra and thus unwilling to accept them. Strangely, the world of opera has not followed suit: from an early stage, black singers have prospered. One can only wonder how and why, since the two worlds are intimately connected, and patronized by largely the same audience.

I regret to say that the picture in my homeland is not much different. So far as I'm aware, there were no blacks in Canadian symphony orchestras when I was young; by the 1940s I was one of only a handful of blacks to do any form of studio work, and later I was certainly one of the very few blacks to appear on Canadian television. And all that poses an interesting question—or, to put it another way, exposes a distressing anomaly. Canadians are very proud of their record in race relations and humanitarianism, and are quick to point to their quiet cities and peaceful racial co-existence. Yet we all know that man is as imperfect in Canada as he is in the USA, and my hunch is that the only reason the white Canadian has not become as bigoted as his American counterpart is that the racial proportions in the two countries are vastly different. The average white Canadian is not as forcibly aware of his black brother in even major cities like Toronto or Montreal as he would be were he in Washington or Philadelphia. Consequently, he cackles smugly when racial problems arise in the USA, pretending that such things could never happen in Canada. Well, maybe not; but—to return to my beginning—the music picture is little better than it is in America, especially when it comes to television.

Television has supposedly opened up a whole new field of opportunity for talented performers, and a huge one. Not so for the black performer; particularly not so for the black *jazz* performer. America has always actively disregarded jazz, and its television companies have merely perpetuated that oblivion. Jazz "specials" are rare, and seem only to be programed when there's absolutely nothing else available; contrast that with the countless "cultural hours" of this or that aspect of the world of classical music. Those who sought to promote jazz on television were told that audiences would not sit still for an hour of music, and yet I have seen many hour-long recitals by classical orchestras and chamber groups. Furthermore, these have featured only the sparsest announcements and have been distinguished for their sensitive and artistic camerawork: Vladimir Horowitz's recitals were admirable epitomes of such taste and thoughtfulness. Again, contrast that with a typical "TV Jazz Show," complete with absurd wide-angled shots of the performer's feet that make him or her look like some creature out of Spielberg's *Star Wars*.

The ever-proliferating "Talk Shows" offer another depressing case in point. With very few exceptions their hosts have proved themselves highly reluctant to present jazz. Over the years I have watched Johnny Carson on many occasions, and have noted with interest how classical artists, for example Itzhak Perlman, are not only accorded generous performance time but are then invited to join Johnny's panel for the night; virtually every jazz performer, on the other hand, gets to play a brief solo piece before being applauded off by Johnny with the same bland remark, no matter how individual the musician may have been. (Buddy Rich was an exception; but then he was a close personal friend of Johnny's.) To be fair, there are one or two oases amidst this desert. Merv Griffin was one of the most sympathetic and appreciative hosts of any show I've been on, and I've done more than a few by now; I rank him with Dick Cavett and London's Michael Parkinson in his sensitive and knowledgeable treatment of musical guests, for all three are genuinely interested in music rather than labels. Mike Douglas was another aware interviewer, and true music lover.

It's no better in Canada. I've never been given the opportunity by American television of doing a full-scale, all-out, hour-long spectacular; neither has any Canadian company obliged. South or north of the 49th Parallel, TV executives simply do not believe in jazz as a saleable entity, and so it is in effect suppressed. Furthermore, there is a lot of bigotry still around, as I found during my campaigns against tokenism in Canadian television commercials. I came up against everything—from belated shame to outright racial resistance—from company executives who were nonetheless seeking to sell their product to everyone, white or black. This is typical of the cynical complacency one finds in my country, for executives of this ilk know two things about Canadians: one, their smugness about race relations; two, that market research confirms that their bigotry is quietly supported by the white community. I cannot believe that the latter phenomenon will go on being true in our major cities, however; maybe such manipulators are in for a rude awakening in this new century.

Jazz has also been poorly served by education. I am aware that education strategies in all Western nations are under constant budgetary constraint, and also that cultural programs are the first to be threatened when economies are required. Even so, it is depressing to find our educational institutions adopting much the same attitude to jazz as television has taken: it simply is not respected as a culture in its own right. And there is a squalid irony to this, in that jazz is often required to subsidize classical music: it not only has to fund itself but music faculties in general, and many teetering symphony orchestras on our campuses owe their continued existence to "jazz relief." In view of this, it is perhaps not surprising that most of the so-called jazz programs of study are half-hearted and bland, a vague nod in the direction of "modern music" rather than a properly cogent consideration of jazz's unique properties and rich history. Only a very few institutions have developed an articulate and definitive curriculum that covers the origins and genesis of jazz with suitable comprehensiveness and without apology.

The world of commercial music is, from a jazz point of view, the saddest matter of them all. Once again, ignorance reigns. Because blacks have not produced the raft of classical virtuosi that the commercial world anticipated, it has assumed that blacks are capable only of "light entertainment" or pop work: yet another section of our society that has failed utterly to realize that blacks have produced their own classical music—jazz. Or perhaps they *have* realized this, and found it not to their liking. Either way, it has ignored jazz in a deliberately destructive way.

The music industry, in both Canada and the USA, has for a long time controlled broadcasting (aided, in America, by the Mafia, who have long had an interest and an influence in the recording business). Once this control was established, it was clear that jazz was to be at best sidelined and at worst jettisoned altogether. I've already commented on the paucity of jazz on television; FM and AM radio have become even worse, featuring an endless diet of what is deemed "commercially viable" music. And when it comes to Music Award shows (the Grammy-fest, for example), any jazz player who wins can by no means be certain of acknowledgement. Such shows are in essence designed as showcases for just one kind of music—chiefly because the sponsors (soft drinks and fast-food companies) wish to strengthen their appeal to the young, and thus insist that rock-and-roll (under various names such as "smooth pop") is associated with their product.

It's hard to say when this dismal state of affairs took full root. Rock-and-roll started in the mid-1950s, but for a while jazz retained its audience and its interest level; the rot set in some ten years later, in my view. Pop music suddenly took on the force of a hurricane that had found its prime velocity and decided to come ashore to wreak havoc. Almost overnight assorted groups were basking in the spotlight that Elvis and the Beatles had switched on for them. Talent was irrelevant: anything that could sell papers, magazines, and, of course, records was the sole criterion of success, and inane new terms ("pure gold," "Platinum") were coined to feed the hype.

In addition, these "new stars" received massive artist support, which astounded and enraged jazz players, most of whom now had to struggle to get recorded at all, let alone in circumstances that could be called generous or sympathetic.

This kind of commercial obsessiveness has led to a glut of "funny-time" groups all over North America; the added irony is that many of them hail from abroad, especially Britain. It is both funny and disquieting to hear these youngsters aping the language of the ghetto (often in an Uncle Remus-ish way that would appal many blacks!) and then, in interview, to find that they sound like members of Mr Blair's cabinet. Perhaps the saddest thing about these groups and the music they've produced these last 20 years is that there is no place for the soloist any more. Group sound and weight of volume, along with an overdose of distorted guitar, became everything, and only recently have a few musicians made their presence felt as individuals. Some of these have flirted with jazz, or, more accurately, exploited some of its features; that's how "Fusion" was born. My personal definition of "Fusion" would run: a search for a line of demarcation; a movement without base or direction; *Con*fusion, rather than Fusion!

All this leads me to reflect that the royal house of jazz is in deep trouble. The passing of such monarchs as Ellington, Basie, Eldridge, and Gillespie is sad enough in and of itself; what makes it a lot worse is the dearth of any obvious successors. No princes or princesses in the wings—just a mélange of Johnny- and Jill-Come-Latelies. Among the many pretenders to the throne are some whose efforts are genuinely Trojan, marked by dedication and literacy, but the majority start and end with an image, paying no heed to the attributes needed, and pronouncing themselves "jazz players" even though they wouldn't know a blues chorus if it bit them in the leg. All you need, they seem to say, is an instrument, a hair-do, and an attitude.

Many have gained their first successes in pop and rock, and finding that field musically stultifying after a while, have attempted to leap-frog into the realm of jazz. This process has nothing to do with aesthetic commitment and everything to do with self-styled public relations— which requires certain very carefully measured steps. First, if you get to appear on a TV talk show, you have to make it clear to the host that you are a jazz player and are to be announced as such. Second, you must arrange to appear on at least half a dozen of the most important jazz festivals around the world in order to cement your image. Third, you must regularly sit in with the Paul Shafer group. Fourth, you must somehow contrive an appearance on a Grammy show alongside a famed jazz vocalist. Fifth and last, you must *never*, on pain of the instant death of your career, share a bandstand with anyone of the calibre of Clark Terry, Freddie Hubbard, James Moody, or Hank Jones.

If those words seem waspish, I can temper them somewhat by saying that life for any honest jazz talent is very hard nowadays. The scenarios I've just outlined are daily and nightly facts of American life; in addition, they are tyrannical in their exclusiveness. Any youngsters wishing to play jazz and who eschew the media route will perhaps get as far as a college band, and if really lucky may find that band invited to one of the major festivals. In all other respects, their growth is stymied. They can release albums, it's true—there is a host of independent labels these days, in America and Europe—but they then run into a classic Catch-22 dilemma. An album has to be heard to sell, and radio and TV air-time is rarely accorded to albums that are not already selling. Moreover, an in-person slot on one of the night shows is almost impossible unless your album is a definite "hit."

And there is no other way now. With the almost total disappearance of the jazz clubs that abounded in the 1950s and 1960s, the training grounds have gone. There is nowhere to learn one's craft and hone it nightly in an undiluted, dedicated, and competitive milieu—just a succession of one-off appearances in the global festival circus that has become the jazz world. The young can undoubtedly play—standards of technical expertise have never been higher—but where and how can they develop true authority and independence of voice? Will there ever again be saxophonists as unique and various in their sound as Ben Webster, Stan Getz, Johnny Hodges, Hank Jones, Dizzy Gillespie, Pres, and the Hawk? At this time I cannot envision it.

So what is the future of jazz? And why do I go on playing? The simple answer to the second question is that I still love it, and am as devoted to the piano as ever. When I began studying classical music, I did it as whole-heartedly as I knew how; when I made the switch to jazz my commitment was even greater, because I realized I had found a medium that offered me full creative freedom. My study-time increased rather than otherwise, for I was determined to be as dedicated and comprehensive in my endeavours as any classical virtuoso.

The less simple answer also takes in the first question. The state of jazz today may be bleak, but jazz itself will remain a noble and unique art, and as long as my performing and composition skills are up to it, I shall want to celebrate and commemorate that art in my work. For despite everything I have listed and described above, I believe jazz will survive, even rise again to new life. In spite of racism, in spite of the desire of music magnates to establish tyrannical control and dismantle all that jazz means and has achieved, it retains a devoted following throughout the world, and its vast legacy of recordings will never be forgotten.

Jazz has suffered betrayal, calculated assimilation, and attempted annihilation, and its current status may not seem very healthy. But I do not believe you can wholly demolish a creative culture. You may subdue it, you may even fragment it; but if time has proved it valid and durable, it will continue to rise again and again.

PART FOUR

MATTERS PERSONAL

84

TRUE MOMENTS OF GREATNESS:
THE OUTDOORSMAN

S tories I first read as a child fostered in me a lifelong admiration for the frontier makers, *les habitants*, the great Indian scouts, *les coureurs du bois*. These gallant men and women were the shapers of history: their courage and tenacity in rolling back the frontiers of the New World created the beginnings of our present civilization. Their hold on my imagination has always been fierce, made all the more intense by my immense love of the wild and my perennial desire to get closer to nature. The episode I am about to relate arises from this yen for the life of the bush.

Quite a while after I had my cottage built, I thought how marvellous it would be if I could use it as a base for forays into the bush. My admiration for those heroes and naturalists notwithstanding, I have never been too keen on just pitching a tent somewhere and ending the day by sleeping on the ground: that's not my idea of perfect comfort, and there's absolutely no chance of all-night room service. With all that in mind, I decided, after discussing it with several friends, to buy a camper. Not just any camper, either: the kind I'm talking about is a box-like affair that needs a one-and-a-half ton truck underneath it to drive it from place to place. Some of my friends argued strongly against it, while others thought it a good, if somewhat whimsical, idea.

The next week or so was spent shopping for said camper, and after many sorties through many lots looking at many campers, I finally decided on one. It was a beautiful rig. It could sleep four comfortably, and came equipped with a fridge, a cookstove, a shower, and a toilet. I immediately began planning the music department and set up some small speakers to give myself some hi-fi in the wild. A few days later I was on my way home in my new truck, the camper proudly locked into its bed. I spent a predictable amount of show-off time driving it from one friend's house to another and allowing them to take their Cook's Tour of it, while I assumed the "camper's stance" outside—leaning against it while fiddling with the various fittings and lock-downs, none of which I yet knew anything about. I had memorized all the normal data I thought they would ask, such as weight, speed of the truck with the camper on board, water capacity, and so on; had anyone asked more penetrating questions, such as how to dump the toilet, I'd have been at a loss. I survived all their queries somehow and was soon happily back unscathed at home. I started fitting out the camper with such necessities as linens, dishware, cutlery, and the like, and within a few days considered the unit roadworthy.

Then a friend called me up and suggested we all take it out on a "shakedown cruise." I thought this a fantastic idea: the weekend would be a great opportunity to test the unit for any bugs, glitches, and idiosyncracies, and we settled on late Friday afternoon as our starting time. My excitement was almost unbearable! I was about to embark on the realization of a lifelong dream—my first trip into the unknown wonders of the pure wild.

We drove northward until darkness fell, and then decided to stop to eat and find a good place to park for the night. We must have been a good hundred miles northeast of Toronto when we found a nice clearing that didn't seem to be part of anyone's land. We briefly reconnoitered the immediate area for trout streams, and then sat down to a very enjoyable supper, after which a good night's rest seemed in order. That's what we thought; it wasn't what the night's passing motorists had in mind for us. It seemed that every last vehicle had to say some sort of hello or goodbye to us, a greeting that consisted of leaning on the horn well before they reached us and holding it down until they were far down the road. Inside the camper this creates the feeling that a train is bearing down on you at full tilt. Oh, great! It has an especially virulent effect when you're just dozing off, welcoming the lull in holiday traffic: you slide blissfully into the comfort zone—and suddenly, here comes the Super Chief at full throttle! "My God! We're on the tracks!" Up off the pillow comes your head, out comes the cold sweat; then as the train's horn swirls up and whooshes past, you sit there feeling like a total idiot—only to have the experience repeated again and again.

We shook off the horrors of the night by cooking a hearty breakfast and then took to the road. We stopped at several streams during the next couple of days and tried our luck with our fly rods. In the evening we sat by the camper discussing its behaviour and the general feeling of the whole weekend. One thing I brought to everyone's attention was the noticeable lack of dumping stations along the way. On a couple of occasions we had specifically gone in search of them, only to find they weren't available or were still being constructed. Once, in a small town, we were told to use the town dump, but when we arrived we decided that to empty our toilet tank there would be too environmentally unfriendly. The problem continued to prey on my mind after I had dropped off the other couple at their house and was heading back home with my wife Sandy. Fifty gallons of human residue! What was I going to do about it?

At the time I lived on the top floor apartment building overlooking Lake Ontario. The parking lot in the yard below comprised two diagonal lines of parking, one against the building and one against the neighbouring fence. We arrived at around midnight and parked against the fence between two other vehicles—one of the last slots available. Unloading everything took several trips in the elevator; after the last one I was enjoying a drink with Sandy and re-living the events of the weekend when I once again brought up the dreaded subject of the toilet tank. I was nervous about leaving it overnight: by morning a fair old stench might be rampant. She tried to reassure me, recalling that the tank was chemically treated against such a likelihood. I was not to be consoled, however, and after wrestling with it all for a further hour I announced I was going to rectify it.

"How?!" she asked in disbelief. "How, at one o'clock in the morning, do you intend to empty a 50-gallon tank with nowhere to dump it in sight? Surely you're not thinking of the lake?"

"Of course I'm not thinking of the lake!" I replied testily, resenting her sarcasm. "I can solve it in a few trips with this," I went on, holding up my faithful aluminum bucket.

She gasped incredulously and spent the next ten minutes trying to dissuade me from this stupid venture. "Don't you realize," she asked angrily, "just how many trips you're going to have to make with that little bucket up and down six floors in order to empty that stupid tank?"

I took no notice of her pleas to give up this madness. I had changed into shorts, sport shirt, and a pair of those famous slippers that I affectionately called "fuzzy-wuzzies." These are the huge jobs that look like bears' paws and are just as woolly. Thus rigged out, I stealthily approached the left side of the camper, where the tank-drain was located, and stood near the white automobile parked on the left, trying to recall the salesman's instructions about emptying the holding tank. Sandy appeared at the side door of the building, repeating her entreaties that I give up this lunacy. I waved her off and got down to business (to coin a phrase).

I held the bucket under the pipe that came down from the base of the camper and then made a left-angle turn, giving it the shape of an "L." I removed the protective cap, and then remembered that the salesman had said something about pulling a lever to release the flow. Dutifully I pulled said lever and waited, bucket poised under the pipe facing the white vehicle. Absolutely nothing happened. Nothing, that is, for about four seconds; then, just as I was about to reach down and check if I'd pulled the correct lever, there was a click, followed by a tremendous "Whoooosh!" To my utter consternation, the tank was now voiding itself at full tilt and under full pressure, contemptuously bypassing my trusty bucket and splattering all over what had been the white vehicle, but was now quickly becoming a greenish-brown monster. In a state of shock I decided that the only recourse was to hold the bucket up into the spray and catch it that way. Wrong! The stream was so powerful that although, yes, it went into the bucket, it then came out again even faster, wrenching the bucket out of my hands and covering everything—me, the camper, the once-white vehicle, and the entire parking lot—with noisome slime. I backed away in horrified disgust. The exhaust drain was still running at maximum power, and I knew there was no way I could get to the switch and turn it off, so I was forced to let nature take its course. I stood there as it emptied itself, covering me from head to fuzzy-wuzzies in a brownish-green avalanche.

Sandy helped me upstairs and we managed to clean me up somewhat; the rest of the night was spent laundering the white car and spraying the parking lot with what seemed like tons of disinfectant. When I awoke next morning and went out onto my balcony to view the damage, I saw the superintendent looking at this huge green stain in the parking lot, scratching his head. He never did ask me if I knew anything about it, and I thought it wise not to volunteer any information at any time.

Thus ended my great expedition into the wonders of camping. From then on I decided that any communion with Mother Nature would be restricted to using my fishing boat and enjoying her glories from the comfortable distance of my cottage!

85

THE GREAT HOTELS OF THE WORLD

After spending more than two-thirds of my life on the road I think I have a good idea of what the word "hotel" means, in both the best and the sorriest senses. I started off like any other roadrunner of my time, accepting more or less all the misfortunes and inconveniences inherent in such a way of life. As a beginner in Canada

I tended to ignore the shortcomings of the less impressive hostels in which I stayed, and it wasn't until my American travels with Norman's troupe that I raised my expectations, which at times led to arguments with the management of various establishments, not least over racism.

When I first arrived in New York for my appearance at Carnegie Hall, Norman was living at a hotel called the Royalton; I visited him there, played the concert, and returned to Canada. On my next visit, Norman tried to book me into the Royalton and was told they didn't want me staying there; he immediately moved across the street to the Algonquin. The unpleasant episode had a most happy consequence, for it heralded a long association between JATP members and this famous hotel, and I was totally enamoured of it from the start. Its marvellous feel and family atmosphere captivated me, as did the warmth and sincerity of the welcome extended on one's arrival. Just to hear that "Hi, Mr Peterson. Welcome back!" from the desk clerk means a hell of a lot to a roadrunner: it gives you a special life that helps to heal some of the bumps and grinds of a long and gruelling trip.

After a few trips in the United States, I decided that in order to remain sane I would have to abide by one irrevocable rule: never to stay in any hotel, motel, or whatever that in any way at all fell below the standards I was used to at home. Norman endorsed this belief, and helped me to fulfill it.

A travelling performer can end up with a ridiculous amount of "dead time" on his hands. A concert takes roughly two-and-a-half hours; a night-club appearance approximately five. Usually the last set would be over by 2.00 a.m. and you would not be due on stage again until 9.30 the following evening. In those night-club-hopping years, our sit-down periods would be anything from one week in a city like Philadelphia to four weeks in Chicago or Toronto, where the clubs favoured the more extended booking policy. The group as a whole— and now I come to think of it, most musicians—preferred longer engagements: it gave them a chance to rest, to rehearse new tunes and increase the repertoire, and to deepen friendships with various women that might otherwise have been only fleeting one-night stands.

However, even these more comfortable extended sojourns left a lot of time to fill, and that led me to make space my chief priority. That way I could bring my "toys" or hobbies on the road with me, and also increase my working knowledge of things like photography, astronomy, and early-stage electronics. It wasn't long before I needed an extra room to accommodate them all.

I knew of course that such a step was going to be expensive, but it was worth it. I at once lost that caged feeling that invariably oppressed me when in the confines of a small, single room; simple as it may sound, just to be able to enjoy breakfast in my living-room gave the road a much different complexion. Another plus factor concerned interviews. Beforehand, I had always felt that allowing interviewers and photographers into my bedroom—no matter who they were or which magazine they worked for—was an invasion of privacy; to be able to conduct these sessions in a sitting-room was infinitely preferable.

I quickly grew to prefer the older kind of hotels to the shiny new plastic palaces, whose modern furniture was never comfortable and always in the way, and most of whose gadgets never quite worked. As I've said, the Algonquin, with its period decor and friendly after-theatre gatherings, has remained a favourite from my earliest days; so too is the Fairmont in San Francisco—provided I can live in the older section, whose charm and warmth engulf you as you enjoy the large bathrooms and spacious bedrooms. I have many wonderful memories of the Fairmont, especially from the 1950s, when JATP came through every year. We would spend upwards of a week playing concerts in the Bay area, and our evenings invariably ended in the Papagallo Room, run by arguably the world's most amiable host, Al Williams.

To say that Al enjoyed his proprietor-host's nightly tasks would be the understatement of the century. Aided by his pretty wife, he reigned over that room much like a maharajah over his kingdom. He knew exactly what was going on in every corner and somehow managed to keep everything in hand at all times. Once he learned of my romance with the world's various cuisines, he instructed his staff not to bring me a menu but instead went to the kitchen himself to fix me up with unusual Mexican concoctions. He revelled in trying to find dishes that would set my palate on fire, but was unsuccessful: he hadn't bargained for my West Indian heritage, and settled for trading stories about legendary performers. However, with a little help from me, Al's Mexican fire certainly got to Ray Brown.

Ray was one of Al's regular customers. He had a habit of circulating throughout the room in much the same manner as the host, greeting friends and engaging in general patter and camaraderie. One night, after accusing him of trying to upstage Al, I spied Ray making his rounds once again. I called him over, knowing that he was going to insist on tasting whatever Al had prepared for me; that particular night, it so happened that the dish was very hotly spiced. Ray duly arrived, said hello, and demanded a mouthful. I loaded up a huge forkful and fed it to him. He staggered back from the table, gasping and coughing, his hands holding his throat, while I of course folded over in a laughing fit. Brown groped his way back to his own table, and wouldn't speak to me for two days.

What makes hotels special is the little favours and treats unavailable elsewhere, or even to other guests—selfish, maybe, but undeniably something to be treasured. London's The Inn On The Park had a manager astute and thoughtful enough to arrange special security and surveillance for me during one of my periods of marital upheaval. Then there's Michael, the very gentle night porter at the Connaught Hotel in London, who was so attentive to the needs of my newborn son Joel. I vividly recall checking into the hotel with six-month-old Joel and his mother. The first thing we asked for was some warm milk to be brought to our room each night for Joel's 4.00 a.m. feed—a pretty steep request, but one that experience had taught us was essential. No matter how beautifully peaceful his abode, this young child would, on awakening at 4.00, climb to the top of his crib and give us approximately three minutes to get some manna to him. Should the schedule fail, for any reason at all, there would be no room for negotiation. The mouth would open to full extension, the lungs would be inflated with a full tank of air, and out would come sounds to make

Cat Anderson or Maynard Ferguson envious. Then would come the rush to the telephone and a frenzied call to the night desk for help!

Such a nightmare never happened when Michael was on. I was appearing at Ronnie Scott's club at the time, and would arrive back at about 3.30, allowing me just enough time to shower and hit the sack for that first round of sleep. Many were the mornings that I would be awakened by an ever-so-gentle tap on the door, and I'd come to sufficiently to see Joel's mother open the door and receive a silver tray with a pitcher of warm milk on it. Michael had come through again!

Michaels are rare in even the best hotels—people who have that special intuitive perception about their guests. On one of my visits I had a long chat with him late one evening and found that he was from what used to be Yugoslavia: Belgrade to be exact. After World War II he escaped to France as a refugee, there to meet many of the jazz masters whom he idolized—Coleman Hawkins, Ben Webster, Louis Armstrong, and others. He spoke of them with great affection and reverence, which, I sadly reflected, is not too common amongst today's yuppies, who may pay plastic homage to the jazz world in the form of T-shirts and other tawdry icons, but whose understanding of the culture itself is about as deep as topsoil after a tornado. Michael's reminiscences revealed a profound and harmonious musical understanding of these giants, which in turn made me understand why I had been so warmly treated and looked after. I was honoured to have earned the caring respect of this gentle bespectacled man behind the porter's desk at my home away from home in London.

I first learned the word "concierge" in an early French class in Montreal, but it wasn't until I met Alfred, the concierge at the Hotel Lancaster in Paris, that I got to see the concept in full operation. Alfred was a big man with a voice to match, and with a French accent women dream about. He was never at a loss for information and immediately eased any problem you might have. In fact, he often seemed to know what your question would be before it was asked.

Alfred figured centrally in one of the more bizarre episodes of my career. The Trio had left Paris to play a concert in a smaller French town, but a big problem developed with the promoter, who refused to fulfill the terms of the contract. I called Norman, who had stayed behind in Paris, and his solution was simple: the promoter had breached our agreement and we should return to Paris at once. I replied that this was easier said than done: although it was still early, there were no flights out of the town until the next day. Norman told me not to worry, and that he would have Alfred call me. Sure enough, about half an hour later, I was listening to his unique tones: "Monsieur Petaarson, please be at the kiosk in the airport in an hour and a half. Your pilots will meet you there."

The beauty of all this was that the promoter didn't believe me when I said I would not play the concert. He had a sold-out house, and was clearly banking on the fact that there were no flights to Paris that night; so out he came to the airport to watch what in his mind was a futile attempt on our part to leave. One-and-a-half hours later, almost to the minute, two young men walked up to me. "Bonjour, Monsieur Peterson. We are your pilots for the trip back to Paris. Are you ready?" The recently cackling promoter was stunned into silence. Alfred the Great had struck again!

I can't carry my home with me on the road, and I can't duplicate it city to city. But the great hotels of the world and their quietly magnificent people provide havens of solitude and comfort that I—and so many travelling artists—depend on.

86

THE CONTINUAL SEARCH
FOR TRUE FRIENDS

A lthough it can appear to some people that a performer's life is one of revelry, lightheartedness, irresponsibility, party-time USA, and so forth, I can assure you that this is not the case. Show business of any kind can often be a very lonely existence. Being almost continually on the move makes it extremely difficult to develop truly meaningful relationships of the kind that settled, static people regard as the norm. Even so, I have managed to form some very deep and rewarding friendships while on the road; my major problems have been with relationships at home.

The biggest, and constant, hassle whenever I would return home was fatigue. I'd get back half-twisted, only to get a string of calls from a variety of people, reminding me of this or that pre-arranged date or function, not sensing that I was in no shape to fulfill them. I would call on our friendship for understanding, but they were instead invariably hurt and disappointed. It took me a long time to realize, thanks to many admonishments from Norman and other friends in the profession, that I must insist on my privacy for a few days, to recoup my sanity and balance and to readjust to my home environment.

My greatest disappointment of all has been to discover that some "friends" were motivated mainly by greed. Their devoted cultivation of me had more to do with gaining access to what they thought were unlimited resources than with anything genuinely affectionate and honest. Such "friendships" had a definite pattern, exemplified by this next story.

Early on in our relationship, one particular gentleman expressed concern that I was becoming too involved with trivial details that I "shouldn't even be bothered with." He reminded me time and again of my position in the music world, and lectured me about my foolish readiness to be "thrown in with the wrong people, people who are below you." He was even more insistent about this once I had received the Order of Canada, but I took little notice; his harangues were not comfortable to listen to, but I believed he meant well and that our friendship was deepening. We became fishing buddies, we hung out together, and I was there financially whenever he got in a jam. I even hired him to work on houses of mine.

I trusted him completely, even though I was becoming aware of some glaring weaknesses in him. As a friend I scolded him about them, cautioning him that other people would not be as forgiving as I was. I put our friendship on the line after I had concrete proof that he had been dishonest, but even then—despite the worried disillusionment of other friends, who by now were warning me almost daily that I was being used and, indeed, taken—I would not give up the friendship. But it did come to an end, and abruptly. I was presented with irrefutable evidence that he had lied about the costs he had submitted, doctoring figures outrageously. When I confronted him with this, he predictably swung round on me, accusing me of being a sneak in checking out his costs and betraying a friendship in which he had given himself so unselfishly.

I had been more stupid than I care to admit. And I still found it impossible to understand such bare-faced lying about incontrovertible facts; it takes all sorts, I suppose. But I was, naturally, deeply hurt: I was appalled that someone who claimed to be such a great friend would be so warped that he could cold-bloodedly try to con me, while expecting me to look on him as someone with only my deepest interests at heart.

There's one consolation, however. The final outcome of that kind of despicable behaviour is ignominy: the predator has to live with his or her actions because they're now known to the community—all the more so if the victim has been one such as myself who is in the public eye. Oddly enough, the same thing happened again quite recently:

another person whom I had trusted as a friend turned out to be much more interested in my income than in my friendship. He, too, will have to live with the role and stigma of a viper.

Troubled years, with disloyalty, even treachery; how much worse they might have been had it not been for such friends as Bob and Margaret Streeter, whom I met shortly after moving to Toronto. Bob, a six-foot-four, blustery, country-honest man, was rapidly becoming one of Toronto's leading photographers, which itself accelerated our friendship, as I was totally absorbed in the photographic world as an amateur. They had a studio in Toronto's West End, within walking distance for both of us. When back off the road, I was virtually a fixture there, and Bob taught me more about photography than it would be possible to itemize. Bob and Margaret realized instinctively, I think, that I needed such normalcy which show business could not provide, and we became fast friends. In addition, Bob appealed to me deeply as a born prankster. He and I have put each other on more times than I can remember, and the invariable outcome is a double laughing fit of cramp-like intensity, the tears rolling down our cheeks.

I remember one night at my cottage, when Bob and his sons, Jim and Rick, and my two nephews, John and Ron, were visiting. It was around 10.30 at night and the rain was bucketing down. The kids had a tent pitched on a couple of landings near the lake, and Bob announced that it was time for all young males to be in bed as he had a lot of work for them next day. After they departed grouchily for the tent, Bob, Marg, my sister May, my wife Sandy, and I chatted away, and someone observed that it was like a night out of *Frankenstein*. An idea hit me. I told Bob to grab a raincoat and come with me down to the tent. We tiptoed over and listened as best we could through the heavy rain, and it soon became evident that the four boys were in the midst of a discussion about parents and their shortcomings. They were acting like a couple of husbands away from home, mouthing off as Michael Machos when in fact they were Casper Milktoasts. "Watch me stop all of this!" I whispered to Bob, who gave me a quizzical look.

I went over to the tent and ran my hand down it while emitting the fiercest growl I could manage, in imitation of a grizzly. Either the rain was too heavy or the growl wasn't loud enough, because the talking continued and nobody seemed to have registered anything. Nobody, that is, except Ronald, who has a slight speech impediment: he stutters. Wouldn't you know that I had chosen the very corner where he was? "S-s-s-say fellas," we heard him ask in desperation, "D-d-d-did you h-h-hear th-th-that?" The others talked on, oblivious to his concern; Bob and I collapsed in the mud, constricted with cramps as we tried to hold in our laughter. We recovered somewhat and crawled back over to the tent. I decided to increase the treatment, scratching the tent in the same way while summoning up the most hideous growl I could. "Th-th-there it is ag-ag-again!" Ron screamed, diving away from his corner into the middle of the group. Bob and I started our muck-and-mire roll around act again, while the boys debated who was going to go outside to find out what was going on. Bob and I still laugh about it today.

Early on in our friendship Bob came over to give me a "reading" that I've never forgotten. "Pete," he said, "There's one thing that you can rest assured of as long as we're friends. You'll always know when I agree with the way you act, but you'll also most certainly know when I disagree. There's no in-between with me."

Bob—and Marg—have proved over and over again that they mean what they say and say what they mean. They epitomize true friends. We've argued, we've laughed, we've played the fool, and we've cried, but we have never fallen out. It's a simple thing to say, but they have given me those things that no amount of money could ever buy.

One summer, Bob said he would act as "advance party" for my vacation at the Haliburton Highlands cottage, turning on the water, power, and so on, so that all was ready for my arrival. When I got there, I found a newly painted cottage, a completely landscaped garden area, a new dock, and various other things that added to our summer facilities and necessities. Moreover, they had rid the cottage of the mice that had invaded that spring through a couple of holes left uncovered by the plumbers. Knowing that I'd be going to the cottage after a lengthy tour, tired as usual and not ready to cope with such purges and repairs, they'd done their utmost to see that the cottage was spick and span inside and newly lovely outside. Such planned, loving care moved me immensely, and I will always treasure and bask in their friendship and love.

Other dear friends must also be mentioned. For over 35 years Morey and Daisy Kessler have supplied me with quietly resilient backup friendship. I remember going to Morey when one of my marriages was breaking up and he said, "Do what you honestly think is the best thing and the right thing and set yourself at ease. There is nothing more to be done. Once you know that you've been true to yourself, regardless of the situation, there is absolutely nothing else to be done." Those words did not just serve me well then; they have always done so.

Eric Smith and Joel Michaels—and their lovely wives—have remained close and valued buddies for many years, even though they live in Los Angeles and we only see each other every few months. We have come to specialize in "getting one another": at any given time, one of us would be conjuring a put-on for the other two, in varying permutations. The enjoyment lies in the elaborate planning and the cunning awareness of the particular victim's psyche and his likely reactions. I have been known to exacerbate this already complex setup by playing traitor to both sides.

Eric often calls me up with some plan he intends to spring on Joel. I listen sympathetically, and suggest a few finer points he could add to make his little scam smoother and more plausible. Within a day or so at most, Joel will call me to say that he knows Eric is about to pull something, and lets me in on his counter-plan. Again, I offer little refinements that I know will convince Joel that his riposte will be even better. In short, I sow enough seeds to be sure that when the two guys' plans collide disastrously, at some point they will both stop dead in their tracks and yell, "Oscar! I see his fine hand in *all* of this—both sides!" Of course, by this time I'll be incommunicado in a city far away!

The enjoyment, suspense, mental fulfillment, and hilarity that these miniature CIA plots always deliver give me an important sense of belonging to a normal, everyday world. That also holds true, in fact, for the less happy incidents with people who were not genuine friends. It is a pendulum of loss, restitution, and final balance: even as it swings to the dark side of fruitless relationships, there is the glowing reassurance of knowing that it will swing back to the warmth and truth of the Bobs and Margs and the Erics and Joels.

87

NIGHT CHILD

"O scar, I feel funny." From the moment that I heard those words from my wife at that time, Charlotte, I knew something special was happening to us. Prior to this occasion I had only been present at the birth of my first daughter, Lynn. The birth of all the rest of my children had found me at various places in the world, but now I would be there, experiencing it as if I'd never done so before. A dear friend, now deceased, by the name of Bick came over to be with Charlotte and to help in reassuring her. Bick was a very special lady to me. She and her sister Dorothy, whom I fondly nicknamed "Bad News," have remained dear to my heart.

I had just received a brand-new electric piano and was caught up in this different sounding keyboard. I asked Bick when she thought we'd need to leave for the hospital, and when she replied that we still had a little time, I sat down at the new piano, turned on a recorder that was sitting there, and recorded what is now *Night Child*. The song poured out of me as I added bar after bar, and when it was finished, Bick came over to me and said she thought it was time to go.

Although it was then mid-afternoon it was not until nearly 4.00 next morning that Joel made his appearance in this world. It was an overwhelming moment for me: a human life had come into being and I had been partially responsible for it. Fatigued, but still glowing with joy, as soon as I arrived home I went to the cassette machine and played the tune whose title, *Night Child*, had since come to me. Strangely untired, I worked into the night, adding the synthesized string parts, until it was finished.

When Charlotte returned home from the hospital some days later, I played it for both her and little Joel. As it played I sat there deeply moved, holding this tiny bundle of humanity whose little head bobbled from time to time. In fact, we almost released that particular cassette as the lead track on the *Night Child* album on account of its sincerity and tremendous feeling. Unfortunately, it was just too noisy to be put on a record, and so it was re-done with the Trio in London sometime later. Because of the musical structure of the piece I can envision it being done with strings and electric piano, and intend to issue another reading of it in future. I think it is a special tune, just as I still feel Joel is a special guy.

88

MARRIAGE AND FATHERHOOD

Although one deals musically with emotion in jazz, many of us have found it impossible to deal with it in real life. Because jazz artists concentrate on acquiring control skills and, in general, can more or less "call their own tempos," they perhaps develop a greater perception and sensitivity in music than they bring to life itself. This is particularly true of marriage.

My first mistake was to marry too early. It was a selfish decision, compounded by my additional selfishness in pursuing my musical ambitions to the utmost. I knew this would involve amongst all else a great deal of travelling, but I failed to realize that this would cause problems in my marital life. I didn't take enough time to attempt to solve them; as a result they multiplied and led eventually to the marriage's dissolution.

Probably the worst problem for my first wife, Lillian, and myself was the loneliness we both had to endure. She was sequestered in our new flat in Montreal, quickly forced to cope with a growing family while missing dreadfully her new husband, who was often away for weeks at a time. Meanwhile I was similarly prey to that dark spectre of loneliness, trying to fight it off via the constant bustle of travelling and nightly concerts, but finding it to be a more-or-less constant companion.

I once wrote a poem (now long lost) that traced the uncomfortable sequence of events that characterized a performance night. The arrival in town in mid-afternoon; orientation—the quiet time that helped me focus on the concert to come; the personal pump-up just before the curtain; and, at last, the pressure of the show itself. In the poem I described the exhilarating joy of the performance, the response of the audience, and the lasting satisfaction of a musically successful night, along with the nightly realization of how much I was learning from the great musicians I accompanied. The sharp descent back to reality would begin almost as soon as I left the performance hall; by the time I reached my hotel room I would be depressed enough to need to call home immediately. It was not uncommon to run up a weekly phone bill of hundreds of dollars in an attempt to preserve a sense of being part of a family; on top of that, I would write letters home that ran to 20 pages, trying to describe my extreme loneliness, and also my feeling of having lost my family during my absence.

At first Lil tried to understand and adjust to all this, which I know was frighteningly new and strange to her. But eventually we reached the point of no return: my absence and the ever-growing problems she had with the children drove her to the end of her endurance. I started to detect a lethargic response to my letters and calls, which only increased my insecurity on the road, and almost inevitably led to the next stage—trying to compensate by seeking female company. This naturally only made a bad situation worse, and we were both rapidly becoming aware that things were hopeless. Then, on returning from one trip and becoming enmeshed in several uncomfortable disagreements, I decided that the marriage was not working for either of us. We divorced and I moved from the house after breaking the news to our children, which was the harshest event in my life thus far.

My second marriage was very different. My new wife Sandy accompanied me on nearly all my tours and appearances, so loneliness was never a problem. However, she was a very strong character—she had been an operating theatre nurse—and had a temper almost as bad as mine; furthermore, I know that she increasingly felt unfulfilled. As my own career progressed and I started to win awards, Sandy became both envious and resentful, thinking of the career she had given up. Such a fierce battle of wills could only end one way, although we somehow managed 15 years together before the marriage came crashing down around us, precipitating a tumultuous, acrimonious divorce. Our time together was also marked by periods of tremendous elation, excitement, and free-wheeling love, but we never achieved true serenity or acceptance of the differences between us.

This second divorce got to me badly, although my musical career continued to prosper, and I now think my third marriage was very much "on the rebound." Charlie, who had been an airline hostess, was much younger than I, and although we were blessed with a son, Joel (whom I thought we both adored), the marriage ended in catastrophe. The break-up was bad enough—exceptionally sour and sardonic—but the aftermath was even worse. I had hoped that from this wreck I could at least salvage a relationship with Joel, but was devastated to discover that, contrary to our divorce agreement, his mother had moved away from Toronto. Rather than trigger another long and painful legal battle, I gave her no opposition; they now live somewhere in eastern Canada. This has been a dreadful loss, and was the sad inspiration for a tune I wrote entitled *He Has Gone.*

The cumulative pain from these marital wounds prompted me to consider the wisdom of the baseball rule "three strikes and out," and I decided I would never marry again.

Happily all that went by the board when I did a concert in Sarasota, Florida, and met Kelly Green, now my fourth wife. From the moment we met in the lobby of a restaurant (which she was managing at the time) I felt unusually close to her, and our romance blossomed—first on the phone, then when she visited various cities where I was performing, and finally at a luncheon with Norman and Grete Granz. The setting was breathtaking: on the shores of Lake Annecy, in a bistro called Père Bise, arguably the best restaurant in France. Norman spoke of how highly he thought of Kelly and suddenly broke out, "Why don't you ask her to marry you?" He went on to say that even if I'd had three failed marriages, there was no doubting the depth and tenderness of how Kelly and I cared for each other, and that he had not seen such qualities in my previous relationships. I proposed to her that evening, and when she accepted, Norman and Grete said that they would like to take care of our reception as a gift to us.

It was a magnificent day. We were married in a suite at L'Ermitage Hotel in Beverly Hills and the reception was held in one of Norman's favourite haunts when he lived in LA, Chasen's Restaurant. The array of such close friends as Ray, Herbie, and Clark Terry made it one of the most exciting and heart-warming days of my life. Even greater happiness was to follow.

It would be absurd to suggest that Kelly and I planned to have a child. She learned that she was pregnant during a trip to Japan, and her first thoughts were those of concern—she felt the news might upset me, or cause me upheaval during the tour, or both—and she only told me when I was sympathizing with her over another bout of what of course proved to be morning sickness. Much to her relief, I was overjoyed and at once caught up in the unique magic of expectant parenthood. I also sensed that Kelly had wanted this more than anything in the world, and all in all it was a time of profound jubilation.

MATTERS PERSONAL · 363

Sadly, I missed Celine's birth. I had already contracted to do a three-week tour of Europe in the summer of 1991, and Kelly delivered two days after my departure. It's hard to describe the impatience and frustration I lived through during those days away. The only time I felt remotely relaxed was on stage, performing; the rest of the time, it seemed, I was on the phone to home, asking what I now realize must have been the most inane questions imaginable about our new joy. I went shopping almost every day, but no longer remember what I bought for Celine, and behaved in other weird ways until I at last got back to Toronto and caught my first glimpse of my new daughter. This was during the shooting of the documentary *In the Key of Oscar*, and I recall answering with an angrily decisive "No!" a request by the then director of the film that this first glimpse should be recorded on film. This was a sacred personal moment, to be shared with no one but Kelly and Celine.

It was also a very important moment for me in other ways. Many of my values and priorities changed radically: it was as though virtually everything in my *Store of Life* had been re-appraised and newly priced. Certain things tumbled in value; others escalated enormously. Things I had wanted badly now seemed worthless, as I basked in a sense of calm I had never known and which I had thought unattainable. I had been a father on six previous occasions, but this was the first time that I fully understood and revelled in what I had helped create. I had thought I knew a lot about creation and creativity: after all, a musical composition can have remarkable depth and almost endless potential. But its life depends on other people, other artists; this new life was independent and emotionally alive in her own right, capable of changing from day to day, even moment to moment. All this may seem a commonplace distinction, and indeed it is; the real point is, however, that it took Celine's birth in my 66th year to make me properly aware of it.

This new awareness and vision were, ironically, strengthened by my need for a lengthy convalescence following two separate hip operations, experiences that one would not normally welcome! I did not perform in public for 15 months from January 1992; more importantly,

I was also away from all my groups, and devoted my musical efforts almost entirely to composition. I cannot pretend that such a lay-off was not frustrating in some ways, but it was also distinguished for the tranquillity I felt, and the many subtle pleasures that arose from having my days governed by my baby daughter. I also found myself getting much more tolerant than before: she was remoulding both life itself and my attitudes to it.

Musically, too, I became more mellow. Such recent compositions of mine as *Nighttime, Should I Ever Dream Of Being Without You, Valse Mauve,* and *Summertime* came very easily, flowing naturally out of my newly serene inner life; and the piano itself inspired me even more, seeming to have grown even grander and more majestic that before.

If I attribute my new perspectives primarily to baby Celine's entrance into my life, there is another factor that has been at work— ageing, and with it the final (and welcome) loss of immaturity. In my earlier marriages my priorities were very different, and I was never able to respond to the arrival of my other children in a way that I now see I should have done. This is not altogether blameworthy: when young, one is prey to uncertainty, to fear of failure, to the pressures inherent in scuffling to provide, and to the anxiety of the need to feed yet another mouth. (This last fear is particularly prevalent amongst young jazz players, for that profession has always been an uncertain, even risky one.) All these factors get in the way of what should be an unbridled joy in being a father. And I was relieved, talking recently to Quincy Jones (himself a new father at 60), to hear him say, "Now that I think back, OP, I realize what a lousy father I was earlier on!" An exaggeration, I'm sure, but I very much shared his recognition of how various pressures and distractions impeded his life as a parent when he was younger.

I feel assured and confident as a performer now, and I feel this will make me a much more stable parent, now capable of giving back some of the joy, serenity, and maturity that Celine's birth has given me. And I hope, too, that I can now give my earlier family the full attention and understanding that they continue to deserve, for I want to enjoy them all to the full.

89

SURGERY; RESURGENCE;
STROKE!

I n the previous chapter I spoke of my 15-month sabbatical, when I neither played in public nor even worked out with my various groups. It was a period that found me very much torn. On the one hand, the deep joy of my new life with Kelly and Celine prompted me to think of retiring permanently, in order to devote myself to them and to enjoy Celine's day-to-day growth and development. On the other hand, I was still preoccupied by the piano, and two things haunted me as I lay in Toronto's Orthopedic and Arthritic Hospital recuperating from my first hip operation. The first was the worry that my enforced lay-off might already have led to the loss of some of my pianistic skills and powers of invention. I had always maintained that once a certain level of instrumental control has been accomplished, it ought not to be necessary to subject oneself to the arduous hours of practice that had been essential in one's formative years; now, I was nothing like so sure. The second was the thought of how much trauma I might suffer if I were never again to play with Ray or the other guys.

The more I thought, the less decisive I became. Retirement offered other pleasures than those of being with my family every day—like saying goodbye to the rigours of the road. No more airline clerks who really don't care if you miss your plane, even though your initial flight was delayed by their airline and this is your last chance to make tonight's gig. No more hotel people who couldn't care less if your room is less than comfortable and clean. No more room-service personnel who knowingly serve you cold or incomplete meals. No more maids who have no thought for your comfort or even for whether your bathroom is hygienically safe for use. And no more airports—ever! In addition, it was not as if I would be musically inactive once I came off the road. Many friends had suggested that, since I now had my own composition studio, the loss of doing live performances would not be quite such a let-down as it might have proved earlier.

Against all that was my undying knowledge of just how much I relished the "fix" of performing live. Would I be happy to exist without the regular musical challenge that Ray, Jeff Hamilton, and Clark Terry provided? Could I serenely douse the fires of competition that had burned in me all my life? Working in one's own studio is all very well, even very marvellous; but nothing can replace the exhilaration of comping for soloists on their flights of musical invention, or the unique highs of running my own musical thoughts along every available rhythmic and harmonic highway.

A second hip operation followed later that year (1992), and in the end, feeling newly able and much refreshed, I came fully to terms with something I had half-suspected all along: I could not retire yet—the lure of live playing was still too strong. So I contracted to do a three-week tour of Japan, fulfilling engagements at the Blue Note Clubs in Tokyo, Fukuoka, and Osaka. The group would consist of Ray, Herbie, and Jeff; knowing them as I do, I realized that the tour would offer me a definitive challenge, and I looked forward to it with an almost equal mixture of anxiety and delight.

I was, of course, accompanied on the trip by Kelly and Celine. The flight over was most enjoyable with Celine in her element, laughing and playing with the crew for the most part. The only bad moments for her came as we began our descent for Tokyo, where we encountered turbulence and a violent hail storm, which upset her: she was indeed terrified, and tried to leave her seat. We somehow managed to comfort her and she was quiet and calm throughout the ride from Narita airport to downtown Tokyo, which is tiresome enough at the best of times, and Kelly soon managed to get Celine down to rest. We watched her in something like wonder: children seem capable of overcoming any given trauma by surrendering naturally to the sandman. She set a good example: Kelly and I were soon ready to crash out, and I left instructions with my road aide not to call us until he heard from me. I was mindful of the fact that our tour would comprise two shows a night with only Sundays off, and I wanted to be ready.

Prior to our first appearance, the guys had been busy kidding me about my supposedly weakened and rusty state, and how much severe musical damage they were about to inflict on me as a result. However, I was confident. For some reason, this time out I did not seem to have suffered at all from jet lag, and I had no last-minute jitters as I stood in the wings; my only concern was wondering what tunes to call.

As soon as we kicked off into the first selection, *Falling In Love With Love*, I was conscious of a great inner warmth. I seemed to be enveloped in a huge cradle furnished by the guys, rocking me back and forth in cadence with the song, while also prodding me forward musically. This gave me an immense sense of security, and the phrases I brought off could not even have been attempted without such confidence. I was vaguely aware of a tingling in my hands that is a regular reminder of my bouts of arthritis, but it mattered little at that moment, as I was more immediately concerned with meeting the guys' challenges. In all truth, during the evening I did experience some difficulty with some of the things I tried to execute, but I chalked most of that up to my recent extended inactivity. As each night progressed I grew in strength and assurance; the group responded in kind and in full, and by the end of the three weeks we were reaching highs that would have seemed impossible at the outset. Then it was back to Toronto and a few days' rest before our opening at New York's Blue Note. The house was packed with charged-up music fans (amongst them Bill Cosby), and we roared into it from the start, building on where we'd left off in Japan.

And then, towards the end of the week, a weird and terrifying thing happened. We were into the closing theme (*Blues Etude*), and suddenly I found myself missing on the boogie-woogie passages that climax the arrangement. To begin with, we all thought no more about it, figuring that I'd simply fumbled this particular performance: such things do happen occasionally. However, when it happened again on the second show, a look of worried disbelief clouded Ray's face, and he asked what was happening. All I could reply was that I was at a loss as to what was going on—I just felt strange. I begged him not to say anything to anyone, certainly not to Kelly (who was in the club that night). He agreed, and we finished off the set.

But Kelly was worried. Initially, I tried to allay her concern by complaining of travel stress and fatigue; she persisted, however, and even asked if I needed a doctor. I pooh-poohed the idea, repeated my remarks about how tired I felt, and headed for bed. I now know, of course, that I was being foolish, that I could have done myself irreparable damage. I didn't think it was that urgent: I had no inkling that this "feeling strange" had, in reality, been a stroke.

90

THE PERFECT RETREAT

I have been remarkably fortunate in being able to visit so many nations and places all over the world. All have invigorated and fed me—some in a culinary way, others artistically, and several have made me grateful that I am Canadian and live in a civilized country. These global wanderings have sometimes made me toy with the idea of living elsewhere, but nowhere has given me more contentment or desire to remain in one place than my experience on a visit to Barbados in 1999.

I had decided to take the family—my wife Kelly and our daughter Celine—on a midwinter holiday. Through the Internet we chose what seemed to be a very comfortable and beautifully sited retreat called The Sandpiper. I took a keyboard with me, for I was engaged on a commission for the Canadian government to commemorate a new environmental highway that would run the length and breadth of Canada, from Vancouver to Newfoundland, right up to the Arctic. The trip turned out to be not only musically productive but also one of the most enjoyable holidays of my life.

Almost as soon as we arrived I found that the atmosphere, the people, and their prevailing attitude to each day had a remarkable effect. I shed most of the "cooped up" tension I'd been feeling and gave myself up to absorbing the island's atmosphere and its beautiful weather. Before I knew it, I was into a daily routine that I could not manage at home in Mississauga. After a good night's sleep I would awake to find Kelly and Celine getting excitely ready to hit the swimming pool. Following morning greetings and kisses, they would make coffee for me and set out some sweet buns and the like before leaving for the pool. My continental breakfast over, I would start composing at the keyboard. Sitting there in the living-room of our suite and able to gaze out at the colourful beauty of The Sandpiper's garden and pool, I had no problem throwing myself completely into my Canadian project.

After a few hours' writing, I would get on my scooter and, taking my camera along, spend the rest of the morning photographing the awe-inspiring beauty of the plants, trees, and bushes which would not survive in a Canadian climate. Then I would join Kelly and Celine at the pool for lunch, followed by further photographic sorties in the afternoon. After that, back to the suite for some more writing and, eventually, getting ready for dinner. Dining there was not only a great culinary experience but allowed us the opportunity to listen to local singers and musicians. I was intrigued and delighted to find how many of them were deeply involved in the jazz idiom: it re-endorsed my faith in the form to which I've dedicated my life.

Sometimes we would just hire a van and tour this beautiful island. Its culture is a wonderful meld of African and British cultures and manners, seasoned with an American curiosity, sprinkled with the grace of the old empire. I loved it all, and the trip affected me profoundly. The restful atmosphere did wonders for my roadrunner's jagged nerves; the friendliness, honesty, and warmth of the people calmed my family and me in a way we had never experienced anywhere else in the world. I shall always look forward to returning to Barbados, hoping that each visit will allow me to discover more of my inner self. I wonder if it is just the natural aura of this beautiful island that makes me feel that way, or whether it might be some kind of subliminal hereditary attachment, since my parents were both raised in this West Indian environment.

91

THE ELUSIVE CONTROL
OF EMOTION

The most fundamental challenge for many musicians and artists is the control (even at times the sublimation) of their personal emotions, coupled with the ability to project to their audiences without being overtly maudlin the momentary highs that they manage to attain in performance. The greatest players that I have known, even though unable at times to control their own lives, manage to redirect whatever internal turmoil they are experiencing into the immediacy of the music. Jazz, being essentially an improvisatory medium, can offer the listener the innermost revelations of the artist; there can be no secondary editing of what has been played, no opportunity for the ego to polish the invented lines with falsehoods. It is at this moment that the true creative statement—good or bad, pretty or ugly—is made.

My own approach, throughout various periods of turmoil in my life, has been to focus first on my love of the piano itself, then on the love of my group, and lastly on the selections chosen. I am the first to admit that in the search for that "normal existence" that many of us strive to achieve within our careers, we at times run into a lot more than we bargained for emotionally. It is also true that many artists seem to handle these misfortunes less well than other human beings involved in more "everyday" occupations; however, the extreme joy of creative satisfaction that we experience as players far exceeds, I suspect, that of people in those same everyday occupations—a theory demonstrated by the joyful exclamation Barney Kessel produced after this first evening in my trio. He came over to me after the last set, shook his head, and said with that Oklahoma accent, "Oscar, that was better than sex!"

Perhaps only a player who has reached some of the heights that a talent like Barney Kessel has reached could understand the full significance of his exuberant reaction. I am constantly asked by various players and listeners what it really feels like to arrive at certain plateaux in music; my reply is that there is an aura or stratum that can be achieved by certain players in jazz that is unlike any other experience I know of. It is like shifting into Mach 10, for within its scope there is a glide path that one can reach which opens up new galaxies that only we as players can imagine as attainable. The only restraining factor is the amount of time you are permitted to wander through these new harmonic and rhythmic worlds.

Depending on the situation, you are either the captain of this particular flight into space, or one of the exhilarated passengers or crew members. I say this to emphasize that at times the space vehicle was captained by people like Lester Young, Dizzy Gillespie, Charlie Parker, Roy Eldridge, and Ella Fitzgerald, and I have always enjoyed to the full and with maximum involvement being merely a contributor in a rhythm section providing the fuel for that flight into space. The exhilaration when one accelerates into special orbit is almost indescribable. There were many, many moments of this nature on JATP, and countless others with my varied trios.

92

THE WILL TO PERFECTION

As I sit on the balcony of my cottage in the beautiful Haliburton Highlands, reading over the many stories and portraits that make up this autobiography, I am struck by how *current* they seem to me. These events and vignettes—some of them from over half a century ago and more—remain as fresh in my mind as if they had happened today, and that is important as well as gratifying: it helps give shape to my life. Each experience left some permanent residue, be it anger, remorse, strength, enlightenment, happiness, or maturity, and some kind of pattern emerges as a result. The pattern is neither complete nor regular: some things seem to cohere; others conflict or exist in isolation. It is somewhat akin to listening to an orchestra tuning up: one's initial impression of mere cacophony alters as certain sounds make sense and cohere with others, together with moments of ugliness, humour, and surprise.

It would be untrue to say that I am completely satisfied with my life so far. No player still performing could—or should—ever claim that, for every performance has its shortcomings, its moments of self-discontent and unrest. All artists spend their creative lives trying to find out how high it is possible for them to climb before their time is over, and however majestic their achievements may seem to others, they are never satisfied. Only perfection will do.

Some jazzmen got as close to that ultimate as makes no apparent difference: Ellington, Tatum, Eldridge, Hawkins. Yet they knew that they had not quite reached that stratum, for such a level is, in the end, a mystical one. Paradoxically, however, its very elusiveness gives it an immense radiating power, feeding artists with a prodigious will and driving determination to reach new plateaux of discovery. I remember, for example, how Coleman Hawkins would run off one of those unforgettable solos that combined linear beauty with astonishing harmonic depth and then, as his audience gazed in awe at such perfect facility, he would shake his head, rattle the keys of his horn, and mutter to himself in displeasure over some phrase or idea that hadn't quite come off as he'd intended. No matter how literate and appreciative, no listener can ever entirely grasp a musician's aims and conceptions; or, to put it another way, perhaps no serious musician can ever be absolutely serene about what he or she has created. Total satisfaction exists only in the ear of the listener.

This "will to perfection," as I have termed it, seems especially prevalent in *jazz* musicians. Creating an uninhibited, off-the-cuff musical composition in front of a large audience is a dare-devil enterprise, one that draws on everything about you, not just your musical talent. It requires you to collect all your senses, emotions, physical strength, and mental power, and focus them totally onto the performance—utter dedication, every time you play. And if that is scary, it is also uniquely exciting: once it's bitten you, you never get rid of it. Nor do you want to: for you come to believe that if you get it *all* right, you will be capable of virtually anything. That is what drives me, and I know it will always do so.

INDEX

Bold type indicates a more significant section.